The Man I Didn't Know

My Father's Hidden Struggle with PTSD

Dean O. Smith

Annandale Press

Published by Annandale Press

Spokane, WA 99224

Copyright © 2023 Dean O. Smith

All rights reserved

No part of this book may be reproduced, or stored in a retrieval system, or transmitted in any form or by any means, electronic, mechanical photocopying, recording, or otherwise, without express written permission of the publisher.

ISBN-13: 978-1-7364534-4-5

Printed in the United States of America

For inquiries, contact Annandale Press at annandalepress@gmail.com

This book is dedicated to Everett E. Smith (1911-1972).

Suzanne Merrill and Everett Smith

Contents

Acknowledgments..v
Preface..vii
The Trove..1
The Early Years...12
The Gap...31
The Double...51
Desertion...75
Days of 59..110
Thoughts of Death..135
Transitions...154
The Springs..185
Remnants...219
The Return...250

Acknowledgments

I should like to thank family members and colleagues who have provided invaluable support and encouragement over the years. They include my brother Curtis Smith, sons Curtis and Corey Smith, and wife Karlene Hoo for her support and encouragement during the preparation of this book. Posthumously, I wish to thank Suzanne Merrill for the love and support she gave my father. And, I acknowledge Barney, my beagle, who provided faithful comfort as I worked on this project.

Preface

I thought that I knew my father. Although my parents were divorced and I lived with my mother, I spent all day Saturdays with him for 11 formative years, from ages 8 to 18. And I continued to communicate with him by weekly letters and occasional visits for another ten years until his death. He was a good father: attentive and loving. But, then, 32 years after his death, I discovered his diary and myriad short stories that he had written. As I began to read the volumes in this trove, I quickly came to a startling revelation: the author of the diary and the stories was unrecognizable: a stranger, a father I didn't know. This stranger was beset by the insidious demons of post-traumatic stress disorder (PTSD), demons that were foreign to the father I knew, respected, loved. Distraught, I was compelled to read further, hoping to resolve this disconnect between the fathers I knew and didn't know.

This became a study of a man's recovery from acute mental illness. The study derives from personal memories of my father and two interlacing narratives: my father's diary and his short stories written under a pseudonym, Ellis Worth. Over time—12.6 years to be exact—they follow the contours of my father's mind. They tell about his nervous breakdown, his hospitalization, his bouts of insulin- and electro-shock therapy. They tell about his conscious thoughts as he interacts with psychiatrists, colleagues, family, and lover. And they tell about his dreams: unconscious nighttime dreams and conscious daytime dreams, dreams of becoming a successful writer, dreams of marrying the woman he loves.

Pedagogically, *The Man I Didn't Know* blends nonfiction and fiction. On the one hand, my own memories are axiomatically nonfiction. They are true products of direct observation, subject to erosion with the passage of time. On the other hand, the diary is also axiomatically nonfiction, a true authoritative account of my father's thoughts and experiences. The fictional Ellis Worth short stories most probably derive from my father's real-life thoughts and experiences. ("Write what you know.") So, in a sense, they recount nonfictional events, embellished with artistic license. Yet, neither the man described in the diary (nonfiction) nor the stories (fiction) conform to what I know is truly nonfiction, my own memories. Regardless of what's real and what's not real, somewhere in this obscure interface between nonfiction and fiction resides the compelling story of a father I didn't know, a man struggling with the remnants of mental illness.

The etiology of my father's illness is hazy. Amidst the haze, three possibilities stand out. As a young boy on a farm in Minnesota, he experienced the sudden loss of his father from a heart attack and the loss of attentive affection from his widowed mother as she coped with maintaining the farm and family. These losses at a formative age could deprive a boy of his sanity. But maybe that wasn't the cause of his illness. As a soldier during World War II, he experienced atrocities in battle and in liberated Nazi concentration camps that could easily deprive a man of his sanity. Or, the third possibility: maybe the childhood losses and the wartime traumas acted synergistically to deprive my father of his sanity. Nowadays, each of these possibilities would be diagnosed as a potential source of PTSD.

Seeking clarity, *The Man I Didn't Know* explores these possible causes. During this exploration, I posit that the childhood trauma inflicted damage that might warrant psychiatric attention at some point in time but not debilitating damage. Innate defense mechanisms formed a protective scab that allowed him to emerge from childhood to lead a normal life. Until World War II, that is. The wartime trauma—interacting with Nazi perpetrators of medical atrocities at the Dachau trials and whatever else occurred on the battlefield—inflicted damage, much worse damage, resulting in the precipitous nervous breakdown. Shock therapy expunged the toxic memories of this trauma, enabling an escape from the pernicious grasp of acute insanity. But, despite continual psychiatrist talk therapy, he was not fully healed. In my father's gripping narratives, vestiges of acute illness recurred for many years.

The book opens with two introductory chapters. The first introduces my late father's friend and lover, Suzanne, who plays an important role in his recovery. It then tells how I discovered his diary and a trove of Ellis Worth short stories, the bases of this book. The second introduces my father via an Ellis Worth story, highlighting events leading up to his nervous breakdown.

After these introductions, the narrative of my father's recovery begins. Chronologically, it follows the timeline of his diary, with its episodic sojourns into the past—his childhood, the War, his hospitalization. Successive chapters recount various facets of mental illness as they appeared during the course of his recovery: dual personality, delusional paranoia, suicidal thoughts. They also recount his disillusion with the legal profession, his acceptance of a new job in Colorado Springs, his discomforting relationships with most women, his enduring relationship with Suzanne. Time passed: the diary entries manifest fewer and fewer remnants of his illness. As the diary comes to an end, the final chapters document his return to the Minnesota farm of his childhood, marking the conclusion of his ascent from the maelstrom.

This book is intended for a general audience. It does not presume any background knowledge about mental illness or its treatment. A more focused audience interested in PTSD may find the book particularly absorbing because of its first-hand account of the disease and its appearances at various stages of recovery.

The Trove

The light bulb in the hallway had burned out. In the dark, I could hardly see the keyhole. It was difficult enough carrying groceries up three flights of stairs, but being unable to unlock the door easily made the situation even more difficult. So, I had to report the outage to the building manager and, hopefully, get a replacement bulb quickly.

Although I had met the manager once before while moving in, I wasn't sure which apartment was his. While searching through the building directory, looking for his apartment number, I saw the name Suzanne Merrill. Curious, I thought. That was the name of my father's lady friend of twenty years. It must be coincidental. This is Wisconsin, but she and my father lived in Colorado, where he died ten years ago.

Nonetheless, spurred by curiosity, I rang her on the building intercom. A woman answered. I introduced myself as a neighbor and asked if I might speak with her for a minute. Yes, she invited me to come up to her door. When I arrived, I met a woman who appeared to be about eighty years old. Despite her age, she was trim, dressed smartly, and seemed poised. And, she spoke with a slight French accent.

I asked the question directly: "Do you happen to know my father Everett Smith?" She flushed immediately and said "Yes. Please come in." We sat down on the sofa, and I introduced myself with more detail. Although my brother and I had known that our father had a lady friend, we had never met her and knew very little about her.

"May I serve you a cup of coffee?" I said "Yes, please." As she prepared the coffee in the kitchen, I remained on the sofa, pondering whether it would be appropriate to call her Suzanne or if I should retain the formality of Ms. Merrill. How familiar can a son be with his deceased father's lady friend and, most probably, lover? Before I could think this through to a satisfying decision, she reappeared with coffee and a basket of shortbread cookies on a tray. "Thank you, Suzanne" came reflexively from within me. The decision on what to call her had been made.

Time passed quickly as we discussed what brought us to Madison, Wisconsin. For me, the answer was simple: a good job with the University. I was now an associate professor with tenure, quite content in my career. For Suzanne, the answer was equally simple, as well: her son who lived in Poynette, about 30 miles to the north. I remembered vaguely that my father had mentioned her son in Wisconsin, but I knew nothing more about him. Suzanne wasn't inclined to provide any more information, so I surmised that they weren't particularly close.

But, her simple answer became more complex as we continued the conversation over a second cup of coffee. "Shortly after your father died, I had a stroke. His death was a tremendous shock to me. It was so sudden, so unexpected. I cried for days, stopped eating, and slept with difficulty. Finally, my body gave out when I collapsed in the hallway with a stroke. I spent a week in the hospital and another two months convalescing at a nursing home in Denver. My son insisted on bringing me to Wisconsin, where he and his wife could care for me. I always liked Madison, so, here I am, ten years later. My body has recovered, but my soul has permanent scars from the loss."

As she told the story, I looked carefully at Suzanne, at her movements, her facial expressions, her posture. If she had a stroke, I surely couldn't tell. She didn't have any obvious signs: no facial abnormality, no slurred speech. A slight limp, perhaps, but that could be from arthritis or some such malady of age. How old is she? As I remember, Suzanne is about ten years older than my father, and he would be 71 this year. So, she is at least 81. As I thought about this, I realized that Suzanne actually looked quite good for a woman of that age. She must have been very attractive in her youth. I remember my father speaking to her in French on the telephone, calling her *mon petit chou*, my little cabbage. What a funny term of endearment. I couldn't understand anything else that was being said, but I couldn't help noticing the smile on my father's face as he spoke to her.

A ringing telephone snapped me back to the present. Suzanne went into the hallway with the phone, spoke a few words, and returned. "That was my son. He will be here in ten minutes to take me grocery shopping." Since I had no particular desire to meet him, I thanked her for the coffee, promised to keep in touch, and took leave. Besides, I still had to find the manager to report the burned out light bulb.

Suzanne lingered in my thoughts for the remainder of the day. I knew so little about her. At most, my father had mentioned just a few cursory details. She was divorced and lived alone in Denver. They met at a meeting of the French cultural society, the *Alliance Française de Denver*, shortly after he moved there from

Kansas City. At that first meeting, they discovered serendipitously that they lived in the same apartment building on Bannock Street. Her apartment was on the first floor, and his was on the third floor. I don't know how quickly the romance began, but they developed a pattern: my father would take her shopping for groceries and she would cook dinner, which they shared in her apartment. Occasionally, my father would tell my brother Curtis and me various details about a dish that Suzanne had prepared, and at Christmas, my father would give us each a small gift "from Suzanne." But beyond that, she was a stranger to us.

About a month later, I looked up Suzanne's telephone number and called her, asking if I could visit with her again the next Sunday afternoon. A flutter of excitement passed through me when she said "*mais oui*, of course." Guessing that my father would give her flowers now and then (it seemed like a French thing to do), I presented Suzanne a bouquet of flowers, red roses, as I entered her apartment for a second time. I thought that I detected a slight blush when Suzanne accepted the roses; she smiled and thanked me in French: "*merci beaucoup*." The blush triggered a memory: as a student in Germany ten or twelve years earlier, I learned that in European culture, red roses were for lovers. Not white, pink, or yellow; specifically red. I suspect that she detected a delayed blush on my part as well.

As Suzanne was putting the roses in a vase, I looked around the apartment. Nothing had changed in a month. Of course, I thought, why should it? Then, on a buffet table, I noticed three photographs of Suzanne and my father. Were they newly placed there, or had I just missed them last time? In each, they were standing together, with his arms around her waist, in front of some scenic Colorado mountainous backdrop. I didn't recognize the locations. But that wasn't the main feature of the photographs. The most prominent feature was their smiles. In fact, I smiled while gazing on their expressions.

We spent another hour or so, still getting to know each other. She told me about her job working for a trade association representing Colorado ski resorts, her son's job working for a trade association representing credit unions, and various details about her move from Denver to Madison. I told her about my college background and professional training in Europe. She seemed interested in what I had to say, but, in retrospect, I suspect that I wasn't telling her anything that my father hadn't already told her. Back and forth, we shared experiences while drinking coffee and eating shortbread cookies.

Ultimately, the subject turned to my father's death. I brought it up while discussing my years studying in Munich. "I'll never forget that evening when I got the phone call from my brother, Curtis.

'Dad had a heart attack.'

'Is he okay?'

'He's dead. He didn't show up for work, so his boss called me asking if Dad was sick. I called him, but there was no answer. So, I went over to his house and looked in the window next to the front door. There he was, lying on the living room floor. I went inside and called the police. When the policeman arrived, he kneeled down to confirm that Dad was dead and then hurried outside to vomit. I guess that he was a rookie, unfamiliar with death. Anyway, the coroner came over and made arrangements for an autopsy at the city morgue. He suspected that it was a massive heart attack."

As I told these details, Suzanne looked intently at me, and I realized that she was hearing something new, something that my father could not possibly have told her. I looked for tears, but she had none, just an absorbed stare in my direction. I continued with what I knew about the event of his death.

"I booked a flight back to Colorado the next day, December 21st. On Christmas Day, Curtis and I looked through Dad's things, sorting out payroll stubs, tax returns, insurance policies, and the like. Although Dad was a lawyer, he didn't leave a will. At least, we couldn't find one.

"While poring over these business-like things, I noticed a book that I had sent Dad for Christmas, a picture book of Bavaria. Curtis said that Dad apparently had this book in his hands when the heart attack occurred. Dad was in Bavaria during World War II, although he seldom talked about those days. But, I wondered at the time if this book somehow triggered the heart attack. I'll probably never know."

Suzanne slowly got up. It was getting late, so I took that as a subtle hint that it was time to leave. I started to put on my coat, when Suzanne took my arm. "I miss your father." Nothing more was said. She let go of my arm and looked down. I'm sure that we both suppressed tears as I left.

Several weeks later, I called on Suzanne for what turned out to be the last time. As usual, she greeted me with a smile and, for the first time, a hug. I presented her a bouquet of flowers (spring tulips of various colors, not red roses). Again, as before, Suzanne's genuine appreciation of the bouquet evoked a warm, comfortable feeling in my heart. I liked giving the flowers, and, as far as I could tell, she liked receiving them. Over coffee and shortcakes, Suzanne's smile faded, however. Her son was insisting that she move closer to him and his wife. So, they had arranged for her to move into an assisted living facility in Poynette. The movers were coming in two days. I sensed that she was unhappy with the move but resigned to it. We both made promises to keep in touch, but, thinking retrospectively, our farewells had a premonition of finality. As I was leaving, Suzanne picked up the small Persian throw rug in her front hallway. "Your father gave this to me. Please take it." After writing her a thank you note for the rug several days later, I realized that I hadn't gotten her new address. Nor did I know her son's address. I sent the note to her Madison apartment, hoping that it would be forwarded. But, I never heard from Suzanne again. She was gone.

On my next visit to Colorado Springs, I told Curtis about my serendipitous encounter with Suzanne. Like me, he knew about her but had never seen her in person. We decided to look for pictures of her in several boxes of papers and *objets d'art* (as my father called them) that Curtis retrieved from my father's house when he died. We found several color pictures of her alone and them together similar to the ones I had seen in Suzanne's apartment, scant records of their relationship.

While looking for the pictures, Curtis pointed out five particular boxes of varying sizes. "No need to look there. They contain Dad's writings, mostly old unpublished manuscripts. I looked through some of them right after he died but now they're just taking up space. You might find them interesting. Why don't you take them?" I didn't need any encouragement, but I wasn't sure where I would keep them in my small apartment in

Madison. So, we agreed that he would send them to me when I had a larger home with more storage space.

To make a long story short, it was thirty-two years before my brother finally sent me the boxes. I was retired, living on a ranch in Bozeman, Montana, and now had the space to store them and the time to go through them. Shortly after they arrived, I opened them. Inside one box was a trove of musty folios with short stories, lots of them. All of them were typewritten carbon copies on onion-skin paper under the pseudonym Ellis Worth. One small box had fifteen unopened envelopes, which, eventually, I got around to opening. Each contained an original typewritten short-story manuscript on bond paper along with a rejection notice from some small literary magazine. According to the postmarks, these must have arrived in the mail within three weeks after his death. In addition, one box contained at least twenty articles about the law, under his real name, Everett E. Smith. I knew that he had published five or ten legal articles, so I wasn't surprised to discover more. I set this box aside, thinking that they were probably out-dated. Besides, I'm not a lawyer and probably wouldn't appreciate these legal essays.

I hadn't counted all of the short stories carefully, but I guessed that there were at least fifty manuscripts. I was startled. I knew that my father had written short stories under his pseudonym, but I had no idea that he had written so many. I knew also that he had modest success in publishing them; as far as I knew, about a dozen or so were published by small literary magazines. In fact, however, one particularly musty box, stained and misshapen due to water damage, contained about fifty magazines featuring either a fictional short story by Ellis Worth or a legal essay by Everett E. Smith. This inauspicious box encapsulated my father's dream: recognition as a writer.

As I sorted through the manuscripts, I recognized the titles of several stories that my father had proudly asked me to read when I was a teenager. Partly from filial rebellion and partly from indolence, I seldom read them carefully, usually just skimming hastily towards the end and passing cursory judgment: "it's okay." Setting those embarrassing memories aside, I decided to curate the entire collection of manuscripts and re-read them all less hastily. That proved to be an auspicious decision: I enjoyed reading them.

Inspired by what I read, I assembled two anthologies of the short stories, *The Sonora Springs Tales: A Collection of Ellis Worth Short Stories* and *Once Upon a Farm: Tales of Discovery*. Both books have now been published (Annandale Press, 2021). Although these stories are works of fiction, I suspected that they sketched the story of my father's life: reminiscences embedded within enjoyable tales about fictitious characters in equally fictitious settings. As Mark Twain asserted "Write what you know." Accordingly, I surmised that my father wrote what he knew using his nom de plume, Ellis Worth. In this fictitious context, his stories relate his own experiences, personal discoveries, and outlook on social mores of the time, the mid-twentieth century. Or so I thought at the time.

But, the most surprising discovery in this trove was not the stories. It was his diary, 72 spiral notebooks that spanned 12 years. Each notebook had 50 pages with hand writing on both sides of the page. I counted about 7 words per line and 36 lines per page. Multiplying all of these numbers yields about 1.8 million words. How could I possibly read all of this? Well, I did. It took me almost a year, but I read every word.

For the most part, the writing was engaging. Topics flowed smoothly from one entry to another, and his writing style tended to pull me along. To be sure, the reading was not always easy or pleasurable. Sometimes, he ranted unendingly about an event in his childhood, sometimes he harangued mercilessly about colleagues, exhausting my patience. Sometimes he wrote in abstruse metaphor, beyond my understanding. Sometimes I found myself gliding incomprehensively over the text, necessitating a re-reading, maybe two re-readings. Regardless, I began to look forward to reading the continuing episodes in this man's life, my father's life, his reactions to daily encounters with other people, his unspoken thoughts, his dreams.

Significantly, I came to realize that the Ellis Worth stories and the diary present entirely different accounts of my father's life. The stories present fanciful narratives of quite troublesome events and interactions with people in various situations described in the diary. The narrative license makes the stories easy and enjoyable to read. But, without this license, the nonfictional diary often provides a far less pleasurable chronicle of the same events, the same people, the same situations. Thus I came to the realization that fiction and nonfiction present two different images of my father. Moreover neither of them matched the image based on my own personal recollections.

I was confronted with three very different views of my father. Which was real? Axiomatically the diary is based on fact, so I had to accept its image as more realistic than that of the stories. But my memories are also based on fact: they are based on what I witnessed as a son, which resembled what I read in the stories more than in the diaries. Quite simply, I was faced with three conflicting versions of the truth. I was compelled to ask myself: who is this nonfictional man in the diary? Ostensibly he is my father, but through the lens of his stories and my memories he is virtually unrecognizable.

The richness of this trove of fictional stories and the nonfictional diary offered me the opportunity to interlace these images of my father with my own memories. Indeed, I was driven by a sense of literary obligation to reconcile these three accounts and to chronicle my efforts. As a son, I got to know aspects of my father — his struggle with mental illness — that had eluded me as a child; as a reader, I came to appreciate the blurred interface between fiction and nonfiction. As a chronicler, I perceived a gripping story of one man's descent and subsequent ascent from the maelstrom of mental illness.

The Early Years

The diary began on May 26, 1956, when my father was 44 years old. I was just turning 12 years old at the time. As I began reading the diary, I realized that he often referred to his experiences at a younger age; many of them occurred before I was born. I knew very little about those earlier years of my father's life, certainly not in sufficient depth to appreciate fully his diary entries. I needed help, but by now, most potential resources (for example, my mother, his siblings, and so forth) were deceased.

Fortunately, help came unexpectedly. While sorting through the stories, I found a folder containing six chapters called *"The Eldon Jones Sextet,"* written by Ellis Worth. (The complete sextet is in the Ellis Worth anthology *Once upon a Farm*).[1] I hadn't seen this collection before, but the table of contents implied that it was a biography of its protagonist, Eldon Jones. That evening, I skimmed the first chapter, *The Legend of Drowsy Hollow*. In my haste, I barely got its gist, but that sufficed to evoke a curious reaction.

Intuitively, without rational cause, I sensed a compulsion to re-read *The Legend of Drowsy Hollow* more carefully, much more carefully. It was, indeed, a biography of Eldon Jones—whoever that might be. After a

---

[1] Ellis Worth, *Once Upon a Farm: Tales of Discovery* (Spokane, WA: Annandale Press, 2021). Pp. 1-89.

few paragraphs, I began reflexively to take notes and mark interesting passages. The story intrigued me, as it meandered from anecdote to anecdote about Eldon Jones' childhood in Minnesota. Was Eldon Jones a pseudonym for my father, and was this the autobiographical help I needed or simply a fictitious story set in my father's homeland? I wasn't sure, but when I had finished this second reading, again without rational cause, I prepared a summary, an abridgment of sorts, by combining my notes and highlighted passages.

The story begins at the beginning, the birth of Eldon Jones. "There are times in any hero's life when he is pretty unheroic—for example, when he's being born. So it was with Eldon Jones. Though in later years Eldon claimed to have dim intimations of life before birth, he never had the nerve to pretend he recalled his first breath or the doctor's slap on the buttocks that started it. His birth was in the hands of others, as was much else afterward."

With that unremarkable beginning, Eldon Jones came into the world, a world of hard work on the family farm, Drowsy Hollow. His father, Farmer Jones, worked tirelessly clearing the land, breaking the sod, tilling the fields, taking delight in the hard work of a farm. And he tells about his mother, Anna, who seemed to have regarded strenuous activity as part of the Divine Order of things. She was busy from morning to night in the house: sweeping, scrubbing, making beds, churning butter, baking bread, cooking, washing dishes, washing clothes, knitting socks and sweaters, making shirts and dresses, darning and mending, and all of the other things that needed to be done in the home.

As a young boy, Eldon was expected to contribute to the hard work of running the farm. He was assigned daily chores: watering the chickens, feeding the cows, and so forth. However, Eldon was not particularly enthusiastic about farm work, occasionally drawing a parental rebuke for neglecting his chores. He preferred to roam the woods, fish and catch frogs in the ponds, hunt rabbits and trap weasels, observe the clouds, enjoy nature. His father would joke half-seriously that Eldon's older brother was good for work, his younger brother was good for play, and Eldon was good for nothing.

Eldon grew up in a multilingual setting. His father's ancestors had migrated from England and, of course, he spoke English. His mother, like many neighbors in the region, migrated from Germany and continued to speak German in her native dialect. Eldon had little interest in the language, with its topsy-turvy diction: "Throw the cows over the fence some hay." He preferred listening to the sing-song pronunciation of the Swedish language spoken by Scandinavian neighbors.

Eldon's formal education began in a two-room schoolhouse located in Cold Spring, over a mile away. He enjoyed the walk to school. It was fun to drink from the spring at the river's edge by the bridge. In the spring, bloodroots and mayflowers blanketed the roadsides. In winter, it might be possible to walk over the crusted snowdrifts. It was worth a try and the next best thing to walking on water. Also, it was great sport to hook a ride on the runner of a passing sled or sleigh. There might be, if one were fortunate, a vociferous dog to silence with stones or snowballs.

Then, while in school on Armistice Day, two years after the end of World War I, tragedy struck. Eldon received the sad news that his father had died suddenly from a heart attack. Eldon was numb. The earth's foundation had given way, sunk from under his feet. The world was no longer the same and never would be. His father's death was unnatural, totally unacceptable. Life went on, of course, but not as before. It went on dully and only slowly gained a semblance of reality and cheer. If anyone had asked him the day before Armistice Day, 1920, if he and his father were close kin, he would have answered "Not especially." The day after, he wouldn't have been able to answer at all. While he lived, Eldon's father had been fallible. Even Eldon had doubted his father's judgment that automobiles were a passing fad because flat tires were too hard to take off, patch and replace (all done at the roadside). In death, his father became Father, infallible, faultless.

After his father's death, Eldon continued his schooling. In grade school, he finished at the top of his class. Then, he went to high school in Avondale, seven miles from Drowsy Hollow. In mild weather, he walked the distance, sometimes hitching a ride, but in winter he stayed in a boarding house, going home only on the weekends. He excelled in most subjects and, at age 15, graduated from high school.

It was vaguely understood by the Joneses and their neighbors that high school was not the end of the scholastic road for Eldon, but he spent the summer following graduation undecided about the next move. Meantime, he threw himself into the various activities of the local 4-H Club for farm youth. His project, a small flock of big black chickens, was to rate a blue ribbon at the county fair, but he scarcely took note of that. That wasn't what he wanted to do before leaving the farm. What was it? He wanted to do what his father had always spoken about doing but never had time to do: plant an evergreen windbreak on the west side of the farmhouse. So, Eldon gathered myriad young evergreen trees and planted the windbreak as a lasting memorial to his father. He was now ready to accept the challenge of the Big City—or rather two cities, the Twin Cities. Thus ended *The Legend of Drowsy Hollow*.

After re-reading and summarizing this first chapter of the *Sextet*, I hesitated, unsure whether I would read further. The story ambled along in a humdrum writing style. But the content piqued my interest: the rustic lifestyle, the formative years of a young Minnesota farm boy, marred by his father's sudden death. It was all vaguely familiar. So, I read the next story, the next, and the next, until I had read the entire sextet.

Subsequent chapters continued the rambling tale of Eldon Jones. At age 15, he moved to the Twin Cities, where he went to business school and then to the University of Minnesota, where he earned a law degree. He received less formal introductory education in the pleasures of women from the Elfstrand twins, who lived in the same boarding house as Eldon. Apparently, he learned his lessons well, for Ellis Worth tells about Eldon's romantic relationships with numerous other women during the next two decades. After law school, Eldon took a job in a Minneapolis law firm, where he worked during the Great Depression. All-in-all, these years in the Twin Cities were years of learning, of growing into manhood.

In 1936, Eldon joined a colleague in Washington, D.C., taking a job as a government lawyer. Shortly after his arrival, he rented a room from a French family that spoke only French in the house. Consequently, Eldon learned the language fluently. During the ensuing eight years, Eldon rubbed elbows with influential statesmen, caroused with women, vacationed in Europe, quaffed cocktails overlooking the Potomic. In short, he enjoyed the life of a young civil servant, a bachelor, a *bon vivant*.

All of this came to an end when World War II broke out. In 1942, at age 31, Eldon became a soldier in the Army. While stationed at Camp Custer in Sonora Springs, Colorado, he met Mildred Quam (Millie), whom he married in 1943. A short time later, Eldon enrolled in Officer Candidate School, located in Ann Arbor, Michigan. According to Ellis Worth, "The time there seemed to pass with the sudden violence of armored columns. Corporal Jones — or Candidate Jones, rather — became Lieutenant Jones, and a few months later, he was ordered overseas." He was assigned to the Judge Advocate General's Corps in the Third Army, commanded by General George Patton. He landed in Normandy on July 14, 1944, six weeks after Millie bore their first son.

Ellis Worth provided few details about Eldon's wartime experiences, none at all about battle. Indeed, his most extensive passage tells about an imposed vacation on the French Riviera. After the brutal Siege of Bastogne, the Third Army had plunged into Germany but had not yet crossed the Rhine when Eldon — now Major Jones — was ordered to take a "rest leave." I inferred that this leave was ordered because Eldon had incurred significant traumatic stress during the battle, for he mentions that "he knew a sergeant who had gone to pieces nervously and been evacuated through medical channels." Eldon wanted to remain until the Rhine had been crossed. No. He preferred to go to Paris. No. He was to be on a plane that was taking a group of "restees" to Cannes. The sojourn on the Mediterranean was a wonderful change, for it provided an opportunity to relax, which was good for Eldon.

When he returned to Headquarters, the Third Army had crossed the Rhine and launched its drive across Germany, headed to Bavaria. Soon afterwards, the war ended, and the Third Army became an army of occupation. Eldon's duties "alas, took him a number of times to Dachau, one of the Nazis' infamous extermination camps."

Eldon's military service came to an honorable end in late October, 1945, with a reputation as a war-hero. By transport ship and troop trains, he returned to Colorado. The soldier was home, free to see his wife and his eighteen-months-old son. He was home and he was free but not yet a civilian in the same sense he had been some three years before. That would take time. "A farewell to arms is a slow process, not a quick wave of the hand."

Indeed. At age thirty-five, Eldon was back from the Crusade in Europe, back in the civilian clothing he had doffed in 1942, back in the Capital City on the Potomac that he had left as a draftee. He had left these familiar surroundings as a bachelor. He returned with a wife and an eighteen month-old son. Within a year, the Joneses had another son, their second, and a beautiful brick home on Endicott Street. Thus, previously an apartment-house tenant, he was now a suburban householder with a GI loan. Once he had been a humble civil servant who drank beer with his colleagues before he went home. Now he belonged to a car pool that departed for the Maryland suburb promptly at five after five o'clock.

Eldon was still a lawyer but no longer a government attorney. He had a new job, Secretary of the Glick Art Museum, a foundation set up by a retired, millionaire brewer from Cincinnati. The founder had bought a grand residence on Massachusetts Avenue just off Dupont Circle, installed his art collection in it, called it a museum (mainly for art students), endowed the institution, and left the peculiar business in charge of Gil Carreau, the Director. There was a Chief Curator, too, a respectable gentleman named Clell Putney, who formerly had been Mr. Glick's valet. Eldon, the third man of the triumvirate, was chosen for his vague duties by Gil Carreau.

This was a prestigious job for the newly discharged war hero. But Eldon found himself woefully underemployed, especially after the unending challenges he faced in the military. To relieve his boredom, he made work for himself: consulted with Gil on the slightest pretext and pointed out the potential legal dangers in everything around and about the Glick Museum. Waxed floors in the galleries? People slip and fall on them. This necessitates careful procedures lest the Museum be sued. After all, the books are full of slippery-floor cases. Eldon piddled on various lawsuits, but Mr. Glick's own lawyers had the chief responsibility for these. For example: an ex-wife of Mr. Glick claimed the old boy had wronged her somehow when he transferred his art collection and money to the Glick Art Museum without getting anything in return; because of the Glick's restrictions on public attendance, the taxing authorities of the District of Columbia kept challenging the Museum's tax exemption; an artist that the Museum had discharged before his term of employment expired for his Socialist ideology and polygamous tendencies sued for breach of contract. Eldon did his part in these and other suits by giving off-the-cuff ideas and suggestions to Mr. Glick's lawyers when they called, on occasion, from Cincinnati.

But they had the lead role, leaving Eldon with a dissatisfying passive role in the museum's legal affairs. Gil recognized Eldon's dissatisfaction with the job but didn't expect Eldon to leave the Glick Museum. No other place would pay so much for so little, and Eldon needed the job to support his family.

As time passed, Eldon became less comfortable with the strange world in which he lived. He was hailed a war hero, but he now began to doubt that he had been decorated as the Army's special orders read. Furthermore, he was being paid more for negligible services at the Glick than Presidential cabinet officers were paid for the onerous duties cast on them by the Cold War with Russia. Eldon became disenchanted with his boss, Gil Carreau, whose abilities were inferior to his own, was paid more by the Museum, and cut a wider swath in society. Without wit or a sense of humor and absolutely devoid of originality, Gil was made to shine on the TV quiz programs of that era, winning rich prizes that way. Gossip columnists who calumniated others praised Gil as an authentic genius.

Eldon ceased to be comfortable alone in his private office. He feared some unknown enemy might brush aside his secretary and enter suddenly unannounced. He wasn't at ease even when his secretary, demure and deferential, came in to take dictation. He was finding it increasingly difficult to draft a memorandum of procedure for the shipment of paintings or sculptures on loan with the same care as if the memo were an important state paper.

At home, he couldn't explain the difficulties of the day to his wife. Difficulties in a job almost without cares, not to mention crises. Then he began to have trouble sleeping. He would awaken in a cold sweat and would find his wife awake, afraid. He started seeing a psychiatrist, Dr. Langley. Thanks to the doctor, he suffered less from sleeplessness, but his sleep was haunted by nightmares. His days were calmer, but he made no effort to pretend there were important things to be done. He was too drained of strength and vitality to make the effort. His calm was that of exhaustion.

In the summer of 1949, Eldon was feeling better. His wife took the two boys on a vacation trip to see her family. Eldon was to join them later. Gil Carreau and Clell Putney, both of whom were ignorant of Eldon's malaise and supposed their able colleague was as stable as an elephant, took their vacations, leaving Eldon in charge of the Glick Museum for a month. The Jones's house on Endicott Street had only one house near it, the Johnson residence. The Johnsons, whom Eldon knew fairly well, had left for the seashore. Eldon was alone, quite alone, physically and emotionally.

In this aloneness, Eldon's life took a tragic downturn. He perceived himself as being mocked in all his leisure moments. His mental health was becoming less and less stable. A turning point occurred when he attended a performance by college players of *The Tempest*, and perceived that the monster Caliban was modeled after him, Eldon Jones. He would have to tell the psychiatrist that on his very next visit. After the theater, home alone, he remembered the awful scene in *King Lear* when one of the characters—he couldn't remember which nor find it in the text—had his eyes gouged out. He was sure that scene was in *Lear*, and he was certain his own punishment here below was predicted. Then there was Othello, a black man. "Surely the English playwright had looked down the centuries and foreseen E. E. Jones. Eldon's skin was white but by no means blond. In his ancestry somewhere, according to Shakespeare with whom Eldon agreed, there had been infusions of Negro blood. He had blue eyes? African violets are blue. Such dizzy, crazy, disjointed thoughts flicked, skittered, through his mind like scenes from one of those early, silent movies; and he could not sleep."

It is a wonder Eldon was capable of driving his car over to the psychiatrist's office the next morning, but he succeeded in keeping his early appointment. He told Dr. Langley of his newly-discovered identity, Caliban. The doctor wanted to think his patient was joking, but, alas, Eldon's intensity and conviction, his pitiable abasement, his plea for mercy prevented any such suppositions.

Dr. Langley said, "But doesn't your good sense tell you better?"

"No."

Dr. Langley put in a long-distance call to Eldon's wife: "Come back." He called a local physician with whom Eldon had worked and gone to school years ago in Minnesota. "Come over." There was no struggle to get Eldon to a hospital. He was as aware he was sick somehow, just as he was convinced he was Caliban—and an African violet.

At the hospital, Eldon was given a physical examination by a young doctor whose verdict was "You're in perfect physical shape. I can't say the same for your mind." As a patient realizing he couldn't come and go as he pleased, Eldon supposed he was locked up for some heinous crime. He tried to imagine what that was, what it could be. He did not accept the doctor's pronouncement that his mind was awry, although he could see plainly that his fellow patients were quite erratic. In fact, he wasn't at all sure the young doctor was a physician and not a prison official.

His wife called on the phone once in a while but seldom came to see him. "Doctors" came and went through the halls, but, at first, scarcely noticed him. He was herded with other patients about the extensive green grounds of the sanitarium, where he saw beautiful fields of corn such as he had seen as a boy on the Minnesota farm and a wondrous river like the one that had run along the boundary of Drowsy Hollow Farm, his boyhood home. These serene dreams were occasionally interrupted by what the attendants called "hydrotherapy": pin-point sprays of alternating hot and cold water were shot at him from a distance.

Was this stay at the hospital to be endless? No, that was unacceptable. He demanded to see a doctor, any doctor. "Why certainly, Mr. Jones." The doctor in charge, Dr. Hinton, listened to Eldon's plea for release but said little. It was as if he had no more authority than the hospital attendants, those husky, white-suited young men who shepherded their charges in the wards, at meals, and on the excursions around the hospital grounds. So Eldon was obliged to wait.

He bided his time at occupational therapy where he played around with high-speed power saws in the carpentry shop and contemplated suicide by sawing the arteries in his wrists. He felt certain his captors desired his self-destruction. Otherwise, why would they have allowed him access to such destructive tools? In the leather-working shop he turned over in his mind projects for hanging himself with a rawhide thong from one of the building's overhead, horizontal steel beams. However, neither wrist-slashing nor hanging appealed to him as a means of exit from his situation.

To drown in the river which ran along the edge of the hospital grounds: that was the way to take his leave. On a Sunday walk with other patients and the ever-present attendants, Eldon made a break for it. He was caught just short of the river's brink. No one asked him what he intended to do. They knew. A panel of doctors was assembled to ask him why he sought to do anything so final, so permanent. As if they didn't know, thought Eldon. As if they didn't want just that. Or, did they, perchance, covet for themselves the infliction of the fatal blow?

The next day two attendants escorted Eldon to a room which was empty except for a narrow hospital cot. They told him they wanted to tie him to the cot and give him a shot of insulin. "No." He refused to cooperate. More attendants arrived on the scene, and the struggling Eldon was tied down on his back, with feet and arms spread. "This is it," Eldon said to himself. "This is the end."

After this first, experimental or test shot of insulin, Eldon submitted to the others which were given every day for more than a month. At least, he had breakfast in bed when he awakened from the deep coma; and what good breakfasts they were; and what delicious fruit juice. After breakfast, all the insulin patients showered, which was all right. It felt good. Lunch came soon afterward, and before long Eldon was beginning to feel overfed and sluggish. Accordingly, he objected to taking the pill that was offered just before lunch. "What's it for?"

"To sharpen your appetite." It was the pretty, short, blue-eyed nurse who spoke. However, a pugnacious-looking but little attendant was hurrying up beside him.

"I already have a good appetite."

Now Eldon's arms were seized from behind by an attendant he hadn't seen coming up. The other attendant, the slight bantam rooster, said, "Now take your pill!" The nurse put the pill in Eldon's mouth and, giving up the fight, he swallowed it.

Toward the end of the course of insulin-treatments, the thick fog, the all-enveloping gray mist that had clouded his existence during the past months began to dissipate, rise, and finally clear away. He commenced, too, to see one of the hospital doctors regularly, Dr. Haigler. At their first meeting, Eldon mentioned that "My nose is tender, and a little blood comes out."

"Yes. That's from the electric shocks you're given."

"I thought I was getting insulin shock."

"Yes, both."

Later, on one of his periodic visits to Dr. Haigler, he complained, "One of my ribs hurts. It feels like it's broken."

"Yes. One of your vertebrae is broken from the electric shock-treatment. I think it will be all right. Let me know if it doesn't get better." A while later his back was broken for a second time.

Spring had come. Now, he had the freedom of the hospital grounds, unattended. He could wander along the river and watch the swans gliding on it. Daffodils tossed their heads "in sprightly dance." Birds sang. Nature exulted.

A few visitors came to call. Eldon's wife, Millie, made several calls. She was tense, nervous, restless. She had undergone great hardship with Eldon away. Much of their money in the bank had melted away. His salary, thank goodness, had continued. She even had received a kind note from Mr. Glick. Gil Carreau, while on his way to a weekend with some TV celebrities, stopped by. "I suppose you'll be getting out soon," Gil said, as if Eldon had been serving a term in the state penitentiary.

"I hope so."

"I'm sure you will. You're looking tip-top."

"Thank you."

When Eldon saw Dr. Haigler, he asked, "Will I be allowed to go home soon?"

"Maybe. There are a few things you ought to know first."

"What?"

"For one thing, you won't have a job."

"I just saw Gil. He didn't say a thing about that."

"He asked me to tell you."

"I see."

"That's enough for today. You think about it."

The two discussed Eldon's leaving the hospital on a trial visit at length during several consultations. Eldon insisted he was ready to leave.

"What about a job?"

"I'll get a new one. I want a new one, anyway."

"It might not be easy to get one."

"It won't be easy. I know that."

"How long has it been since you've seen your folks in Minnesota?"

"Several years."

"Will you go and see them if you're given a trial visit?"

"Yes."

"I told you once there were several things you needed to know before you left the hospital on a trial visit."

"Yes."

"One is that you don't have a job."

"Yes."

"But we haven't yet talked about your wife."

"What about her?"

"I think she wants to leave you. I discouraged that idea, but I don't think she was convinced. She had consulted Dr. Langley and another doctor. And, she's talked it over with a few friends. I have a hunch everyone advised her to stick with you. I don't know what she's finally decided, but you ought to know she might not be there when you get home; nor the children, either."

"I haven't seen the boys in all this time."

"I know."

"I hadn't figured on this."

"I know."

In the middle of May, Eldon was released from the hospital on a "trial visit" home. He had been in the hospital for almost a year, and the grip of old habits and old associations and friendships had been loosened if not broken. "Naked came he into the world, and now he was starting again from scratch." Seeking the comfort of family, he went to Minnesota for two weeks. On his return, he lived in the family residence on Endicott Street in one of Washington's Maryland suburbs. The house was full of furniture, but his family was gone to parts unknown. There was no note on the mantle, no note anywhere. He figured he'd find out where they were in God's good time.

"Eldon Jones made a comeback, but not without delay, anguish, and heartache. He had descended into the maelstrom but had now returned. None of those who escape this hell is ever the same afterward. Nor was

Eldon. It didn't matter. He had come up from the depths. That was enough, enough for hallelujahs."

He found a job in the least likely of places, the Internal Revenue Service. He never really understood how it was that the hard-headed officials of that Service would take a chance (really not so great) on him. He was an egghead, which was against him, and was in his late thirties, whereas the System's recruitment aimed mainly for young men, young lawyers. Finally, he had a medical history which was enough to alarm the most timid (which is to say almost all) employers. Fortunately, Dr. Haigler had recommended him for the job without qualification. That he knew. Friends of his in the Service may have said a few kind words. Maybe somebody up there liked him. Anyway, he went to work in August, 1950.

Eldon was assigned to the Kansas City office, where he stayed for a year. During that time, his wife Millie, who now lived in Colorado Springs in a house owned by her parents, obtained a divorce. By agreement, Eldon retained full interest in the Maryland house and, in return, bought from her parents the Colorado Springs house where she had been living and gave her the house and custody of the two boys. He retained only, as the decree put it, "the right to visit them at reasonable times and places." With no wife now to encumber his title to the former family residence in Maryland, Eldon sold it and put the money in a selected list of stocks. He was homeless but not penniless.

Toward the end of 1952, the Truman Administration created a Revenue District Headquarters in Denver which needed several lawyers. This was a magnificent opportunity for Eldon to be still nearer to his two sons if he could be appointed to one of the positions in the

The Early Years

Denver office. He pleaded his own case and won. He was transferred to Denver with the title of Chief Trial Attorney. The title was splendid, but trials were so few that he was the chief of only one trial attorney. Furthermore, the election of a Republican president in November made it doubtful whether the Denver District Headquarters created by the Democrats would be long-lived.

Sure enough. In six months the Eisenhower Administration abolished the Denver District Headquarters. Eldon refused to be transferred, and in another six months he was forced to resign. No matter. He had established a pattern of weekly visits to his sons in Sonora Springs every Saturday, and he would let nothing disturb that arrangement. He opened an office for the practice of law in Denver. Clients stayed away in droves. His practice was a dud. But, he kept at it with a borrowed typewriter, a second-hand desk, and a piddling collection of books.

The story, *The Eldon Jones Sextet*, approached an end. Eldon Jones had returned from the maelstrom, the depths of acute mental illness. He found a job, moved to Denver, lost that job, and started a private law practice. In the final few pages, Ellis Worth compressed time, relating short anecdotes about interactions with his sons as they grew into young men. He concludes this long tale with a bittersweet reminiscence:

"In a remarkably short time Eldon was the father of grown sons. His burden of care and support, which really hadn't been a burden, was less, but the joy of leading and teaching two healthy young boys of intelligence and good will — that immense and inestimable joy — had vanished forever."

With that sentimental ending, I sensed empathy, as if Ellis Worth had been telling his own tale.

The Gap

Within the first several paragraphs, I had realized that the *Eldon Jones Sextet* constituted a short biography. No, more accurately, I suspected that they constituted a thinly disguised autobiography, my father's autobiography. The *Sextet* didn't cover his entire life, nor did it go into great detail. Nonetheless, just as a skeleton defines the basic form of a person's body, these stories appeared to define the basic events in my father's life.

I sought validation of my suspicion that the *Sextet* was, indeed, an autobiography. My mother, who would probably know enough details about my father's early life, had died nearly twenty years ago. Perhaps my father had discussed these stories with my brother. But that was not the case; my brother could only surmise that they constituted an autobiography. Perhaps Suzanne had read them in his presence. I wanted to talk about them with her, to discuss my father's life, to parse the various events. But, that was a pipe dream.

Regardless, on reflection, I convinced myself that the *Sextet* was, indeed, autobiographical. My father is Eldon Jones. Of course; I recognized some of the details presented in the *Sextet*. For example, I knew that my father was born and raised on a farm in Minnesota. He had talked occasionally about raising chickens, milking cows, catching frogs for fish bait. And, he told us about his mother who had immigrated to the United States from Germany as a young girl. I met her, my grandmother, only a few times and remember her primarily as a heavy-set woman with a thick German accent, so thick, in fact, that I had trouble understanding what she said. I knew that his father, the grandfather that I never met, had died suddenly from a heart attack when my father was nine years old. He seldom talked about the impact of that loss, but I suspect that it haunted him, just as it would any normal human being. As my brother and I were growing into our teens, my father once confided that "it's hard to be a father of teenagers when I didn't have a father of my own as a teenager."

I knew that he had served in the Judge Advocate General's (JAG) Corps as a lawyer in the Third Army under Gen. George Patton during World War II. In fact, my father idolized Gen. Patton. Although he received several decorations for valor (with colorful medals and ribbons), he never talked about actual events during his years in the army. I knew that he had been deputy counsel for the National Gallery of Art, and I knew that he had a nervous breakdown while working there. Occasionally, he spoke about his mental illness and visits to a psychiatrist. My mother told me about his "paranoid schizophrenia" and how he had threatened to kill my brother and me, his own sons. Ostensibly, that is why she fled with us back to the safety of her parents in Colorado. Importantly, though, I knew from my own experience that my father loved my brother and me. He made that clear by his actions, his devotion to us as we grew into young men.

In contrast, I didn't know several details presented in *Eldon Jones*. For example, I didn't know that my father left the farm and went to business school in Minneapolis at such a young age, fifteen. Certainly, I didn't know about his sexual exploits with women, like the Elfstrand twins. In fact, I am amazed at my father's interest in women; he had always seemed somewhat indifferent to them. I didn't know that he lived with a French-speaking family. That explains his fluency in the language. I didn't know that he landed at Normandy, as the Third Army invaded Europe. I didn't know that he contemplated suicide while in the mental hospital or that his law practice was so unsuccessful—a "dud." And, I didn't know a handful of other less consequential fine points in the *Sextet* not worth mentioning.

For several days after reading about Eldon Jones, I pieced together the first forty years or so of my father's life, merging the details in the *Sextet* with details stored in my memories going back to infancy. The timeline of events began to fill in. The progression from one event to the next began to make logical sense. Metaphorically, the skeleton began to resemble an intact man.

But, there was one cavernous gap in the timeline of events: the transition from a seemingly stable young man to a patient under suicide watch in a mental hospital. What events set the stage for the nervous breakdown, and when did they occur? In *the Sextet*, the first hint of any instability doesn't arise until after Eldon Jones had returned from the war to his new family and job at the art museum. It happens when he mentions that he "ceased to be comfortable alone in his private office." Paranoia starts to manifest itself, as he "feared that some unknown enemy might brush aside his secretary and enter suddenly unannounced." These comments clearly indicate that his mental health was eroding.

To bridge this gap, to understand what caused the mental erosion, two pivotal questions required answers. The first is straightforward: Did traumas of war disrupt the brain's normal synaptic harmony, inducing the disorders of mental illness? I suspected that the war was a major disruptor. However, the second is more complicated: Did the traumas of war tear off protective scabs from childhood traumas, releasing latent disorders of mental illness? Neither the *Sextet* nor my memories provided answers to these questions. In the *Sextet*, the sole indication of mental stress during the war was when Eldon Jones was ordered to take a "rest leave" shortly after the Third Army entered Germany, but there is no explanation for this prescribed rest. My brother knew a few more details about my father's past, but like me, he knew very little about his wartime experiences. Again, I couldn't ask Suzanne these questions, and my mother is dead. I alone would have to find the answers.

The quest for answers required homework. I began by studying the history of the Third Army's activities in World War II. The goal of my studies would be to account for my father's military experiences during the war. If some particular experiences were particularly traumatic, judging vicariously, I hoped that I would recognize them. Studying the history of the Third Army's activities in World War II, took me back to my undergraduate college years. I collected several books recounting the liberation of Europe, the exploits of Gen. Patton, and so forth. Quickly, I learned that old habits die hard. As in college, I would read assiduously at first, drift into shallow sleep within ten or fifteen minutes and then promptly forget many details of what I had just read.

Some things stuck, however. What stuck was the Third Army's role in the Battle of the Bulge, where, under Gen. Patton's command, they repulsed the German army in the Siege of Bastogne. The battle was bloody. All told, the Americans suffered 75,000 casualties in the Battle of the Bulge, the most of any battle during the war. Despite my efforts to trace my father's whereabouts during the battle, I couldn't ascertain whether he was actually anywhere near the front lines. Lawyers in the JAG Corps were more likely stationed behind the lines, in the rear echelon, the "back office" so to speak, not involved directly in front-line battle, except in particularly intense battle conditions. In any event, the ferocity of the Battle of the Bulge surely presented many potentially traumatic experiences. The Battle's impact on my father simply remains unknown.

    What also stuck even more firmly was the Third Army's role in the liberation of Nazi concentration camps: Ohrdruf, Buchenwald, and Dachau. The soldiers who liberated these camps in April, 1945, encountered unimaginable Dantean atrocities. They had survived the war with its bloody battles and were preparing to go home, remarkably naïve about Nazi abominations. At these three camps, however, the soldiers "peered into a frightening abyss," as one account described the encounter. Within and surrounding the camps, they saw death of the most gruesome sort: starvation, disease, violent murder; dead bodies stacked like fire wood, ready to be burned, destroyed, expunged from this world. They saw deteriorating human carcasses, dead and nearly dead with gruesome white maggots writhing from every orifice, every open wound, burned flesh and bones caked in industrial ovens, waist-deep ash from incinerated corpses. They smelled the nauseating byproducts of rot and putrefaction, a stench that abused all human senses, detaching the brain from reality. They inspected mechanisms of torture and cruelty. They cleaned up cesspools of inconceivable filth. They nursed hopeless survivors infested by lice and covered by excrement. They witnessed the horrors of Hell on Earth.

Firsthand descriptions of these camps document their traumatic impact on the unsuspecting soldiers. The initial response commonly involved revulsion: aversion, disgust, horror, nausea. Even battle-hardened Gen. Patton recoiled as he first entered Ohrdruf, quickly retreating outside to vomit. Of course, every soldier reacted uniquely. But, according to accounts, few could escape the darkness of depression cast by these atrocities.

Was my father there? Did he witness this Hell on Earth? Definitive military records proved elusive. Many military records, nearly 80 percent of them, were lost forever when, in 1973, fire destroyed the Military Personnel Records Center in St. Louis. In the aftermath, the Center salvaged a rudimentary record of my father's military service, but it has no specific details about his whereabouts in April, 1945. The Center recommended contacting people who served with my father at that time. Unfortunately, by this time, they had all passed away—at least, those that I knew about. The *Eldon Jones Sextet* provided a clue, however, when Eldon notes that "His duties, alas, took him a number of times to Dachau, one of the Nazis' infamous extermination camps." Although my father never mentioned Dachau to me, he told my brother that he was "very disturbed" by Dachau. That was all he said: no further explanations or clarifications.

During my homework, I discovered a decisive clue while poring through transcripts of the so-called Dachau trials. These were a series of military tribunals of concentration camp guards, members of German military and police units, and various German medical personnel indicted for war crimes. They were conducted by the United States Army between November, 1945, and December, 1947, at the site of the former concentration camp at Dachau. The first major case, *United States of America v. Martin Gottfried Weiss et al.*, charged 42 Nazi officials with cruelties and mistreatment of non-German civilians and unarmed prisoners of war: killings, beatings, torture, starvation, abuse, and other indignities. Significantly, these charges included abusive medical experiments performed by Nazi doctors. All defendants were found guilty; 36 of them were sentenced to death on December 13, 1945, of whom 23 were hanged on May 28-29, 1946, including the commandant, Martin Weiss and the camp doctor, Karl Schilling. The rest were sentenced to various terms of imprisonment.

To my surprise, the official review of the proceedings of this trial was written and signed by Colonel Charles E. Cheever, who I knew had been my father's commanding officer during the war. If Col. Cheever was there, my father most probably also was there as a participant in the military tribunal.

My father was there! He witnessed firsthand the testimonies describing these horrendous acts, probably in much greater (and more gruesome) detail than transcribed in the official tribunal records. His participation in the Dachau trials also sheds light on another comment he made to my brother: he was deeply disturbed by hearing the Nazi war criminals speak German, just as his mother and childhood friends had.

By inference, my father suffered from what is now called PTSD triggered by his military experiences and, particularly, witnessing the Nazi atrocities. Accordingly, I researched PTSD in books and blogs that defined its causes, symptoms, treatment, et cetera. Notably, most resources asserted that PTSD symptoms may start within one month of a traumatic event but sometimes not until years after the event. In my father's case, the symptoms manifested themselves three years later in Washington, D.C.

As far as I was concerned, my father's presence at Dachau bridges the gap between his military service and his nervous breakdown. Sure, the evidence isn't definitive, but it sufficed in my mind. That is a qualified assertion, however, for it leaves unanswered the second question about my father's illness: Did the Dachau (or other wartime) traumas cause my father's mental illness directly or indirectly by awakening demonic progenitor traumas that had lain dormant for years since childhood? Hypothetically, the common use of the German language by heinous war criminals and his mother may somehow have destabilized normal mental processes.

The search for answers took me back to my father's diary. I would re-read it, looking for clues. My first reading of this enormous document had been cursory, skimming along simply to get the gist. During this second reading, I planned on taking notes, marking pages, and digitizing handwritten text in passages that seemed relevant to my quest. Although I didn't look forward to this daunting task, I suspected intuitively that it would payoff in the long run. I would learn more about my father's past. So, I began re-reading from the beginning.

The first entry, dated May 26, 1956, provides a chit-chatty introduction to my father's Saturday routine. He would drive from Denver to Colorado Springs to spend the day with my brother and me. Despite her anxiety, my mother Margaret, or "Margie" as my father called her, condoned the visits, for they allowed her to spend the day teaching violin lessons at a downtown music store without worrying about child care.

Apropos my mother: before proceeding further, I should introduce her and her relationship with my father, her estranged ex-husband. Vilified for her desertion in the *Eldon Jones Sextet*, my mother played a minor role in the diary, seldom receiving more than cursory, uncomplimentary attention. But, she played a significant role in my brother's and my upbringing, and, in that respect, merits this introduction. As a violinist, my mother made her living teaching music in the Colorado Springs public schools, giving private lessons, and performing in various musical venues. These three jobs consumed most of her days and evenings, leaving my brother and me to eat and amuse ourselves without her; we were what are now called "latchkey" children. But her musical performances introduced us to a variety of ideologies, people, and institutions. For example, often, we accompanied her to Sunday services at various churches ranging from Unitarian to Catholic where she played during the services to earn a few dollars, and we learned their particular religious doctrines. She hosted ad hoc rehearsals for visiting concert artists at our house, ranging from popular musicians such as Nat King Cole, Johnny Mathis, and Ray Bolger, to classical masters such as Manoah Leide-Tedesco. At the apex of her musical career, our mother became concert mistress of the Colorado Springs Symphony Orchestra. She was widely recognized as one of the best violinists in the State, and we were quite proud of her. All was not music, however. She was still a third-generation Colorado native and an avid outdoors enthusiast. On her occasional vacations, she rented a rustic cabin in the mountains or simply set up a camping tent for a week or so and taught us lessons about survival, fishing, and enjoying the Colorado wilderness—lessons that she had learned from her parents and grandparents while growing up in Colorado Springs. From her, a Colorado native, and my father, a Minnesota farm boy, my brother and I learned to appreciate the great outdoors.

In their parental roles, our mother and father complemented one another. Although she became a professional musician, my mother majored in botany as a student at Colorado College. She accentuated the relevance of science, unlike my father, who much preferred the humanities with little appreciation for science. As my brother and I progressed in school, we gravitated to humanities (mainly music) and the sciences, respectively. True, as a musician's son, I learned music: to play piano, French horn, clarinet, oboe; to sing in the school choirs and musical performances; to read and transpose scores; and so forth. It was expected of me. But, I didn't practice often, so I had a limited future in music. My future lay in the sciences. My mother encouraged me in designing science fair projects, reading popularized science books, learning the names of plants and positions of stars in the night sky, et cetera. In contrast, my brother learned to play one instrument, the piano, quite well. Unlike me, he did practice—a lot. As a result, he became very accomplished and received accolades for his playing. With our mother's active guidance and father's encouragement, he became a concert pianist and well-respected member of the local musical community.

Although my father was not a performing artist of any sort, unlike my mother, he was a lover of the classical arts, and he shared that love with us. While driving in the car during our Saturdays together, he always insisted on listening to the weekly matinee broadcast of the Metropolitan Opera. Occasionally, he took us to the Colorado Springs Fine Arts Center or the Denver Art Museum to view their collections. On birthdays, holidays such as Christmas, and so forth, he always presented us not with standard Hallmark-variety cards but with cards featuring classic paintings from collections at various art galleries. And, as birthday and holiday gifts, he usually gave us books by acclaimed authors. My brother and I learned to appreciate these cultural attributes; they became an important part of our formal education.

Our mother and father seldom spoke to one another. Indeed, they avoided contact. Neighbors occasionally taunted my brother and me about their apparent hostility, asking why our mother and father couldn't reconcile their differences and get together again. Subtly, we may have wished it to happen, but realistically, we knew that it wasn't in the realm of possibility. Although we spent all-day Saturdays with our father, rain-or-shine, we were nonetheless the children of a broken marriage. Accordingly, most of what we knew firsthand about our father came from the Saturday visits: no evenings at home discussing issues of the day; no family dinners or vacations, no social interactions with his friends; no conjugal displays of affection between husband and wife. Consequently, our knowledge of our father was quite limited. And, most probably, vice versa; my father's knowledge of his sons was based only on what he gleaned during these weekly one-day visits.

Returning to this initial diary entry: as my father was en route from Denver to Colorado Springs for his weekly visit he noted that "Going to the Springs, the bright, light green leaves of the aspen on the hillside made an attractive contrast with the dark pines and spruces. After I had turned off the main highway into the city, a feeling of sadness came over me which I fear lasted for some time after I arrived at the house. I've forgotten why. I think Emerson's poem 'Good-bye: Thou art not my friend, and I'm not thine,' etc.

"When our day was over, I left the boys at the house before Margie got back and began the drive back to Denver as the sun began to set. The sunset was brilliant. For a while there was one of those scenes I enjoy so much: sun shining onto a splotch of cloud which gets bright around the edges. Later one of the narrow horizontal clouds over a mountain peak became a bright, shining golden."

And so the diary began: upbeat, in a major key, speaking musically. By the second entry, however, the diary took on what was to become its more characteristic minor key signature, with downbeat musings about one thing or another: social and cultural norms, stressful interactions with other people; money owed to his psychiatrist Dr. Walker; editors' rejections; languishing law practice. Many passages narrated mundane concerns, but I read them carefully hoping that they might ultimately provide insights, however subtle, into my father. As in this initial entry: "My morale was low today. I have no new writing project. This feeling of disapprobation naturally is strongest in me when I have received a rejection notice from a publisher; when there has been no call upon me for my legal services. I did have one call today. But for that, my morale probably would be even lower. Were my practice to show some notable improvement, my cold disapproval of the world of skinflints, chiselers, robbers and moochers would probably undergo a change. I'm going for a walk. I need to get out of this firetrap."

The diary seemed on the verge of telling a story, a somewhat gloomy story. Hypnotically, I read further. By and large, it held my attention, beyond my usual span which is customarily interrupted by occasional cat naps. Indeed, surprisingly, I rarely nodded off or found spurious reasons for setting the diary aside. Nonetheless, progress was slow, and the stack of notebooks seldom seemed to change in height. I had the time to read them all, but it would be slow going.

Characteristically, the diary entries narrated events and emotions in my father's daily life. He told about legal articles and short stories he had written. He told about disillusion with the law and his ultimate rejection of it as a profession. He told about his romance with Suzanne, his reluctance to marry her until he was more secure financially. He told about his sons maturing into young men bound for college. He told about his repudiation of mercenary *bourgeois* values, about his solace in nature, free of social constraints. But, he never told about the traumas of war.

He narrated dreams as well. He told about his daytime dreams, his daydreams of recognition as a writer, financial success as a lawyer, being a good father of two sons, as well as thoughts, images, and sensations occurring during sleep. He told about his nighttime dreams, stories from the unconscious mind. He dreamt about his parents, strangers, German soldiers, thieving rats, coiled snakes, woodpeckers and other fantasies of the sleeping mind.

Also characteristically, my father analyzed these narratives of daytime experiences and nighttime dreams. The daytime experiences usually involved interactions with colleagues or clients at work. To my disappointment, Suzanne was not an exception. My father would analyze dialogues, often with pejorative assessments of some perceived innuendo or banality. I did not enjoy reading entries like these; they made me uneasy, perhaps because they portrayed my father as an angry, unhappy man with few, if any, friends that he could admire. The nighttime experiences involved dreams, many dreams. In some entries, he would document two, three, even more dreams from the previous night. My father would scrutinize them, looking for symbolic meanings of events and individuals. Unlike the daytime experiences, I enjoyed reading about the nighttime dreams. Often, they were nonsensical, like dreams sometimes are. But, I assumed that they manifested my father's subconscious attempts to make sense of his past and present daytime experiences.

As I read more and more of the diary, I found myself asking "Who is this man in the diary? I don't recognize him. He appears as a stranger, so unlike the father I knew." To reconcile these two images of my father, the unknown and the known, I realized that I had to understand his mental illness far better than I did. So, like a detective, I pored over the diary entries, his narratives, his analyses, seeking clues to the etiology of this disease. In early August, 1956, about three months into the diary, I came across what might be the first noteworthy clue, an indirect reference to his wartime experiences. My father referred in passing to a planned Ellis Worth story, *A Case for Commitment*, which would chronicle a German military tribunal. Intrigued, I set the diary aside, found the manuscript and read it forthwith.

The Gap

The story, now published, was about a "little known court case during the Dachau trials."[2] Worth elaborates: "When I say little-known, I mean less well-known to most people than the famous Nuremburg trials, but I knew a lot, in fact too much, about them. You see, I had been there—Dachau, I mean—during my years in the army as a member of the Judge Advocate General's Corps."

In his diary, my father summarizes this story about a military tribunal set in Dachau as a former Nazi physician Dr. Franz Lieber is on trial for rejecting Nazi ideology. The plot involves interrogation of a witness by a prosecuting attorney before a sometimes-daydreaming judge. The witness, a psychiatrist, asserts that Dr. Lieber is insane, beset by delusions, and should be committed to a hospital for the mentally incompetent. The delusionary symptoms of Dr. Lieber are unclear. "Perhaps he has a split personality, feelings of guilt, worthlessness, inferiority. He fancies people are accusing him of being a communist and of telling his patients that they are not dependent upon property acquisition for acceptability in the sight of God. He has fired his secretary, has his recorded dictation typed by a public stenographer, only one copy. Then he takes a photo of the original for copies.

"Good grief. Writing the above has given me a headache and almost made me vomit. I'll have to change the subject."

Assuming that the story has a basis in reality (again, "write what you know"), I hypothesized readily that my father had been a prosecuting attorney assigned by the JAG Corps during the preliminary phases of the

---

[2] Ibid. Pp. 90-100.

first Dachau trial, the one involving medical atrocities. The story's setting (the Dachau concentration camp), the trial (military), the defendant (a physician): all could derive directly from my father's wartime experiences. I may have exceeded the limits of factual inference, but the hypothesis made sense to me. It conforms to what I know and what the story implies. Moreover, it bridges the gap between normality and insanity. It places my father in a setting certainly conducive to trauma.

Nonetheless, prudence bred by years of professional training reined in my enthusiasm for this hastily constructed hypothetical explanation of my father's mental illness. Yes, it may be true. But, I required more factual evidence before I could rule out other potential explanations, such as childhood trauma. Realistically, the hypothesis remained just that: a hypothesis, a starting point for further investigation.

My father's memories of Dachau in this context elicited my own memories of Dachau. As a young man, long before I had read this story and the diary, I worked as a medical researcher in Munich for a number of years. I lived in an apartment one block from Dachauer Strasse, the main thoroughfare between downtown Munich and Dachau, not far from the infamous concentration camp. I visited the camp several times, usually with curious guests from out-of-town. Although the German government had sanitized the grounds and buildings, the site still evoked an unsettling chill. When I asked my older German neighbors and colleagues whether they knew what was transpiring at the camp during the war, they all denied any knowledge, any suspicions of the atrocities being committed. End of conversation. As far as they were concerned, that was history and just as well forgotten.

The Gap

My memories of Munich and Dachau drifted further to a time when a German colleague told me that: "Germany executed six million Jews during World War II, and they should have executed the remaining six million while they were at it." Shocked, I asked "How can you say such a thing?" He replied that: "They were enemies of the State. How could the German government function with so many enemies of the State?" There was no point in arguing, so I simply walked away.

Oh, I would have liked to discuss these unsettling experiences with my father, but he was dead by then. So, I never had the opportunity to bring up memories of Dachau and Bavaria—his or mine—with him. He never mentioned his to me when he was alive, and he had died soon after I moved to Munich. My only communication with him after moving to Munich was a short note telling him about my new address and so forth and a coffee-table picture book of the city and its surroundings. Besides the stunning views of Munich set against the Bavarian Alps, this book also had several full-page photographs of the Dachau concentration camp: the gas chambers, prisoners in striped pajamas lying in their tiny bunks, emaciated bodies stacked in piles awaiting cremation. My father died from a massive heart attack with that book in his hand. I sometimes question whether stressful memories evoked by these gruesome pictures resonated with his memories of Dachau, triggering a stress-related heart attack. This remains an insoluble question.

I might add that growing up in Colorado Springs, I had limited contact with Jews. Neither my father nor mother spoke about Jews to any extent. But, the Unitarian church usually had readings from Jewish scholars during the Sunday morning service, which introduced me to the Torah, Spinoza, and so forth. My first real introduction to Jews was at Harvard. For the first time, I saw Orthodox Jews in their traditional garb, heard about Jewish customs such as the Bar Mitzvah, and encountered their tightly knit social order. On several occasions, a Jewish student turned me down when I asked her for a date: "My parents don't want me dating a goy [a non-Jew]." Off campus, in Boston and New York, I also saw physical remnants of the concentration camps: identification numerals tattooed on the forearms of former occupants. These chilling tattoos brought to life the atrocities of Nazi Germany.

Well, I digress from the topic at hand, learning about my father when he was alive. As I resumed my quest, I realized that the diary and the Ellis Worth stories interlace fact and fiction. I found it difficult to trace the exact boundary between the two accounts, between fact and fiction. I assume that the diary entries have a basis in fact, not in fiction. Surely, the stories have a basis in my father's factual real-life experiences, but just as surely the author, Ellis Worth, has used poetic license to embroider the tales. Thus, the diary and the stories present two related versions of the facts—the real facts and the fictional facts. I faced a perplexing conundrum: do the stories impart factual or fictional information?

Although I couldn't discern the exact boundary between fiction and fact in either *The Eldon Jones Sextet* or *A Case for Commitment*, I realized that the stories were recognizably close to the boundary. Thus, I began to coordinate my reading of the stories with my reading of the diary; I would read a story whenever the diary first referred to it. As I discovered, a few stories proved to be as insightful as these first two, and many of them added subtle details to the composite image of my father. *Vice versa*, the diary often added clarifying details to the story.

Several weeks after the initial entry, my father wrote a cursory entry about the war's impact on his mental health in a comment about the cause of his illness: "the war had something to do with it; so did other things." What other things? He didn't say, but he alluded to childhood experiences: not just the sudden death of his father but verbal rebukes even earlier in childhood.

Following that lead, I began to concentrate on his account of childhood experiences, searching for those that might have provoked trauma. The challenge was to sort out those that caused transitory "hurt feelings" from those that induced serious mental disturbance later in life. It didn't take long to realize the difficulty of this task. Not far into the diary, my father wrote that: "One of the remarks father used to make was 'be useful as well as ornamental.' Probably nothing he ever said to me cut me, wounded me, so much as that. It meant I don't think much of you as you are. You will have to earn acceptance by being useful, i.e. by this or that activity called work. Also much was condemned besides me—the ornamental and the beautiful. Thus those things which I prized most highly were relegated to the category of junk by that injunction. My own tendency is to lump non-ornamental, the non-beautiful, the useful into the category of junk. I do this by labeling it pseudo useful, useful for a purpose, perhaps, but one not presented by existing circumstances. Therefore, useful for nothing."

Clearly, my father suffered from verbal wounds inflicted in childhood, wounds of apparent rejection. As in this example, wounds inflicted by a father cajoling his son to perform chores. Perhaps innocuous peccadillos were misinterpreted, "overblown," by a hypersensitive child. Perhaps malicious invectives were interpreted accurately by a precocious child. No matter, they may have caused emotional damage that persisted into adulthood, damage that required psychiatric attention for years after his acute breakdown in 1949. This much I inferred from a subsequent diary entry: "In thinking about the long interlude before my next meeting with [my psychiatrist] Dr. Walker, it occurred to me that he accepts me as I really am without disapproval. Why shouldn't he? Why shouldn't everyone? Why do some cramped and crotchety paragons of good taste insist that everyone not similarly embalmed is a danger to the body politic? Well, what if they do. I'll put a firecracker in the seat of their pants."

As I read these initial entries, I began to appreciate the intensely personal nature of a diary. In his diary, my father exposes his private realm, his mind's inner sanctum, his soul—regions inaccessible to me except by reading the diary. A momentary doubt coursed through my mind. Am I violating my father's sanctity by reading his diary, by sharing it publicly? Am I trespassing where I don't belong? No; without sound evidence, I surmised that my father left the diary for others to read posthumously. Right or wrong, I shall proceed.

The Double

The early entries in my father's diary introduced a concept that became more prevalent during the next two years: duality. My father perceived two images of himself, two separate beings. He had a double. It was not a look-alike twin, a *Doppelgänger*, or some person with a similar outlook on life. In fact, the double was just the opposite; it was an individual—or, in one case, an animal—representing an alternative aspect of my father. He and his double had opposing viewpoints of society, opposing relationships with people, opposing standards of behavior. And, not surprisingly, the existence of a double was invisible, unknown, to me.

I suspected a priori that the perception of a double related in some way to my father's mental illness. Ellis Worth provided the primary clue to this suspicion in the *Eldon Jones Sextet* when he recounted the events leading to his admission to the mental hospital at Perry Point. After seeing a performance of Shakespeare's *The Tempest*, Eldon Jones likened himself to the swarthy monster-like character Caliban, who possessed two different personalities. On the one hand, he was a savage, grotesque creature of the earth, but, on the other hand, he was also a noble, sensitive native of his island, which he described in beautiful imagery. The next day, Eldon insisted to his psychiatrist that he was, indeed, Caliban. At that point, the psychiatrist committed him to the mental hospital.

Ten years later, in the diary, my father acknowledged his absorption in duality and its adverse relation to his mental illness. "The idea of duality has occurred to me several times lately. What does it mean? The idea of being a one-eyed Cronos has come to me once in a dream. If there is an unhealthy duality in my thinking and feeling, what is it? I know that I try to shut my eyes to my own strength.

"Is this the key? As an infant, I was given the choice: be yourself and forfeit parental approval and starve; or be phony, be as your parents want (for their benefit, not yours) accept the stultifying group standards, and you will be approved and know no want. Well, I couldn't kill my own nature, but I could conceal it. Conceal it I did. I couldn't become a real phony, but I could pretend to be as my parents insisted and to accept group standards no matter how phony they were or seemed to be. What a complex train of evils such an adjustment hauls with it. The feeling of the inferiority and worthlessness of one's own nature; the shock of being unloved in one's own right, as one is basically; the anxiety over the effectiveness of the masquerade; the guilt over the pretense.

"My early experience with my parents convinced me of the asininity of the accepted, authoritative standards of behavior and deportment. Father's religion of appearances left me cold. Mother's yen to manipulate people for her benefit left me colder. So, what others have to teach me is no better than the ill-digested hay cast off by horses. I will learn what they teach, keep it in a separate compartment of my mind so as not to be contaminated by it, and as the occasion demands, I will parrot it to please others and benefit myself.

"Mother was viewed as a predator and parasite, just the opposite of what a mother should be. Hence I have felt like stealing from the predator and preying on the parasite. Father wished to dictate the standards which I should observe and follow. I have wished to dictate to him. I have been inclined to accept the standards they exemplified and then turn them against them—a way of showing the falsity of such standards, an indirect complaint.

"So here I am: on the one side is the surface Everett E. Smith of learning, ethics, and relation to such significant attributes of people as dictated by mores and manners of the time and place, and on the other side is the deeper Everett E. Smith of feeling, experience, and relation to people. In the surface Everett E. Smith, I reacted to the guy's rank in the army, his money in the bank, his standing in the community, his knowledge of the earth and of the world. The deeper Everett E. Smith came no closer to relating to people as they were or to people as they are. The deeper reaction was toward this woman as if she were mother and toward this man as if he were father."

There, in a nutshell, my father identifies his dual nature, the two sides of Everett E. Smith. That is, the two alternative personalities of Everett E. Smith. On the surface side, he is an engaged member of society—interacting insincerely with colleagues on a professional and social basis. But, on the deeper side, not visible on the surface, he is a tormented critic of society—interacting venomously with colleagues as he casts them in the roles of father or mother. Looking back, I now realize that my father indeed had a double: one known only to him and perhaps Dr. Walker and the other known to his children, his colleagues, society as a whole.

In my father's words: "My two worlds are two me's. There is a duality: my own nature concealed from view and the phony front visible for others to see: my true self and my double. Of course, I had this same thought before, but the idea came to me with more force this last time, and with certain further realizations. The natural world, the natural me, is something I rejected after father's death as carrying with it a horrifying destructiveness—my father's untimely death. After that, I endeavored to be as cultured, civil, and tractable as possible, obedient to my mother's will and the social dictates of convention, law, and so forth. Now, the process of psychotherapy has involved the wish to recall as precious what I previously had rejected in my sorrow and mortification. What I then embraced with such pitiable desperation I have been disgorging and rejecting lately, to-wit, the civilized, regularized, routine, conventional, and legal.

"What I need to do now is bring the two worlds, the two me's, into focus and evaluate them. Evaluation does not mean rejection necessarily. Isn't there a place in my life for both: the natural, spontaneous, Godlike; and the civilized, socially approved, conventional? Not through the lens of psychotherapy. I am a witness to a conflict between the real me and my doublet, a witness, that is to say, to the civil war between the natural, spontaneous, real, me and, in opposition, the tractable, domesticated, civilized, double. When the former shall have been completely victorious, it will be compassionate to the loser. The witness will jump down from the fence when there is no longer any need for a vantage point of safety from which to observe. The compassionate human will bind the wounds of the domestic animal."

The Double

My father struggled to resolve this duality by casting off one of his two doubles. But which double to abandon proved to be a difficult decision for him to make, certainly more difficult than I would have imagined given his continual fulminations against social convention and bourgeois values. He struggled with indecision. Indeed, he compared himself to Buridan's ass: paralyzed by its inability to decide which equally-distant bale of hay to choose, the donkey starves to death.

Fortunately, Dr. Walker provided soothing comfort as my father worked through this dilemma. Indeed, his gentle hand guided my father along this pathway of troubled indecision. As my father noted: "My relation to Dr. Walker at the present time is this. I need to express my opinions, my convictions, in brief myself, to someone who accepts and approves of me and does not ask me to meet certain standards as a condition of approval. From repeated insistence on myself without disapproval or closure, I gain confidence that I am worthy just as I am. What I need is faith in myself, my own worthiness. With that, I may trust others more. Dr. Walker asks nothing of me but money. He does not say I shall judge whether you are intelligent or courageous or put money above yourself or fame. He is not concerned to judge. I do not have to observe myself so that I can judge when I fall short or when I exceed the mark or stray."

Vicariously, I, too, felt Dr. Walker's soothing hand as I picked my way through these diary entries. They constituted "heavy reading," to say the least: sentences packed with ravaging emotion, with meaning, with intensive introspection, with revelation. The occasional mention of Dr. Walker provided fleeting relief from the dense heaviness of my father's narrative. He lightened the load.

I had a premonition of further heavy reading in the ensuing diary entries. They had become challenging, strenuous to understand, unenjoyably intense. I was not reading about the father I knew and loved but about a stranger, no more familiar to me than a deranged vagrant huddled in the dark corners of an alleyway. To lighten the emotional load imposed by these diary entries, I thought about skipping forward several years, hoping to pick up the storyline during a more stable period in his life. But, I demurred. With their ranting heaviness, the diary entries thrust forward the hidden story of my father's illness; they bear direct testimony of his mental tumult. I had to continue with them.

Ultimately, as my father inched towards a decision about which double to cast aside, his attention in the diary turned to his profession as a lawyer. In its formality, this professional role manifested the alternative aspect of his personality, the double that he found more and more repugnant. In a series of vituperative diary entries, my father renounced the practice of law and the social structure embedding it. He likened the practice of law to a horrible master that must be overcome. "My difficulty in being a lawyer in the past has been the assumption that law is master; that my practice is my master, a master so horrible I am justified in killing it. A God so vicious I am not bound to worship. From such an evil captivity I am entitled to liberate myself. An alter so tainted and besmirched is deserving of destruction. Finally, the master is weak and of unsound mind. This has been my litany as I have endeavored to steel myself for the final, mighty, mental effort to free myself."

Thus, the fateful decision had been made. Although he didn't explicitly make the linkage between his practice of law and his double—this master which was slavishly based on sacrificial allegiance to an abhorrent society—I inferred that he equated the two and that renunciation of the law equated to renunciation of this double, renunciation of this dreadful alter ego. "I am beginning to get used to the fact that my destined role is no longer that of servant and sacrifice to this master. It is considerably more honorable. While in the past I have seen the imperfection of legal processes, I have been seeing them as flaws in the master, flaws which somebody else should be doing something about. I was looking for someone else to liberate me from the wicked master to become my new master."

By deciding to cast off the double manifest as a lawyer, my father concluded that his future lay in the natural, the spontaneous world. "The conclusion that I am not bound to sacrifice myself for a miserable society and culture and do not owe allegiance to any unworthy cause or person is one which I have been reluctant to draw. The inescapable necessity for the conclusion had to be established in my mind by the overpowering unworthiness of society: the ugliness of its materialism; the irrationality of its goals; the falsity of its organized and taught truths; the phoniness of its strengths. Only after I had recorded the horror of my God could I free myself from his dominion over me."

The decision had been made, but this should not imply that my father stopped analyzing the etiology of his crippling post-traumatic duality. The demon—the dreaded double—had been subdued but not expunged, for it occasionally reemerged into his consciousness. On those occasions, my father would delve into specific aspects of his childhood that might have caused this reemergence. Fortunately, these occurrences became less frequent as time passed, but they never disappeared completely.

Before reading these diary entries, I thought naively that I understood the concept of a double. After all, I had read *The Strange Case of Dr. Jekyll and Mr. Hyde*, *The Secret Sharer*, and several other stories about a man and his double. Not to mention such iconic doubles as Superman and Clark Kent or Batman and Bruce Wayne. But, I had no personal experience with the construct of duality described by my father; it was foreign to me. I questioned whether I am an outlier. Is it normal to have a double? To answer this question, out of curiosity I did a quick internet search of "doubles." Nowhere did I find an answer to the question of normality. But, according to one encyclopedic article on the psychological meaning of doubles, commonly they represent an alter ego projecting into the real world from the subconscious. In Freudian terms, the fantasy creation of the double follows the same principles found in personality splits characteristic of paranoid schizophrenia. That phrase readily caught my attention, because on numerous occasions my mother described my father's acute mental illness as paranoid schizophrenia. By inference, my father's double may be a remnant symptom of his illness, paranoid schizophrenia.

How does a father conceal remnants of paranoid schizophrenia (if that is what he had) from his sons with whom he spends every Saturday playing, chatting, sharing hours together? Once again, I wandered through the vault of memories from my youth, seeking clues to this mystery. There were none. Oh, sure; I remember occasional moments of seemingly irrational irritation at someone such as a disrespectful waiter or inattentive driver, but these certainly didn't rise to the level of clinical abnormality, at least as far as I know. I remember my own naiveté at that age—a young teenager—and question now, as an adult, whether I should even be expected to have recognized abnormal paranoid schizophrenic behavior in my own father. Perhaps, but I didn't. He wasn't overtly "crazy"; he didn't converse out loud with an imaginary person, display aggression towards others, walk funny, or exhibit other behavior that a teenager might interpret as signs of lunacy.

These reflections on improbable "craziness" drew me back to a core question: did the diary actually transcribe my father's factual thoughts? Perhaps the diary was all fiction, an epic story about a tragic character and his double. Not likely; many of the details resembled reality as I remembered it or my mother described it. But fictional stories often have roots in reality. Lacking a simple answer to this core question, I continued to read the diary, learning more about the protagonist: ostensibly my father himself but from my viewpoint an unreal representation, a verisimilitude, of the father I knew.

During this time period, my father continued to write non-fictional legal articles and as Ellis Worth continued to write fictional short stories. My father was modestly successful with the former, as several law reviews published his legal analyses. And, he continued to receive invitations to speak on the law at various venues in the Denver region. In contrast, Ellis Worth was less successful as a writer of fiction. He sent short stories to one literary magazine after another, and their editors usually rejected them with few comments.

In one of these short stories, Ellis Worth wrote about my father's double, aptly titled *My Father's Double*.[3] This poignant tale tells about a young boy who lost his father during the Korean War and his ersatz father, a fantasy double of his imagination whom he called Grandpa. Ellis Worth accentuates duality by portraying the double with attributes quite unlike those of the deceased father. Father seldom drank alcohol, Grandpa often drinks too much; father wore a uniform and a cap, Grandpa wore a gunny sack and no cap. *In toto*, the two fathers were opposites. Whether real or imaginary, the double manifests the duality that my father wrote about in the diary entries of this time period: conforming to society's norms versus following nature's spontaneous impulses.

Amidst this emotional turmoil, my father enrolled in the Bread Loaf writers' conference held in August, 1957, at Middlebury College in Vermont, hoping to improve his fortunes as a short-story writer. I remember his excitement about this first vacation since moving to Colorado. He would be in the company of other aspiring writers like himself, of renowned poets like Robert Frost, of literati like Richard Wilbur and John Ciardi, all who presumably would accept him as a colleague. But, in the diary he tempered this excitement with apprehension. He would be alone, on his own for a month, without emotional support from the army, Suzanne, or Dr. Walker. In that sense, my father viewed this adventure as a test of his ability to overcome the insecurity inherent in his mental illness. This was an unsettling prospect.

---

[3] Ibid. Pp. 191-194.

The Double

While contemplating this trip back East, my father's thoughts turned unexpectedly to the duality — the doubles — represented by his two parents. I had not expected this turn of attention to both parents in the context of his trip back East, but he conjured up a linkage between the two: a linkage that thrust upon him once again the need to make a decision about which double to cast aside, the one manifest as his father or the one manifest as his mother. I thought any decision about doubles had been made when my father cast off the double represented by his career as a lawyer. But, I now realized that my father's disruptive concept of duality existed in several dimensions. It was a multifarious disruption not easily overcome by a single effort.

Accordingly, he found himself confronted by another choice to make. "The prospect of going on a journey has been deeply unsettling. The trip represents, I suspect, a choice between two alternative ways of life. It is an extension of my childhood's painful struggle to choose between two parents, neither of whom seemed to offer me much chance for growth, life, or freedom. When father died, I may have felt that events had dictated my choice. I chose to align myself with the one who had been removed from the scene. Maybe, in fact, he had left abruptly because of my delay in choosing him."

Whoa. My father is now tracing the existence of his double back to his father's death, which he attributed to his own, childish rebelliousness. He was responsible for his father's death! In response to that perceived guilt, my father suppressed his rebellious free-spirit and became an obedient, well-mannered ("tractable, domesticated, civilized" in his words) child, seeking approval from his mother and, later in life, his colleagues.

There they are: the concealed double and the visible double; my father's two personalities. "Now, events are not dictating a choice. I have to make it on my own. This is painful, or at least unsettling, because of its painful background." And, so he decided: choose father and cast off mother.

Again, a decision was made between the two doubles, but not without introspective analysis of its provenance. "In going east on my vacation, I choose father, freedom, masculinity. This is so because of the father figures I will see in Washington, and because Washington is the father of this country. Washington is also where I was drafted and assigned another father, in the form of the United States Army. In that regard, the choice of a father figure was made for me by the draft board, with no opportunity for me to object, much less resist the choice. This time, my own father does not appear to be such a bad choice as when he was represented by the army. The army father left me no more freedom than the hovering protection of mother. Indeed, he was nearly as predatory as mother, taking my freedom and giving me food and shelter in return, and doing that with a roughness which made the other deal seem better. I would have preferred mother. I wanted what I couldn't have when father died—a caring, attentive mother—and now in the army I wanted what I couldn't have, my mother.

"I tried to get around the difficulty by marriage. Thus, I married Margie, a substitute for mother. Then in 1943, I had to leave Margie for Texas, preparatory to going overseas. In a sense, circumstances beyond my control dictated I should go with father, the army. Once again, I wanted what I couldn't have. As I never had felt that I qualified for father's approval, I now felt these same old doubts haunting me and causing me grief. Nonetheless, as an obedient soldier, I went to war and lived up to father's standards fully. I was promoted, decorated, et cetera and declared a war hero. I returned to civilian life and to Margie. This was partly choice and partly fate. The nature of the choice was concealed from me. Then my troubles began. Margie became blurred and then reversed her role by being competitive with me. My marriage fell apart several years later.

"My trouble in all this was that I viewed the world as a child. I looked for parents to choose between. Neither looked good until excluded or removed from the scene. There still are vestiges of a childhood choice now. That is why I am restless and faint. I need to get over the childish search for a parent."

Several months later, the concept of duality took human form as strangers representing an alternative aspect of my father's personality. It began in a 1957 diary entry, where my father writes about perceiving his double while dreaming; his double was a man in the unconscious world of sleep. This dream-world double seized my attention, but soon afterward, a real-world double shoved it aside.

Specifically, in early 1958, a real double appeared in the conscious world while my father and Suzanne were in a lamp-repair shop that was cluttered with used lamps in various stages of repair. This real-life double was not a look-alike fraternal twin but a manifestation of my father's alternative personality. He was a young man who came into the store with his hands jammed down in his overcoat pockets. In my father's eyes, the man was intent on robbery, perhaps armed robbery. He describes his reaction to this stranger in a bizarre entry that later became the element of an Ellis Worth story, *The Thinker*.[4] In his description of the real-life double, my father imbues sinister traits that, frankly, stretch my imagination of the person based on events chronicled in the diary entry. But, for my father, his perception of the double was real, very real.

"At the lamp-repair shop I met my double. He was silent and sinister, with his fist clenched in anger. He was possessed of an ominous, concealed, destructive weapon. In a sense, he was me. His supposed rebellion at the strength of cluttered junk was mine. His rebellion at masculinity, supposedly incident to the menial repair of women's damaged properties was mine. His determination to rob the shop, the situation, of its phony strength, its false pretention, was my wish to strip falsehood of its cunning camouflage. The young man was but a soldier in my war against falsehood and hypocrisy.

"Why did my double show himself there? Because the shop was a junk shop, because the owner-operator had been given a buildup by Suzanne at my expense; because there were in this clutter junk lamps such as we used, prized, and cherished in the farm house in which my tender years were passed; because the repairman had spoken of threading new wire through the hollow stem of the lamp, and the symbolism of the remark was easily evident to me; because lamps symbolize artificial illumination.

"I say I have been left cold by conflicts and competition. Ah, but I saw a terrifying conflict and competition at the lamp shop where none existed. It was a conflict of youth and age, of artifice and maturity, of

---

[4] Ibid. Pp. 278-287.

society and individual, of truth and falsehood, of matter and spirit. Previously, I had seen such a conflict in abstraction. Here I saw it in the concrete, but here I saw it where it did not exist.

"How can I say it did not exist? It did exist. I was there. It existed within me. Given all the extraneous factors, they triggered, they kindled what was in me. My double did not know he was my double. I did a little manipulating a little string-pulling on my own.

"Why did I attribute my own angry feeling, my own competitive rancor, my own destructive spirit to another? Because I did not wish to acknowledge that such anti-social, disapproved qualities were part of me? But society approves competition and hostility more than it does cooperation, altruism, and friendship. Because I wanted to do a little manipulating in approved fashion, while at the same time, I disapproved manipulation? Was it a way to get around my own disapproval? No. I don't know why I created my own double.

"This much I do know. My double was bent on robbery. He was not mocking me; he was not accusing me; he was not persecuting me. I was a minor factor in his intended actions. He was going to take actions directed towards others. Perhaps he was accusing and judging others and was about to destroy others in the sense of robbing them of their false front, their mess of pottage.

"Previously, my doubles enacted roles having reference to me. Here, for a change, was a double about to act with reference to others. This is a step toward the realistic perception and evaluation of external realities, toward a healthier interaction of the internal and the external."

The intensity of my father's reaction to the young man in the lamp shop unsettled me, for my father's grip on reality seemed tenuous as he struggled to separate fact from fiction. Assigning the stranger the role as his double, my father overstepped the boundaries of rationality—certainly of rationality as I perceive it. To my knowledge, no robbery occurred; at least my father never mentioned any criminal act by the stranger in his diary. Accordingly, I presume that his reaction was a remnant of his mental illness, akin to dissociative identity disorder, with two personalities in conflict. I presume further that his psychiatrist, Dr. Walker, recognized this disorder and treated it in their talk-therapy sessions.

Coincidentally, my father's difficulty in discerning the discrepancy between fact and fiction, reality and dream, arose in an equally bizarre event documented in the next diary entry. It occurred while my father was moving from one office to another in the same building.

"Today, I moved to my new office down the hall and did so in a trance. I was moving from an office facing the courtyard to one which faces out onto the world, to one which has daylight. During the move, I thought I had two sets of bookshelves made from bricks, though I know well I have but one. With two, though, I would have balancing bookshelves on each side of my desk. That is what I had before in the courtyard office. *A fortiori*, I would now have the same.

"Why insist there were two sets of bookshelves? I posited two theories. First, I guess I thought the bookshelves should flank me like wings, balancing the opposing forces represented by my doubles: a balancing of forces, a warring of equal factions, thesis and antithesis. I expected this to continue. I would hold the balance between them. Second, the bookshelves stood for parents. Could that be possible? At one time, I used to have two parents that I saw as doubles. There was a great change when one of them ceased to exist, but I wanted to wish the situation of two parents back into existence.

"My two theories are dramatically opposite. On the one hand, I insist on a balance of opposing forces, of warring, conflicting tendencies such as I have known for so many years. The old office stood for that old personality. The office itself had but one set of bookshelves, but my old personality, for which the office stood, had the two, balanced, conflicting forces. On the other hand, I insist on two parents. My old office represents that phase of my childhood before father's death. My change of office coincides with a change in my personal life. It can't be good unless there are two parents, symbolized by flanking bookshelves. A variant of this second theory is that I think of the bookshelves as embracing arms. I insist that I am held in the embrace of two arms. This wasn't true of my old office, but now that I am changing offices (read personalities) I insist on being loved. A change in outlook is a wearisome thing unless accompanied by the embrace of loving arms.

"This much I can't doubt. My insistence that there were two sets of bookshelves is an insistence against the known facts of the old situation and something tremendously important. It is the insistence upon something new. I am trying to strike a bargain. I will take a new outlook on life, but I insist, as a condition, that life take a new outlook on me. Forms of affection henceforth must be balanced by the reality of it. The argument is based partly on the assumption that the more things change, the more they remain the same. If there weren't two before, there can't be two now. The present can't hold more than the past. Therefore, I must give two bookshelves (read form and actuality of love) to the past so that I can have them in the present. I do not conceive of handling the present apart from the past. The past is too much with me for that. To the forms of the past, I shall add content so that I shall have both forms and substance now and in the future.

"Shortly after the move, my new office neighbor, Barney, stopped by to welcome me. When I told him about my mistaken belief that I had two bookshelves, he wondered if I was 'all right.' That I resented. He may have feared me a bit. He left without ceremony, fearing that I was suffering a delusion. Why should Barney fear a delusion, a fixed idea, on my part? Because his own safety depends so greatly on the correspondence of his ideas with the consensus, and he sometimes doubts the correspondence. That is to say, in all likelihood, he doubts himself. He durst not doubt others.

"I doubt others. I do it all the time, and profoundly. I have mistrusted them. I scarcely care about one book case or two. There may have been a reason that I disclosed to Barney my subconscious wish to see form and content joined. Barney was the name of Mr. Miller's old horse, the brown one. I remember him well, even as I remember our Old Bell and Stevens' Old Torn. We killed Old Bell, the strawberry roan, the horse I loved, the horse which loved me.

"I may have wanted to see how a well-domesticated human horse acts or, rather reacts, to a display of human unreason. The domesticated animal fears such a revelation, for he has forsaken his own intelligence, his own mind, in favor of the group mind. The group mind is that of a plow horse. The plow horse is disturbed by the glimpse of life without a harness. In harness, he obeys the reins. What if there were no harness, no reins? To act on his own—how horrible.

"I even accentuated the horror for him. I showed him a mind unharnessed and going wrong, going astray, beyond the forced reservation of reason and sense perception. I do just the opposite from Barney. He renounces his own mind. Reason is what others say. Perception should accord with group judgment. The herd determines right reason and correct perception and sound judgment. I, on the other hand, question all herd recipes.

"The unharnessed mind can go astray because of psychological urges, wishes, fears, factors. So, for like reasons, does the group mind go wrong. How much preferable it is to be making mistakes as a free agent than to be aping the errors of others."

My father attributed the perception of two bookshelves to an "unharnessed mind." But, the event did not conform to his friend Barney's sense of normality. It certainly did not conform to mine either; as I read this, he seemed delusional, or stated more bluntly, crazy. However, my father found no harm in this dreamlike version of duality. To him, the two bookshelves represented a synthesis of his past and future relationships with other members of society: my father will pursue his new, more accepting outlook on life but insist on sincerity in return. I have tried to understand the gist of this metaphorical synthesis, the rationale for the two bookshelves. Alas, my harnessed mind simply cannot comprehend the episode without invoking remnants of his mental illness. Regardless, my father's interpretation of it seemed positive—if not totally rational from my perspective.

About two months later, my father's preoccupation with his double reached a climax when he confronted his double in a dream. A young-man in the image of his younger brother Dean plays the role of his double in a sequence of events: in response to pressure from the Treasury Department, the brother (my father's double) intends to sell a house, but my father intercedes to stop the sale. Upon awakening, my father interpreted the dream. "In the dream of last night, my double is going to succumb to the pressure to sell. It is for me, the dominant me, to put a stop to that and to dictate to my double. When I, rather than the herd, dictate to my double, he ceases to be a double. I wish to be rid of it. The meaning of this dream is clear: if I am to be rid of this accursed double, I must dominate it and not be dominated by others.

"My own wish to rid myself of my double, created in the image of brother Dean, resembles homicide. My double is a rival. He pleases others as I do not. Indeed, doubles are created for the purpose of pleasing others. In fact, some people take great pride in their double. It represents the acme of creative power. They have created a double, and, furthermore, they manipulate it and deploy it as they would others. But, my double has not given me such satisfaction. I have felt dependent on him. Only with his aid could I placate, please, and propitiate others. Without an environment of good will, an atmosphere of warmth and friendliness offered by my double, I could not be secure, safe. My double, my own creation, has told me 'It is smarter to receive than to give.' There are rules for living, a hierarchy of established values. Receiving and having rate high. My double has become a Frankenstein. He dominated me and was, in turn, dominated by others because, of course, he had been created to please others. That was his sole excuse for being.

"The average person, if he has an integrated personality at all, owes it to his satisfaction with his double. He is content with it because he worships those who have ordained it as necessary and prescribed it as the source of his achievements, pleasure and satisfactions. To all practical intents and purposes, therefore, the double and the ego are one. But me! Ah, no. I do not worship those who have ordained a double. Had nature wished me to have a double, I would have had one. My creativity is not to be wasted in building and manipulating a double. But even as I objected, I built one and pulled the strings on him. The double and I were not one. I entered a double in the social, conventional rat race reluctantly. The more cleverly the double performed, the more I despised him and his admirers. And, at the same time, the more dependent I was on him.

"In fact, why must I have a double? Why? Am I not all right just as I am? My front-man double has been a great receiver of learning, advice, aid, food, salaries, directions, orders. He pleased others and received benefits. But, I despised the gifts; hated the givers; was un-reconciled to the necessity for dissimilation. If my double is all people care about, I might as well commit suicide. One who is so worthless he needs a double surely is incapable of the creativity to produce a double of any value. I have despised my double, fought with him, labored to rid myself of him. Sometimes the creator is pleased with the creation which pleases others. I, however, wish others to be pleased with nature's creation, that is, me. My hidden 'me' wants to give. The past week or so it has been borne home to me how much others want to receive from me, not necessarily money but attention, notice, care, caresses.

"Now I go back to reverse the old decree. Now I wish to scuttle the double and take my chances with society and the world. Instead of employing a double to go out and round up business, to court society and win its approval and good will, I stay soberly in my office and say 'You court my good will. You follow me. You seek me out. You ask my aid and approval. I have fired my advertising man, my advance agent, my scout.' I have now to count on my own merit, talents, and superiority. I expect my brother lawyers, whether they read forums like Morningstar, slave for employers, or have simple practices to take notice of me, to seek me out. I will be available, like papa, to whosoever wishes my help, advice, advocacy. I go to see Suzanne, to see my boys, to see Dr. Walker. So far as others are concerned, they'll have to come see me. They'll have to call me for lunch, coffee, or what not."

"The die is cast. I have scuttled my double, my propitiatory parade-masked, double, for better or worse." With this declaration, my father casts off his double, rejects it. The decision will not be without consequences. "Without my double to beckon their favor, some people may scorn me, ignore me, shun me. 'Somebody else has taken my place. Somebody else shares your embrace' runs through my mind. Ah, but it is not I who has lost place. It is my accursed double. He promised me the world, this Mephisto, and he gave me but matter. Contentment, satisfaction, happiness were not at his disposal. The sad song shows that I expect the worst, expect others to bask in the sunlight of popular favor while I walk accursed in the by-ways and alleys. But that is a small price to pay for my happiness.

The Double

"I, like France, have had my Revolution. Like France, too, I had my Reign of Terror. Like my second country, I have labored to reconcile the Red and the Black, the redness of the Revolution, Jacobeans, willingness to change even at the cost of disorder; and the blackness of the clerical and judicial garb, of an ordered, authoritarian hierarchy."

As my father might say, "Thus endeth the double. The double is dead." In the diary, this pronouncement occurs with less drama in the beginning of a paragraph as a question: "Why must I have a double? Am I not all right just as I am?" In answering this question, my father destroys his double. This results from a conscious decision, a rational decision. I presume that Dr. Walker helped my father reach this decision through his counseling, although my father never wrote or spoke about conversations along this line. Regardless, this rejection of his double marked a significant turning point in my father's return from the maelstrom of acute mental illness. It was indeed a revolution.

Ironically, I was completely unaware of this revolution. After reading about this momentous event in my father's life in the diary, I scanned my memories but simply could not recall any change in my father's personality during this period; he was a rock of stability, the same father Saturday after Saturday. Understandably, my father never mentioned his accursed double to me. Although I was somewhat precocious, as a young teenager, my father most probably questioned whether I could understand his inner turmoil as he strove to rid himself of the double, the alternate aspect of his personality. And, rightly so. Even as an adult, I struggle to couple this aspect of the father I didn't know with the father I did know.

Moreover, I wonder whether he discussed his double and its overthrow with anybody other than Dr. Walker. This was not a topic to discuss openly, as evidenced by the limited interchange with his colleague Barney about the two bookshelves. Mental illness was, quite simply, a taboo subject in that era, and anybody suspected of having it was often shunned. I queried whether Suzanne knew about my father's double and his struggle to be rid of it. Could she have gleaned the difference in his personality after he cast it aside? I surmise that she did. And, in that regard, she may have been my father's only confidante (other than Dr. Walker).

I must add a caveat: although I was unaware of my father's struggle with his double, I was vaguely aware of his struggle with mental illness in general, past and present, to the extent that both he and my mother spoke about it. This vague awareness kindled a nascent interest in psychiatry that influenced my career decisions for many of my adult years. As an undergraduate, I intended to enter medical school, specializing in psychiatry. Although I was admitted to medical school, I chose to get a Ph.D. instead, specializing in neuroscience. As a postdoctoral fellow, I befriended several distinguished psychotherapists in Munich, learning about their practice. And, as a young medical school faculty member at the University of Wisconsin, I incorporated the emerging principles of psychiatric pharmacology into my teaching curricula. Retrospectively, all of these career decisions undoubtedly relate to my subconscious desire to understand my father.

Desertion

After the double's demise, my father entered a period of introspection as he sought to understand his illness. Metaphorically, he conducted an autopsy. It revealed wounds inflicted in his early childhood that had scabbed over but not healed. Although my father had discussed these wounds in several earlier entries, he examined them in greater depth this time. I got the impression that he was on the verge of resolving the hurts that inflicted these wounds, of relieving the pain.

Desertion quickly emerged as a prominent theme in this autopsy. Indeed, obsession with desertion became a hallmark feature of his diary during summer of 1957 and well into 1958, when he wrote a series of introspective entries about desertion: by his father, by Suzanne, and interestingly by substitute fathers. In almost confession-like style my father recounted delusional schemes to desert ersatz fathers such as Col. Cheever, his commanding officer in the army and Huntington Cairns, his boss at the National Gallery of Art. Like weft through warp, my father wove these schemes of desertion into the fabric of his mental illness. Indeed, the assignment of a "father-role" to other colleagues from my father's past arose in various contexts, sometimes overtly and other times covertly.

Before proceeding, I should say something about Col. Cheever and Huntington Cairns. They played an important role in my father's life.

Like my father, Col. Charles E. Cheever served in the Judge Advocate General's Corps under General Patton during World War II. With the rank of Major, my father reported directly to Col. Cheever. They became close life-long friends. On several occasions, I met Col. Cheever when he visited my father, and, even as a young teenager, I recognized, I sensed their comradely friendship—a friendship bonded by wartime experiences.

Huntington Cairns, a noted lawyer and author, was Secretary-Treasurer and General Counsel of the National Gallery of Art from 1943 to 1965. As Deputy Counsel of the Gallery, my father reported directly to Mr. Cairns after the war. I remember that my father admired Mr. Cairns. He took particular pride in an acknowledgment of his contribution to Mr. Cairn's classic anthology *The Limits of Art*.[5] Despite his admiration of Mr. Cairns, at the cusp of his nervous breakdown my father suffered delusions of abandonment by Mr. Cairns, who had simply gone on vacation in nearby Kitty Hawk, North Carolina. Diary entries chillingly document those delusional attributes of insanity.

The framework for desertion arose gradually. My father set the foundation with an eruptive discourse on sacrifice: a child's sacrifice to please his parents. In his viewpoint, "my anti-materialistic bent, approaching a compulsion, is a way of saying to my parents: 'You say you will let me live if I submit to your training. You aren't letting me live; you aren't giving me life; you are giving me merely the material necessities; you are completely overlooking my emotional needs. Indeed,

---

[5] Huntington Cairns, *The Limits of Art: A Critic's Anthology of Western Literature* (New York: Pantheon, 1948).

putting it to a child that he lives by sufferance is itself a complete absolute denial that there even are such things as emotional necessities.

"To raise a child to be helpless is to sacrifice the child for the benefit of the parents. The child conceives it as his role to be sacrificed and to sacrifice himself for the glory or benefit of the parents. The idea of a sacrificial role may be very strong—so strong and deep as to shape, warp, and govern all. There may be a perennial search for a master, a father, an authority. As a moth seeks the flame which kills, so the child will seek the piratical parent who will steal blood from his own child. It is, he thinks, his role to be the sacrificial lamb.

"This role, though necessary, is not easy. A gifted child imbued with the sacrificial philosophy may find it hard to reconcile his sacrificial fervor with the worthlessness of the father for whom he sacrifices himself. He may wonder if he is offering himself for a good cause, if he, the sacrifice, is not more worthy than the master of the cause.

"Huntington Cairns raises this type of problem for me. Just out of the army, I needed a father to replace Col. Cheever as an authoritarian masculine mentor who had been a superior officer and a father worthy of my sacrifice for his—the army's—benefit. Cairns seemed to fill the bill. He stood for constituted authority, which is to say false artificial strength. So, Cairns became his successor. However, the whole set-up I had at the Gallery spelled trouble from the outset. I joined the Gallery expecting Cairns to be a second Col. Cheever, a strong father. But, he lacked courage and admitted it (for example, fear of riding in a plane). He was devoid of other attributes of masculinity. He thought he possessed the supreme virtue of intelligence. Worst of all, I soon realized he was inferior in that respect; Cairns, was less intelligent than I, and this seemed important, for he prized intelligence above all else, and I was familiar with that kind of estimation. With worth determined by intelligence, I should be dominant. So, why should I be cast in the role of sacrifice?

"Now the dilemma of my life became acute: I was serving an inferior. I was serving one I could destroy. Great Scott! What manner of man was I if I did destroy him, wreaking havoc, wronging family, etc.? I had no choice; I must sacrifice myself. Father's death must have meant that the role of sacrifice was enjoined upon me. I asked myself if my superior intelligence could save me from this unjustifiable sacrificial role, or could it save me only if I destroyed Cairns? Resistance to this injunction would cause the death of others as it had been the death of father. Such destruction is out of the question; I could not repeat that tragic history. As in a play by Victor Hugo, I was now destined to be the slave of Cairns, a mock master not worthy of being my slave; to sacrifice myself for one inferior to me in two well-known components of worth: physical strength and mental strength. Ceasing to serve was hardly optional; I needed the job. Thus, I felt bound to sacrifice myself as I had before, bound to repeat the role of servitor-destroyer. History would repeat itself.

"Then Cairns went away on vacation, and I was left alone as Acting Secretary of the Gallery. With Cairns gone, I felt that I had killed father—had killed Cairns—and was reliving the tragedy of 1920 all over again. I couldn't bear freedom at the cost of being a killer. I went to pieces. My personal history had repeated itself. My mock master was gone, presumably dead. My world was in ruins. I, who was destined for the role of servitor, had to be my own master. And mastery was a fraudulent enterprise with which I had no acquaintance. Only now do I begin to see that my destiny is to be free, no matter what."

This dramatic entry synthesizing my father's perception of relationships with his parents as a child and with colleagues as an adult was an appalling revelation for me. I now realized that he perceived himself as sacrificial in both settings. As a young child he sacrificed his individuality to appease his parents, starting at the earliest age, well before his father's sudden death. Then, as an employee at the National Gallery of Art, he sacrificed his integrity by serving a boss, a weak father figure, whom he considered inferior intellectually. In both sacrificial settings, tragedy struck: his father died, and Cairns went on vacation; first his real father and then his ersatz father deserted him. In his delusional perception, history had repeated itself. The shocking irony broke my father's grip on sanity.

As I read the entry and later wrote this synopsis, I found myself detached from this tragic protagonist. He seemed fictional, no more real than some wretched character from a story by Edgar Allen Poe. But, he was my father! A man I didn't know. To this day, I continue to have difficulty coupling this acutely ill stranger with the father I know. Filial love has effectively blocked that disturbing association.

My father encountered apparent desertion in a very real guise following a dinner party hosted by Suzanne, who lived in the same apartment building. It began when he went into an unexpected, unwarranted rage, insulting all of the guests—Suzanne's female coworkers. I surmise that this bizarre behavior disturbed Suzanne. In fact, about two weeks later, she ostensibly deserted him by moving to a new apartment located several blocks away from her old apartment and my father's apartment. My father mentioned in the diary her inclination to move to another apartment, suggesting that the rationale for the move was to save a few dollars in rent. Money may have been one rationale for the move, but I would not be surprised if Suzanne wanted to put protective distance between her and this man who had just shown troubling signs of mental instability and hostile volatility at her party.

Predictably, Suzanne's departure affected my father; it hurt him emotionally. "Suzanne is on the brink of deciding to leave 1377 Bannock. Let her go. My move into 1377 Bannock where Suzanne lived was to save money. So people may say. It wasn't to be near her, to pursue her. Now, Suzanne is leaving this apartment building to live elsewhere. I told her 'Well, I used to see you when I lived on Birch and you lived here. You won't be as far away on Sherman as I was on Birch. We'll see each other all right.' This is to say 'I don't consider that you're deserting me.' It could be that just as her father left her when he passed away, she expects me to leave, go away, and having been hurt by a departure once, she plans to do the departing herself this time. She'll save herself from hurt and even hurt me as Papa hurt her. This is part of the plan anyway.

"Of course, I could move along with her. But, if she leaves first and I follow to the same building and pay more than I have been paying, then I am activated by feelings higher than 'base respects of thrift.' This would comfort her in her own thinking and would protect her against the slurs of others. Suzanne feels better about her move not being too rational on the grounds she sets forth. This gives me room for speculating and for being hurt if I choose to be hurt. It gives others an opportunity to speculate and to conclude that she is not overcommitted in my direction. She still has some freedom."

Just as predictably, Suzanne's departure evoked ruminations about previous departures in his life: from Cozy Nook [the farm] to Minneapolis, from Minneapolis to Washington, and so forth. "What about mother? I left the farm and mother as soon as I had finished high school. I wanted to leave mother who had left me–left me in neglect. I left Minneapolis, where the university became my substitute mother figure, for Washington–which was again leaving her who had left me. Washington stood for father, and maybe the government took the place of mother. Then the army became father. I sought for another substitute for mother. Margie filled the bill as the university had in Minnesota and the government had in Washington. In each case, I found a mother and then left her, deserted her as mother had deserted me.

"I always found a credible reason for leaving. When I left Cozy Nook, I had an acceptable excuse. I was going away to school. When I left Minnesota I did so with the plausible pretext of advancing my career. I took leave of Margie to go overseas. I had no choice in that matter, since I was under military orders, which tended to conceal that I still blindly wished to leave her as I previously had left Cozy Nook and Minnesota. Ironically, the orders obscured my own desires to leave her so effectively that they were an imperfect cause for leaving Margie; I was denied my free will in that departure.

"In the summer of 1949, Margie left for a vacation in Colorado at the same time that Cairns left for a vacation at Kitty Hawk. I was deserted. I assumed she wished to leave me as mother had done. This was childhood over again, when father had died and mother had overlooked me. How could I leave these two, Margie and Cairns, who had left me? The bastards! What shadow of a basis did I have for leaving them? I was married to the former and on overtly good terms with the latter. Furthermore, I obviously needed my job at the Gallery. I was apparently powerless to retaliate for their desertion. I was caught in a vise. In the grip of this awful vise I alone could be hurt. What could this mean but that I was singularly monstrous and wicked? Ah, I saw an escape with certain merits. I found a way to desert them. As I had left Cozy Nook for Minneapolis and then Minneapolis for Washington, I now departed Silver Spring where Margie and I lived for Perry Point, a hospital for the mentally ill, an insane asylum. Tit for tat. Blow for blow."

Less predictably, these ruminations quickly enveloped cogitations about his troubled search for substitutes to replace his father following his father's death. "What about papa? I had to find a substitute father, a papa like Cairns, for example, whom I could hurt, slay by deserting him. My desire to find a substitute for my father was based on an unfulfilled need of childhood. My wish to hurt papa by deserting him was derived from the hurt caused me when father died and so deserted me.

"But leaving would not be desertion unless my reliability and my capability made my papa dependent upon me, as a child depends on a parent, as I depended on my father. That is, this scheme of life—finding, deserting, slaying—required that I should be able to establish a semblance of superiority. I always had been able to do that, indulging, perhaps, a little wishful thinking now and then. The superiority had to be in the fields where superiority is recognized as valuable: in the area of man's spider web of business, law, letters, etc. So, before deserting papa, I was compelled to make him depend on me. Then I would desert him as father deserted me. I enacted and reenacted this dream of vengeance. First I would find papa and, by effort and ability, reduce him to the state of minority, of dependency. Then I would desert him, just leave arbitrarily. So had father left me, suddenly, without reason or explanation.

"This well-planned scheme fell apart with Cairns, however. When I finally felt sure that he was dependent on me, my child, my inferior, and so deserving of desertion, he went on vacation. He deserted me! Tables turned! I had not counted on that. This time, I lacked all supports. My deep-laid plans of vengeance, my guidelines in life, had given way, gone awry. Now, topsy-turvy, I felt guilty about wanting to desert him, knowing how much father's desertion had hurt me. I became dissatisfied with my plan for dealing with my own hurtful experience by hurting others through desertion. With no ability to find a better solution for redressing my past hurt, I was driven to Perry Point, defenseless.

"Lately, with Dr. Walker's help, I have begun to retrace my steps back to the point at which I began to follow the path of vengeance, finding a papa, reducing him to infantile dependency, deserting him. I repudiated my father for leaving me. In my anguish and sorrow what else could I do? Now I would call him back insofar as that is possible. Wipe the slate clean. Father left physically, yes. But my repudiation was a spiritual separation. Had he died and my reaction been an attempt to assimilate him and that only, the separation would have been less complete. I divided my efforts. I sought to revive father and, at the same time, I repudiated him. I killed him for dying.

"Where do I go from here? I can't bring father back to life. That's for sure. If the terrible hurt is healed, I can cease to feel angry with him. Now is the time for me to play the prodigal father or, rather, the prodigal son. I can welcome back my father's spirit. So can father and I be re-united, by my being father. I now realize that during the past ten years with a psychiatrist's help I have learned how to take father's death as a grievous misfortune.

"All that time, Dr. Walker did not desert me, I did not desert him. Maybe I will go and see him again after the first of the year. But have I learned how to get along without him? By being responsible for myself, by being father? It would be easy for Dr. Walker to point out to me now that I am obsessed with myself, narcissistic, full of self-pity. That self-pity is a morbid sentiment from which I am not free can be admitted. I have cried, but I had cause. Had I but cried more then, there would have been less grief to ferment into self-pity."

Stunned, I read and re-read my father's scheme for retribution until I had it clearly in my mind. I would never have thought that he was capable of such vengeance. But, here it was: the destructive pathway to his nervous breakdown. I repeated the scheme in my mind, hoping to understand his delusional reasoning. As a young boy, my father equated death and desertion; by dying, his father deserted him. As an adult, my father sought vengeance for the death of his father, for desertion by his father. According to his logic, he achieved vengeance by deserting ersatz fathers, which equated to destroying them, killing them. But, he could desert ersatz fathers only if they depended on him, as a child depends on a parent. Therefore, the scheme involved dependence and desertion, in that order. As I pieced together elements of the scheme, I could understand his relationships with Cairns—at least I thought I could. My father found himself in a dominant relationship with Cairns, cast as a parent to a dependent child, respectively. The stage was set for my father to desert Cairns, according to his scheme. Consequently, when Cairns went on vacation, my father perceived this as desertion of him—just as his father had deserted him in childhood. History had repeated itself. My father's distorted mind could not process this irony; he was catapulted into the maelstrom.

This synthesis of childhood experiences and acute mental illness buoyed my hopes of understanding the etiology of my father's disease. It provided encouraging insight into his relationship with men at the time. Now, I wondered if the synthesis might provide insight into my father's relationships with women, with his mother, my mother, and Suzanne. Quite possibly. The answer lay in a continuation of the diary entry.

"Women in general posed a particular problem for me. In the past, apparently, I have doubted my place in their consideration. I have doubted that they gave vent to any real affection, confederation, or regard for me. I suspected that they held themselves in restraint by an act of will. They couldn't be so lacking in feeling naturally. Another feature of my reaction toward women has been my presumption that their lack of feeling toward me was not merely willful restraint but a reserve withheld for another man, a competitor. The woman's relations with others I have tended to regard as desertion. Yet I wished them to maintain some liaison with others, imputed it if it did not exist. Suzanne's arrangement with other men fitted this view of the situation. I forced her attitude toward Olson, the paint man, toward the lamp repairman, etc., to fit my prepared views: they were competitors vying for her attention. These arrangements I pointed to as a basis for my own reserve. In return for their willful restraint, eye for an eye, I have held my real, powerful feelings in check. I have refused to give rein to my passions and emotions. I have held my women off, treated them, as Gladstone did Victoria, like government departments. I have not considered my role as an aggressor who should determine what I wanted and take it. I supposed that my role was that of a suitor. I was to get what I wanted by pleasing the woman, appearing to work her will but secretly planning to work my own on her, to get her involved and then cease my suit without, at the same time, breaking off diplomatic relations.

"With women I have aimed at desertion in fact or spirit but not in form, and this desertion was not, as the desertion of men, to be abrupt, unexplained, or stark. Rather it was the withdrawal of one who has been wronged, hurt, but too much attracted to withdraw physically. I aimed to hurt men by physical desertion but to wound women by spiritual desertion. Always, however, my goal has been to retaliate and destroy. I would leave women in fact while retaining diplomatic relations, but the diplomatic relations would be with a wrongdoer, one who had deserted me in fact but not in form. I expected history to repeat itself, if given an assist. Thus men were to be reduced to children and women were to dally with other men. Toward women, I worked out this unsatisfactory role of passivity, dependence, and reserve. My hostility encompassed resistance but passive resistance to a superior force with decisive issues always avoided. Like a guerilla force, I would retreat, retreat, avoid an open conflict. I would use them but couldn't be counted on as a friend or lover. I would not give them the satisfaction of being dominant or the satisfaction of being subordinate. I would keep them dangling so I could use them, milk them, etc. Here I planned no role or moment of decisive domination, no moment of destruction. The war was one of attrition. There would be sallies from the trenches. I would counter aggressive movements and try to wear out and weary my inimical friend. I would retreat, etc. I would clinch to prevent an open exchange of blows, an open airing of views and elations. I took it for granted the relationship would be unsatisfactory for me. I tried to make it equally for the other. From a woman I had learned dependence. She had thought the lesson would serve her purpose. I would accept the lesson but thwart her purpose. I would, in addition, make her dependent, insecure, dissatisfied. I would obscure my dependence, obscure the basis of our relation, confuse, thwart, frustrate. I would seek permanence in this murky relationship.

"In general, my relation to women has been based on accepting them, a relation with them, in default of a more satisfying relation with men. *Faute de grêve, ou mange de mêles.* Suzanne, who puts that face on things whether it belongs or not, was not far wrong. Women merely fill in a gap caused by some terrific disappointment. I never hope for much from them. The taking, taking, gimme, gimme motif of women was all I knew. I turned to mother after father's death, not of desire but of necessity. What they offered I always regarded merely as bait for a tender trap, jail bait."

To my disillusionment, the heartrending synthesis of childhood experiences and mental illness pertained to women as well as men. Indeed, the scheme was the same, dependence and desertion, and the logic was the same. In my father's logic, his mother deserted him by denying attention and love. In retaliation, he sought destructive vengeance on ersatz mothers: engender dependence and then desert, destroy. He would court women, render them dependent, and then desert them emotionally by withholding affection. Infidelity, whether real or imputed, was central to this scheme. It provided the rationale for my father's "spiritual desertion." Of course, this scheme precluded meaningfully close relations with women, although I infer that it did not deter his sexual relations.

Suzanne was seemingly immune to my father's quest for vengeance. Although he seldom referred to her in that context, repeatedly he asserted his dominance and indifference to their relationship, indifference tantamount to desertion by attrition. At least, that is what he wrote in the diary. From my viewpoint, however, he depended on her as much as she depended on him, and their mutual dependence did not fit smoothly into my father's scheme for vengeance. In that sense, Suzanne played a unique role in my father's life.

I could not assess whether my mother was immune, for she deserted my father shortly after his nervous breakdown and hospitalization. She fled this unstable man with my brother and me to her parents in Colorado Springs. On rare occasions, my mother spoke about his instability during that period of time. She claimed that he had threatened to harm her and to kill his children — my brother and me — which, of course, frightened her into fleeing for our safety. I remember being pulled abruptly out of a kindergarten class, going back home to pack clothes, parting with favorite toys, et cetera, and boarding a train headed to the safety of her family more than 1600 miles to the west. My mother's fear for our safety in the presence of our father persisted for many years, certainly until my brother and I were in our late teens. My father seldom spoke about my mother's flight to Colorado Springs, but when he did it was always pejorative: for example, "she fled back to Daddy;" "she took you boys and ran"; and so forth.

These diary entries about the scheme for vengeance portray a stark silhouette of my father, a dark image that I had not seen before. Despite my mother's admonitory comments, I saw him as a bright, caring father, not as a shadowy man who sought to injure others — men and women. Naturally, I found this revelation disturbing. I wondered: Was I naïvely blind to this darkness? Did my father camouflage it beyond a child's recognition? I could not answer these questions immediately, and with time, I became less inclined to seek answers, less disturbed by this dark image of my father, as I began to doubt that many of these dark traits were expressed behaviorally. They were confined to words written confidentially in the diary. Introspectively, I also began to wonder if I, too, have harbored dark thoughts invisible to others. Dark thoughts that might startle my own children. Of course I have; presumably everybody has phantasies that they seldom enact. Perhaps my father's thoughts, his scheme of desertion, were simply normal parts of human nature. I certainly preferred that rationalization.

As I pondered the scheme, the logic fascinated me. Structurally, it was sound. It had the elements of a well-reasoned argument: premise (desertion equals death), inference (dependence empowers desertion), and conclusion (desertion equals vengeance). Moreover, the rationale fascinated me. My father sought vengeance, retribution for his father's death. The quest to avenge a father's death is not an unreasonable quest of a crazed villain, for it appears time and time again in human history. In that respect, the logic and rationale for my father's behavior lay within the boundaries of reason. However, the targets of my father's vengeance were unreasonable: ersatz fathers and mothers embodied in bosses, colleagues, girlfriends. In that respect, he crossed the boundaries of reason. He was undeniably ill but not disastrously so.

Pedantic logic aside, this scheme coupled my father's illness to the trauma of his childhood experiences. Was I wrong, therefore, in attributing the etiology of his nervous breakdown to trauma inflicted by wartime experiences? They had seemed so compelling: the Siege of Bastogne, the Dachau trials. But, my father mentions only the emotional hurts inflected by his dysfunctional childhood in the context of his scheme for vengeance, with no mention of the war. If that was my father's explanation of his mental illness, I had little authority to question that etiology. Nonetheless, I felt vaguely dissatisfied with this conclusion. Surely, the war must have played a role. But why wouldn't my father consider it? I was confused and certainly not yet prepared to dismiss this possibility.

Coincidentally, at about this time, Ellis Worth wrote a story about a man's childhood in *My Second Childhood* that added to my confusion about the factors causing his illness. Events in the protagonist's life resemble those in my father's life. Like my father in his diary, the protagonist laments the loss of his father and the inattentiveness of his widowed mother. Moreover, Ellis Worth tells of the man's nervous breakdown after returning from the war and subsequent shock treatment in the hospital. The similarities between the protagonist and my father certainly suggest that this story has an autobiographical core. Indeed, the similarities warrant retelling the tale.

****

My Second Childhood

In my office during the day, I meet the finest people in the world. I depend on them for a living, and I wouldn't think for a minute of complaining. But they all have troubles—a world of troubles. Or they expect to have troubles as soon as they've shuffled off, unless I draw a will dividing their property between a baker's dozen of fifth cousins and specifically providing, mind you, that nothing whatever is to go to Uncle Sam. They've made ample provisions for Uncle in their lifetime what with income taxes and all. I understand that.

When I have heard more than the daily quota of woes, worth scarcely a variation on the theme, I like to start home, on foot, through the park between the Civic Center and the Capital Grounds. The walk is relaxing in itself. Besides that, the park is the favorite refuge not only of myself but of many others who tarry there to appreciate the scenery, to enjoy the late-afternoon sunshine and maybe even to regain their faith in human nature. The plain, ordinary folks who comprise this tiny area's shifting, variable population always are a balm to my spirit, if for no other reason than that they appear serenely unconscious of the agonies of the income-tax bite, the insidious threat of creeping socialism, the horrifying dangers of galloping inflation, and the mockery of those grasping hands of the unknown fifth cousins at Ottumwa.

There may be some risks in casual, offhand conversations with strangers, as my wife is continually warning me. However, I am convinced, especially since yesterday, that the risks are worth taking. It is really because of what happened then that I'm telling all this, for the experiences related to me by my park-bench neighbor have made an impression I'm not likely to forget.

Here, as simply as it was given to me, and omitting only the preliminaries, is the story I hear from the lips of our mutual friend. I wish I could convey some into the man himself, but, alas, I cannot. The story is the man. There was a noticeable strangeness and sweetness in his manner, a solidity in his person, a wild, perhaps poetic frenzy in his eye, to be sure, but such vague impressions scarcely make a description. I fall back on what I have said: the story is the man.

Infancy begins for everyone at birth. Second childhood, however, is a more variable affair. In my case, it came when I was in my thirties. That may sound as if I am claiming to be unusually precocious, but nothing is further from my mind than vainglorious boasting. All I mean is that my first childhood was so unsatisfactory in some respects that I wanted more than anything else to repeat it under more favorable, happier circumstances, and, my fantastic wish came true.

It is not my intention to be more mystifying than necessary. Life is a mysterious, wonderful adventure. One has to take it as it comes; tell about it in his own fashion; and, on occasion, lend a willing, wondering ear

Desertion

to the mysteries of another's life, whether told with much or little art.

For years I had delighted in entertaining people with tales of my boyhood, while they listened with envy and exclaimed "How lucky you were." They were right. I had been showered with blessing. Still, that was but half of the story, for I had been unfortunate in ways which, being human, I had forgotten and didn't mention. But what was buried and forgotten was not dead. It was living and was as vital in a strange way, as the encoffined, temporarily entombed lady, Madeline, in Poe's *Fall of the House of Usher*.

The boyish activities which I recounted to my friends, as I have said, all shared the glistening magic of having taken place in the presence of the smiling face of Mother Nature: the beautiful bloodroots which, beneath the showers and breezes of April, heralded the retreat of winter and the coming of spring; summer's luscious wild strawberries on the hills; the exultant, melodious larks in the meadows; the whimsical flight of the gaily-colored butterflies; the smell of new-mown hay in the noonday sun; the drowsy, evening croaking of frogs in the pasture pond; autumn's bountiful, slow-ripening black currant at the edge of the lake; and winter's hushed wonderland of white.

If and when my intimates asked, I would tell them, as best I could, of my people, my parents; of my hustling, hurrying father, who died when I was nine years old; of Mother, who was so busy churning, washing, keeping house, making meals, mending clothes, tending chickens, weeding the garden, and performing the multitude of other chores which fall to the lot of a farmer's wife (and widow) that she turned over to my oldest sister much, if not most, of the care of the brood of five children. Such recollections were matter-of-fact which I recited slowly, with pauses, being careful that I should get the history straight and do justice to the Fates and, most especially, to my parents, who, undoubtedly had done their best according to their lights and the traditions of the community.

There were, you see, reasons for wanting a second childhood. I can see it clearly now, too. The experience came, however, unannounced, and before I had any idea at all how much it meant, and would mean, to me. It was this way.

After my return from the European war, the doctors said I had a "nervous breakdown," an expression which was Greek to me at the time (and yet remains rather ambiguous). The staff of the hospital decided I should be given insulin shock treatments. Strange as it may seem, the hospitalization in general and the shock treatment in particular were my happier second childhood.

To awaken from a profound sleep and then to be given a sweet, refreshing, strengthening, reviving drink of fruit juice, followed by a hearty, tasty, nourishing breakfast in bed is close to the pinnacle of a child's wishes. The virtually unvarying patient, kind, sympathetic, helpful attitude of the attendants, nurses and doctors, though but dimly sensed and vaguely appreciated then, did make an impression and one which was as permanent as it was new. These things were the essence of my second childhood. There were other details, but these I have named were the heart and soul of my second childhood. My growing up again, complete with "growing pains," is a separate story entirely.

Someone with a keen wit once remarked playfully that youth is so precious that it is a pity it is wasted on children. However that may be, isn't one fortunate at having had his second childhood while he was young enough to enjoy it?

With a smile, the stranger rose to go.

As I was saying at the beginning, listening and dreaming are good enough for me. One isn't proud of being a provincial lawyer, I suppose; but he can be content with it, and the sweetly solemn satisfactions which come along now and then. Many who claim more settle for less, you can be sure.

****

Notably, the Ellis Worth story and my father's diary portray two different versions of a man's recovery from childhood traumas: one sanguine and one gloomy. The story has the protagonist emerging from the hospital as if he had awakened from a "profound sleep" to enjoy a second, presumably happier childhood. The shock therapy had accomplished its purpose. In contrast, the diary entries have my father emerging from the hospital to an antagonistic environment borne of his childhood experiences.

The discrepant accounts beg for resolution. Assumedly, the story is fiction and the diary is nonfiction. More precisely, the storyline in *My Second Childhood* begins on a factual basis — poetic license aside — but ends on a fictional basis, while the diary presumably remains factual throughout. Accordingly, the diary's account must be considered definitive, although (as I have said before) neither my brother nor I was aware of the emotional turmoil documented in the diary. Perhaps the Ellis Worth story projects a wishful outcome, a dreamlike conclusion.

Once again, however, like the diary, the story does not account for wartime experiences. It stages the nervous breakdown after the protagonist's return from the European war but does not imply any causal relationship between the two events. Instead, Ellis Worth implies a palliative relationship between the troubled childhood and the beneficial shock therapy. In that regard, the story (in fact, all Ellis Worth stories) and the diary coincide: the war occurred without mentionable consequence to mental health. That discrepancy continued to puzzle me, for it did not conform to my presumption of wartime trauma. I have read too many accounts of PTSD following traumatic experiences while serving in the military to dismiss this possibility. Quite simply, something was amiss: my father attributed his destabilized mental health solely to childhood trauma, but I cannot dismiss the notion that his wartime experiences contributed to this destabilization. Why does he not acknowledge the war? This vexing question remained unanswered.

On a positive note, as the summer progressed, my father continued to write legal essays with modest success. For the most part, they were scholarly expositions, often critical of the legal system. He submitted them primarily to law reviews and bar journals, with occasional acceptances. I read several of them, looking for relevancies to his mental health. As far as I could tell, there were none; these were straightforward legal articles with case analyses, extensive footnotes, et cetera. They bolstered my father's reputation as a legal scholar in Denver, generating invitations to lecture at various venues, but, on a less positive note, they had little impact on his standing as a practicing lawyer. He had few clients, certainly not enough to make a living.

With hopes of improving his financial position, my father accepted a part-time job with Georgeson and

Company, a public relations firm that specializes in proxy solicitation. As a proxy solicitor, my father telephoned holders of stocks in a company (the client) to solicit their support for a particular point of view in the company's forthcoming shareholders' meeting. This part-time work for Georgeson provided a modest income and a first step in his eventual departure from the legal profession. Symbolically, it meant independence, freedom from a controlling master, the law: "Yesterday, by my decision to work for a public relations firm, I acted on the assumption of freedom from obligation or servitude to law and law practice. I hesitated to assert that proposition. As I go along, I will act promptly on the assumption of freedom, from a position of strength."

Over the next several months, in early fall of 1958, I detected an inflection point in my father's path towards recovery. For most of the year, the diary entries had been about desertion by his parents, real and ersatz, along with philosophical musings about this and that aspect of society, of the world in general, and recapitulations of his legal articles, with an emphasis on his interactions with editors. Notably, however, the discussions about desertion began to focus more and more on his relationships with Dr. Walker and Suzanne. And, I sensed change in the air.

Apropos desertion by Dr. Walker, in September, 1958, my father wrote: "I feel that my relation to Dr. Walker—should I see him again—has changed drastically. He cannot tell me anything which I will regard as authentic, as magic pulled from a hat, as secret, mystic wisdom. He is closer to the all-knowing, all-wise, all-giving forces of the universe than I am. I repudiate such pretense on his part. Should I return to see him, and perhaps I should, I would do so on the supposition that talking to him would be a cooperative pursuit of evidence, a partnership enterprise in which I am the senior partner, an investigation in which I am the directing spirit.

"Is tonight's emotion really a reaction to the fact that Dr. Walker's office has not called me, may not call me? I feel deserted, left alone, unwanted, unnecessary in an incomprehensible, topsy-turvy, crazy world. Perhaps everyone feels lonely, alone in a wide, wide, incomprehensible world. It isn't only that the world is wide. It isn't that it's a desert; it isn't. It is bountiful and beautiful. The confusion arises from the inhabitants. They, in their desolation, loneliness, and sorrow, have agreed upon the most preposterous postulates and on the tremendous importance of these vulgar fables.

"I am beginning to consider anew, or just plain consider, what I have to pay out to see him. My questioning whether he is worth it is, in a sense, new. Previously, I complained he wasn't worth it. His charges were part of the injustice he inflicted upon me, but which in my terrible, desperate need I had no choice but to pay. Now the question is more objective. Will he help at all? Will he help that much? I don't know. The only way to tell would be to have a whirl at it. The one thing which is fairly certain is that the whole picture has changed. Our relations are not the same. I have not missed seeing Dr. Walker. Or, perhaps I should say I did at first, but since then I haven't. The next week may be a test. I doubt that the test will be so severe.

"I always have charged father with leaving me, with desertion. In a sense, I probably level the same accusation at Dr. Walker. He said 'Feel free to call me.' He made his defense by putting on me the onus of continuing our relations. Since this involved recognizing his superiority, I have refused to call him. Dr. Walker thrust upon me the same onus I have thrust upon others. Come to me. Dr. Walker told me, in effect, 'I am available to help whenever you need help. I am not deserting you. I am, however, placing upon you the responsibility of seeking, of knowing whether you need help.' I hate to admit that I am not able to get along on my own. It is clear that Dr. Walker has not deserted me. It ought to be clear to me by now that father did not desert me. I have no intention whatever, at present, of calling Dr. Walker."

That intention became moot a week later when Dr. Walker called my father. "I haven't seen him since June, as he reminded me. I told him we had parted on the understanding I should feel free to call. I had felt free but didn't know that I wanted to do so. I spoke without constraint. If either of us had a studied attitude, it was he.

"I still am not sure that I have a precise, clearly-defined picture of my present relation to Dr. Walker. I should say that this much is certain: desperate dependence is not in the picture. Nor is a reaching out for a lifeline, i.e. helplessness. Whether we are to meet again is for me to decide. I was decidedly blunt in saying I was not sure I wanted to see him. I felt I am in the driver's seat.

"In telling Suzanne of Dr. Walker, I mentioned how patient he had been, and then I added that I felt he had been 100 percent on my side. Dr. Walker filled a formidable need of mine for many years. I didn't kill him. We drifted apart. It now may be that I shall cast off the Old Man of the Sea [Dr. Walker]. Desert him. It isn't a question of whether I can but whether I should. Would I benefit by continuing to go? What of throwing off the

Old Woman of the Sea [Suzanne]? Desert her? Perhaps I have put them both down on their own feet already. I may resume seeing one. I may not. I may or may not discontinue seeing the other.

"As for Suzanne, I don't know. The truth is I have close relations with no one, not even her. Tonight, for example, Suzanne was annoyingly indifferent to me. I told her how I went on a hunger strike when I was at the hospital. Then I said 'I was a pretty sick man.' She answered 'You must have been.' These revelations I have made may embarrass her. I didn't add that I thought the food was poisoned. To such an extent have I revolted at the philosophy of the swine's snout. I have spurned material comfort and food as poisonous, inconsistent with independence, freedom, spontaneity. It is for the thieving mice and rats and the domesticated animals. Then I spoke to Suzanne about the sale of my writing. She suggested that editors wouldn't change their preferences and that, therefore, I would have to change. The short of my answer was 'never.' She might have said that I would have to change to win her favor. I might have said 'never.'

"In truth, I have no intention of pretending to change, of adapting myself to the irrational and debased. Let the lowly rise to my level. I won't sink to theirs. No doubt Dr. Walker would advocate new relations as the best way to escape old ones, as a new skin rids a snake of an old one. So far, so good, but I have hardly needed new ones to rid myself of the old in other instances. I have had to exert myself to keep old friends from flying into limbo. Others I have let go.

"When Suzanne grew argumentative, I said 'Why argue with me? You can order the world, past and present, to suit yourself.' I got up to depart. This probably signifies that the continuance of our relationship depends upon your admitting my dominance. I am not going to fuss or argue about who is boss. If you want to see me or to have me around, you must be willing to capitulate, surrender, acknowledge my mastery. I don't intend to impose mastery. She can submit to my domination or go free. It is for her to decide whether she would rather be my subject or the subject of the herd. She isn't going to be free. That is quite certain. Her choice is between me and an anonymous master. She can't serve both.

"Irrespective of my inclination to leave Suzanne, she brings me pleasure. I enjoy her company like nobody else's, her feminine outlook on life. For example, my potential move to a new apartment has got Suzanne all excited. Here she is able to function as I cannot, measuring windows, noting this and that. As for me, I realize her facility in dealing with such physical things and my own distaste for the manipulation of objects. The immediately utilitarian and hand craftsmanship have an importance. Granted. It is natural, too, for Suzanne to squeeze the maximum self-importance from her connection with the impending tasks. What I resent and resist is any down-grading of my own importance. (What importance have I? My ability to earn a living as a free man is doubtful. As I age, my value as a slave decreases even).

"Why do curtains excite Suzanne so much? Is it, so to speak, blinders on my eyes? Is that, also, what tradition amounts to—blinders? The guy with blinders sees nothing or no one he shouldn't. I do not wish to hear about curtains."

As I read this entry for the first time, I questioned why Suzanne would continue a romantic relationship with my father. His insistence on dominance verged on verbal and emotional abusiveness. But, on subsequent readings, I began to smile at his mention of their petty squabbles—all of them benign—and the comfort offered him by Suzanne's traditionally female attention to homemaking activities. I even caught myself smiling at the thought of my father's insistence on dominance, if he, indeed, expressed that insistence in words to Suzanne. Might she have enjoyed these "caveman-like" remarks from her lover? I don't know now and certainly didn't know then.

These interactions with Suzanne reveal the closeness of their domestic relationship. They were not married nor were they living together. In modern terms, they were living apart together. Accordingly, I now realize how he had shared his affections three ways, between my brother and me and Suzanne. In a sense, he had two lives: as a father of two boys and as a man living apart together with his lover. Because he never alluded to the closeness of his relationship with Suzanne, I never observed how a father relates romantically to a woman. For me, that aspect of growing up was in the domain of movies and books. Retrospectively, I suspect that my emergence into manhood was affected adversely by the lack of a fatherly role model in this regard. But, I'm not sure how and, of course, at my advanced age there is little benefit from dwelling on that aspect of my past.

As the year 1958 drew to an end, my father shifted his attention to his failing law practice. In late November, he wrote: "My writing up to now has been visualized as a scheme for evading the law. The time has come for scrapping evasive, subversive schemes. The hour has struck for bold, decisive action to overthrow the system of ideas associated with the practice of law which have kept me in bondage. Not secretive subversion, not covert evasion, not conspiratorial schemes but bold, overt, forceful, unequivocal action. That is the need. Bold assertion. I am free. I am boss. The world is my oyster.

"In practicing law, I have felt somewhat as though I, and not the client's cause, was involved. I chose, then, to repudiate the judge, that is, to repudiate him as a father figure. You are not my father. I have none. So don't presume to tell me. You have no right. I wasn't carried screaming from the court room, ever. But who can ever imagine the terrible, soul-soaking, hurt, and despair of a child whose father has died?"

And so the diary continued for the remainder of the year. As his law practice withered from lack of clients, my father's disenchantment with the legal profession grew. By year's end, he had decided to quit the bar, tantamount to quitting his practice of law. He would withdraw from the profession gradually, in an orderly fashion. Although he didn't set a specific timeline, the withdrawal and its consequences loomed ahead.

In the final entry of the year, December 25, 1958, my father commented about the privacy of his diary and of himself as a diarist. "This diary is a private affair. It is consistent with my past policy of keeping my thoughts and feelings, comings and goings to myself. Were it to know, society would disapprove. Ergo, avoid disapproval by drawing curtains." This comment provoked reflection, because in those words, my father asserted the confidentiality of the content, the musings in his diary. It was not a draft document intended for publication as I had hypothesized. But I had already decided to share the contents of his diary posthumously in this narrative. If I truly have betrayed his privacy, I bow my head in shame.

In actuality, very few people were privy to the mental turmoil, the internal conflicts, documented in the diary. Dr. Walker, perhaps Suzanne. Certainly neither my brother nor I perceived any hint of significant turmoil—at least none that we can remember. As I have stated bluntly several times, the psychological tumult documented in my father's diary during the past two years did not align with our own perceptions of his behavior.

Admittedly, during that time period, our perceptive awareness may have been clouded, as first I and then my brother entered puberty. For us, the usual physical and emotional hallmarks characteristic of the age accompanied this developmental transition. Another transition, a parental transition, occurred: at my father's suggestion, we began calling him "dad" instead of "daddy," apropos his role as the father of young teenagers approaching adulthood. He, who had no father of his own as a role model when he was a teenager, now relied on instinct to guide him as a parent of teenagers, as a dad.

As I looked back on these years of transition—the doubles, the desertion schemes—and the inconsistency between diary entries and my own perception, I began to question the nature of my father's mental health at that time. In the diary entries, he lamented again and again the pain and dysfunction following his father's sudden death. This anguish definitely troubled him, but I began to question whether it rose to the level of mental illness. Certainly, it was unlike the acutely virulent mental illness that culminated in his hospitalization.

Searching for a better understanding of mental illness, I consulted the American Psychiatric Association's definitive set of guidelines, *The Diagnostic and Statistical Manual of Mental* Disorders *(DSM-5)*.[6] As expected, his nervous breakdown after the war clearly fit the diagnosis of PTSD, a clear-cut form of mental illness. But, the mental anguish associated with his father's death imprecisely fit the diagnosis of a personality disorder, a more subtle form of mental illness. In its description of this diagnosis, the *DSM-5* begins with a definition of personality traits:

> "*Personality traits* are enduring patterns of perceiving, relating to, and thinking about the environment and oneself that are exhibited in a wide range of social and personal contexts. Only when personality traits are inflexible and maladaptive and cause significant functional impairment or subjective distress do they constitute personality disorders."

My father had personality traits that were undeniably "inflexible" but not distinctly "maladaptive." They may have caused "subjective distress" but not "significant functional impairment." In short, he presented a borderline case. So, I read further:

> "The essential feature of a personality disorder is an enduring pattern of inner experience and behavior that deviates markedly from the expectations of the individual's culture and is manifested in at least two of the following areas: cognition,

---

[6] American Psychiatric Association, *The Diagnostic and Statistical Manual of Mental Disorders*, 5th ed. (Washington, D.C.: American Psychiatric Association, 2013).

affectivity, interpersonal functioning, or impulse control (Criterion A). This enduring pattern is inflexible and pervasive across a broad range of personal and social situations (Criterion B) and leads to clinically significant distress or impairment in social, occupational, or other important areas of functioning (Criterion C). The pattern is stable and of long duration, and its onset can be traced back at least to adolescence or early adulthood (Criterion D)..."

Conceivably, a professional psychiatrist might conclude that my father exhibited some of the attributes of these criteria characterizing a personality disorder and, therefore, presented with mental illness requiring treatment. (Cynically: that's how they earn a living.) Consistent with this conclusion, the diary indicates that my father relied on psychiatric therapy to resolve emotional conflicts for several years after release from the hospital. In the diary entries, beginning in 1956 (seven years after he entered the hospital), psychiatric therapy with Dr. Walker focused primarily on interpersonal relations, my father's anger with social expectations and conventional cultural values. But, they do not indicate what symptoms necessitated this therapy. Ostensibly, this need derived from the childhood trauma lamented extensively in the diary, but it could also derive from lingering wartime trauma or even trauma emanating from his hospitalization (for example, insulin- and electro-shock treatment).

In retrospect, I realized that *a priori* I had accepted as axiomatic that remnants of mental illness persisted after his discharge from the hospital. Why else would he have sought continuing psychiatric treatment for another ten years if it weren't medically necessary? Rethinking this, however, I proffered that psychiatric visits were perhaps necessary for a brief period after release from the hospital, but they continued not as a medical necessity but as a luxury, a welcome opportunity to express his controversial thoughts to a sympathetic, non-argumentative listener. Naturally, that opportunity would provide soothing comfort for nearly everyone.

To clarify my thinking, I rethought my father's childhood experiences. At age nine, he suffered trauma when his father died. But, he could not have become overtly ill due to this childhood trauma, for he went on to earn a law degree, launch a career in Washington D.C., and serve with distinction in the army. Granted, the loss of his father when my father was nine years old was tragic, indeed, but not unique. Young boys and girls have been losing one or both parents for time immemorial, especially before the advent of modern antibiotics. Surely, over the millennia, physiological defense mechanisms to allay trauma from these childhood tragedies have evolved, allowing bereaved children to mature, raise offspring, and perpetuate civilization, as did my father, unhindered by debilitating mental illness consequent to the trauma.

Similarly, I rethought my father's wartime experiences. During World War II, he participated in the bloody Battle of the Bulge and the horror-laden Dachau trials, definitely potential sources of serious trauma. Indeed, three years after his discharge from the army, my father fell acutely ill. I attribute this acute illness to wartime trauma, PTSD. In the hospital, he received psychiatric care with insulin- and electro-shock treatment, and the acute illness subsided. After his release from institutional care, he reentered society healthy enough to resume what appeared to be a normal life: establishing a law practice; interacting with other people at work; enjoying social occasions with Suzanne and Saturday visits with his young sons. My father may have harbored remnants of the acute phase of his mental illness, but they lay hidden from view. There were occasional episodes of unusual behavior, but, by and large, his mental health was not demonstrably unstable.

Synthesizing these notions, I posited a hypothetical conclusion. Stated metaphorically, innate defense mechanisms formed a protective scab—a mental scab—over my father's childhood trauma. (How such scabs are formed is an unsolved mystery of neuroscience.) The acute wartime trauma weakened this scab and maybe tore it off completely, elevating my father's childhood traumas to the level of mental illness requiring psychiatric therapy to resolve. Laying aside whatever remained of the protective scab, in Freudian style the psychiatrists probed my father's repressed memories, analyzed his dreams, and brought forth emotions from the unconscious to the conscious realms. Albeit with good intentions, they effectively unleashed the mental anguish that, in childhood, my father's innate defense mechanisms had sealed off. As in his childhood, my father's inherent defense mechanisms were slowly forming new protective scabs *en route* to restored mental health.

At this point, I could accept this hypothetical conclusion and, with satisfaction, bring this study of my father's hidden life to an end—return the diary and Ellis Worth stories to musty storage. Or, I could query how well my father adjusted to society with his newly singular personality—continue re-reading the diary to assess his progress towards complete mental health and, quite simply get to know my father better. I chose the latter course. After all, several issues remain unresolved. Did my father achieve success as a lawyer or as a writer? Did he get a new job? Did he marry Suzanne? Of course, I knew the ultimate answers to these questions, but as I have discovered, I knew surprisingly little about the history of the answers. And, most importantly, did my father achieve the level of acceptance as a colleague and a thought leader that he craved? I did not know the answer to that ultimate question.

Days of 59

As I began reading the diary entries for 1959, I noticed occasional passages bracketed in red pencil. The red marking began in January, 1959, and ended in December, 1959. For some reason, my father had marked these passages for a particularly special purpose. Serendipitously, I remembered seeing a folio among the short stories entitled *The Days of 59 – A Memoir of Personal Discovery*, written by Jeremiah Jones. After perusing this folio, I discovered that *The Days of 59* comprised the red-marked passages from the diary, rearranged by topic and then date of entry.

I wondered why he had chosen these particular entries or, in some cases, specific sentences from an entry. Did they present a particular theme or a particular story or insight? For that matter, when were they red-marked: as my father wrote the diary or after it was completed? I'll never know. Undoubtedly, however, this collection of specific diary entries was intended for publication as a separate, stand-alone document, written using the pseudonym Jeremiah Jones instead of his usual Ellis Worth.

The Days of 59 is a long manuscript, with seven chapters and an appendix. Five chapters are personal in nature, "notes to self," so to speak: commentaries on works of literature that my father was reading; nighttime dreams; interactions with colleagues; philosophical musings about various social and cultural trends of the time; and cogitations about daily activities of his two teenaged sons. While sometimes interesting, they consisted primarily of loosely related conversational snippets and did not provide any noteworthy insights into my father's state of mind. Thus, after a cursory reading, I set them aside. The other two chapters and the appendix were far more relevant in that regard, because they tell the tale of two pending departures: from Dr. Walker and from the practice of law. I have excerpted portions of these two chapters, *Doctors and Patients* and *A Strategic Withdrawal*.

****

Doctors and Patients

I woke up this morning with a touch of the flu: runny nose, raspy throat, headache, slight fever. As the day wore on, I began to feel better. Suzanne invited me down for a bowl of chicken soup and a cup of hot chamomile tea. Afterwards, I lay on the couch while she put a cover over me and offered to do this and that. It was as if she were going back to childhood and saying "Papa, don't die. I'll take care of you." (Her father had died while she was in her early teens.) As for me, I enjoyed, in my sickness, the pleasure of a child being the object of maternal solicitude. Thus, for Suzanne, I was Papa and for me she was Mama.

Several days ago, I had called Dr. Walker's office and made a couple of appointments, including one for this afternoon. Because I was beginning to feel better, I kept the appointment. He and I should meet, and when we do, on terms of equality or near equality. I called the meeting. I can almost hear myself saying, "I called this meeting because...." Here I go confusing equality and domination.

When I went to see Dr. Walker, he looked young, self-contained, a bit like my older brother as he was ten years ago, or as I looked ten years ago. I fancy he trembles or thrills to my approval. I wouldn't be surprised if Dr. Walker was flattered by the compliment I paid the appearance of his office. I ventured to make an approving comment on the dark East Indian vase he has in the office. Also, I recommended to him the Romain Gary book, *The Roots of Heaven*. That is to say, I set myself in position to judge his taste. To be able to approve is to be able, as well, to disapprove.

To a certain extent, I do not talk to Dr. Walker as much as at him. Indeed, my recommendation of the book was rather flung at his feet than handed to him. The difficulty of giving the tip directly is doubt about his capacity to approve what I do. If he picks up what I have put in his way but fails to like the book, then he has only himself to blame.

In today's confab I told Dr. Walker that I felt that I outranked him. He took it not as a challenge but as a statement of fact, the state of my feelings. It isn't that I am better than him or others, but that I see more deeply than most. I told him that I prefer the rule "Don't think" to the reverse and the advice "relax" to "work." I made no genuflection to his experience and specialty and training. I didn't ask him. I told him.

Afterwards, I was sleepy. The resumption of sessions with Dr. Walker marked a turning point toward good health. Deciding to return signified that I wished to integrate within me, to make room in my heart for the forces and factors symbolized by father and mother. They are to be part of me and not vice versa. Dr. Walker is to have a place, but the dispositive power is mine. I am the senior partner.

Days of 59

In this decade of talk-talk-talk with Dr. Walker and his predecessors, I have, in effect, retraced my steps to infancy. I have gone back to my earliest times, to question, to examine, to evaluate, to re-learn. My disposition has been to disdain everything produced by others, anywhere, at any time. Why? Because my earliest experience had taught me that others gave me no credit at all for anything.

During most of my talks with Dr. Walker, I wanted to have things my own way. I kept pulling and tugging, so to speak, to bring him around to my point of view. This process went on for years. I would make few concessions to prevailing modes of thought, which were mainly crazy. It was for the crazy to make concessions to the sanity of my attitudes. Dr. Walker was deluded when he was not wildly mistaken. Several times, he conceded that I was not alone in considering society or our culture as relatively insane and in need of a more realistic outlook.

I used to regard Dr. Walker not as himself but as a mere agent for public opinion: a mouthpiece of orthodoxy; a chameleon reflecting the color of his surroundings. My respect for him as a mouthpiece, an adjutant, a flunky, was not appreciable. Now I get the full impact of others considering a legal adviser as the mouthpiece who interprets, translates and explains authoritative texts, and I don't like it. I wish to speak not as an adjutant, but as a general.

I thought of the possibility of calling Dr. Walker and seeing him again a few times-on "terminal visits." The possibility occurred to me, but it didn't have a strong appeal. What could he do? Some good may come from basking in the summer sun, but none is to be expected from Dr. Walker. In fact, my visits to the park are like going to see Dr. Walker. The green grass is my father-confessor. It is my better self. To it I confess my dalliance with the perverted doctrines and gospels which are dominant in our culture. I have messed with courts and clients and law. I admit it. I have immersed myself in the study of histories and governments and languages. Forgive me, O God of the Green Grass. Give unto me a full measure of thy tender and healing sympathy....

When I was wont to visit Dr. Walker, he gave me fifty minutes of his time. He couldn't give more. It was beyond his ability, for he had commitments to other patients. So now I remind him that I have obligations to others. He is but one of my creditors and, not being a trade creditor, he lacks a preferential status. He is low on the list.

Toward the end of my going to see Dr. Walker, my want-pattern tended to fade out. I began to see he couldn't give me any more than he was giving. I began to see him as limited, human, deficient. His ungivingness was not hostility but lack of capacity. When I saw that, the end was bound to come.

In talking to Dr. Walker, I used to give him short shrift. I carried the conversational ball. It was I who was paying the fee. All right then, I would do the talking. In time it came to be understood that I would dominate the interview. If I did not become attached to Dr. Walker in the years that I went to see him, it was, perhaps, because (or partly because) I did not trust him and his friendliness.

What happened to induce me to give the good-bye to Dr. Walker? When I finally got the idea that he was simply human—human enough to chart his course in life by "learning." Then he lost all authority. He no longer was a threat to me, no longer capable of offering me anything tempting. It may be surprising that I should have imputed great authority to Dr. Walker, but I did so. When I caught sight of the fact that he, in turn, from a similar need, ascribed high importance to the lore and techniques of the medical profession, I inferred that his strength did not exceed mine. His adequacy depended upon his contact with and access to those imaginary, communal reserves.

What my parents told me had been fake. They had bound me into a state of helpless dependency and then force-fed me bunk. Now I wanted Dr. Walker to sit helplessly by while I repudiated the hokum which had been fed me and explored the truth of things. He would have only the passive role of confirming my discoveries. Still, he would have that importance.

From that experience with Dr. Walker and other experiences, I have gained an increased faith in my own capacity to discover, do the valuing, judging and censoring. Could it be that a parent inflicts helplessness on a child when he, himself, feels disabled, incompetent, incapacitated? If so, society pretends to be all knowing in proportion as it is ignorant, helpless, insecure, doubtful.

My relation to Dr. Walker was given its character or quality by me. I cast it in an old-fashioned setting. I gave it a dream or wish atmosphere. "Here we are, Doctor, you and I. You will play the role of my parents. I will be the child, but this time I will do as I always wished to do. I will go on voyages of discovery and exploration. I will learn. I won't be taught. You will observe the learning process. You will see that I need no active assistance. You will merely confirm. When we have exhausted this parent-child relationship, I will leave you. You will have done your duty by giving me a chance to act, to discover, to learn, to grow. See, I won't even ask for encouragement—just for a chance."

Dr. Walker's willingness to let me do as I wished, his assenting to participate in the re-enactment of my childhood on the terms I prescribed for him, indicated his acceptance of me. The role I gave him wasn't bad at all, but it ascribed little potency or importance to him. He had to have a fairly good reservoir of strength to be willing to be relegated to a bit part. Actually every parent is faced with just about this situation. As a parent myself, I do a stint of self-effacing, regularly, for the benefit of Dean and Curtis.

Dr. Walker's example has served me as a guide in bringing up Dean and Curtis. I have been tolerant, indulgent, understanding, sympathetic, not condemnatory. As a rule, I have given them a chance to exercise capacities. I have even gone further than Dr. Walker did with me. I have tried to indicate that my authority and my example are not perfect but susceptible to error. They ought, therefore, not to hesitate to oppose my attitudes with their own.

All of that aside, the notion has slipped into my mind recently that my relations with Dr. Walker have been tarnished and made shameful by the element of payment. His acceptance and my giving of fees made for a commercial relation equivalent to prostitution. He prostituted his talents and training for money. I see Dr. Walker operating within the framework of the customary without misgivings. I see him as small enough to do that. He is content to be in private practice as a psychiatrist—giving of himself on commercial terms.

I daydreamed of writing to him and asking him to write off part of his last bill. My role seems as disgraceful as his. I put out cash for attention and consideration. Evidently I am not, of myself, worthy. With my gold, yes; without it, no. How humiliating! Ah, yes, I also fantasied asking Dr. Walker to recommend another psychiatrist—one who would charge less—or, better yet, arrange for my going to a VA or other clinic.

Until Dr. Walker is paid, I am not likely to visit him again. I am paying him slowly. Money standing between us is what I wish to dramatize for him: your money-orientation keeps us apart. I assume he would like to see me, but would like more, as a creature of his culture, to see money.

Yes, I am closing out this year without any thought of a future resort to Dr. Walker. Whatever my destiny may be, I'll take what comes without asking Dr. Walker to hold my hand.

****

Clearly, my father respected Dr. Walker. By and large, he considered his visits beneficial in many respects. By the end of the year, however, he questioned whether he would have further visits. That does not imply that my father would no longer benefit from his sessions with Dr. Walker. Rather, it implies that my father would dare to sever his dependence on Dr. Walker. He would confront the world without relying on Dr. Walker's supportive hand or, for that matter, incurring another bill.

Although my father occasionally mentioned these visits to my brother and me, he never went into detail about the nature of their conversations. For us, just the notion of our father visiting a psychiatrist caused embarrassment; in our perception as young teenagers, the visits stigmatized us. We never discussed the psychiatric visits with our friends, but in our long-established neighborhood, close neighbors knew about our father's history of mental illness and would taunt us now and then about it. In that limited regard, Dr. Walker was a persistent albatross around our necks: certainty benign but for boys our age a source of embarrassment.

Amidst his musings about Dr. Walker, my father—that is, Jeremiah Jones—abruptly inserted an anecdote about his visit to the dentist. I have included this narrative because it illustrates a cardinal feature of my father's mental fragility: anxiety, verging on panic, when confronted by a member of the medical profession such as a doctor or a dentist. Throughout the diary, comparable anecdotes appear occasionally, anecdotes that I have excluded simply for brevity. But, they all manifest episodes of anxiety and hostility towards medical doctors and dentists.

****

I went to the dentist that day. As usual, I had the impression that I was regarded there as a victim rather than as a patient. Besides, my troubles with my teeth provide an opportunity for financial plunder. But, I had little recourse because I was having trouble with my lower left teeth in general and the eye tooth in particular. Dr. Beckwith it was. His office is fairly close to here. I spoke first to Dr. Beckwith's assistant. I couldn't remember what he calls her. First, I thought of Shelley (as a young man in Sheboygan I knew a girl with that last name) and then Sherry. It actually is Garry. I wanted to make her more feminine: more dear (*cherie*, as the French say).

Dr. Beckwith and his girl played around with x-rays, an electric current, ice. The ice was so shaped as to remind me of a mother's tit; also, somewhat of those rubber finger-ends that file-clerks use. This is to say the ice resembled a nursing nipple, being hollow even.

I was left alone for some reason, and my throat became dry. I spied a glass and filled it with tap water from the sink. Soon after, I was seized by extreme chills. I shivered and shook. I was terrifically nervous and in a hurry to get out of there. As for the process of consumption and excretion, I had an incipient, involuntary bowel movement at the dentist's office. I noticed the odor and thought it came from Dr. Beckwith's breath.

Dr. Beckwith, having returned, took my temperature. "He has a fever," he told Garry. They gave me a prescription for achromycin, and then Dr. Beckwith gave me some aromatic spirits to drink right there and turned me loose to flee this tortuous office.

I was in a hurry to get away. I was shaky, gasping for breath, nearly in the grip of a seizure like those of epilepsy. I was able to come out of there on my own two feet. Despite my discomfort, I walked home, although I almost collapsed before I got there. During the walk, I could think only of getting away as fast as possible, be alone, call Suzanne and tell her of my sudden illness.

That night, I could hardly sleep. I was a bundle of nerves. Sleeplessness had not plagued me since I started working in hospitals years ago. The chicken I had for dinner was slow in digesting.

My eyes burned for days after the seizure. I discovered this when I put a wet towel on my forehead; the coolness felt good to the eyes. Before that, I knew my eyes hurt, and I kept them closed much of the time. I trotted around our dim apartment without any glasses.

My difficulties sleeping went on for several more days, though I kept to my bed a great deal. My vague, obscure dreams were questions: What is real? Ah, I thought, Suzanne will tell me when she comes home from visiting her sister in Omaha. I lay in bed thinking that sometimes the theme proceeds as far as a tentative answer. Reality may be tit-for-tat treatment. It may be a process of consumption and excretion.

The what-is-real theme was awfully upsetting, virtually a nightmare. It occurred to me that this experience and these dreams are reenactments of early infancy. I reject the milk bottle and its cold impersonality. I spurn the validity of the scheme of tit-for-tat: you get well fed if you stifle your anger and sobs or get this if you do that. Ah yes, I felt like weeping at the dentist's office.

As I thought back on this frightful experience, it dawned on me that when taking the drink of water in the dentist's office, I projected myself back and took care of myself in infancy. All I got was water, but that was what I wanted. I determined what I wanted, saw the glass, and got the water. Symbolically, I returned to childhood and trampled over substitutes for father and mother. Slew my parents and supplied my own wants.

****

Incidentally, this particular episode constitutes the basis of an Ellis Worth story, *The Dentist*.[7] The story is set in an amusing context: storytelling by a group of ale-tippling hospital workers. It comes across as a comical experience. But, in the diary, it comes across as a somber encounter with the dentist and his assistant.

Somber indeed. My father [Jeremiah Jones] suffered a panic attack when the dentist left him alone. His reaction fit the formal definition in the DMS-V:[8]

---

[7] Worth, *Once Upon a Farm: Tales of Discovery*. Pp. 131-133.

[8] Association, *The Diagnostic and Statistical Manual of Mental Disorders*. P. 190.

"Panic attacks are abrupt surges of intense fear or intense discomfort that reach a peak within minutes, accompanied by physical and/or cognitive symptoms....Panic attacks may be expected, such as in response to a typically feared object or situation, or unexpected, meaning that the panic attack occurs for no apparent reason."

"Intense fear:" my father experienced a "fight or flight" response, an adrenaline rush, culminating in an involuntary bowel movement. This episode most probably manifests my father's PTSD and not some more general panic disorder. According to the DMS-V, "Other diagnoses and conditions are excluded if they are better explained by PTSD (e.g., symptoms of panic disorder that occur only after exposure to traumatic reminders)."[9]

This diagnosis implies that some "traumatic reminder" triggered the attack. The two obvious candidates are desertion and medical treatments: desertion by his father and atrocious medical treatments by German-speaking Nazi physicians. These traumas continued to plague my father long after their occurrences, insidious demons emerging occasionally, briefly out of their subconscious realm.

I began to realize that by and large, my father loathed dentists and physicians. In the diary, but not in his conversations with my brother or me, he made no secret of his disdain. He considered them parasitical and threatening. For example, my father's visit to the dentist, Dr. Beckwith, resulted in a panic attack so severe that he lost control of his bowels while in the dental chair. This acute panic attack undoubtedly manifests remnants of his mental illness, of some traumatic episode in my

---

[9] Ibid. P. 279.

father's past. Although I could not yet pinpoint the source of this manifestation—the events in early childhood or during the war—I intended to keep an eye open for clues in subsequent diary entries.

Likewise, my father loathed the legal profession. In the tersely written chapter "*A Strategic Withdrawal*," he (that is, Jeremiah Jones) pronounced dissatisfaction with the practice of law, with lawyers, judges, and their "retinue of flunkies." And, with that, he quit.

****

A Strategic Withdrawal

I want to get out of the legal profession, but that is not all there is to it. I must stop taking on clients, relinquish my office, announce my departure from the profession. To all intents and purposes, however, I am out. Indeed, I turned away two would-be clients today. The cases did not appeal to me at all. My office door continues to carry the words "Law Offices," but I do not consider myself as practicing law any more. That is a thing of the past, that humiliation and sham. The practice of law represents for me the worship of false gods for money: the sale of the mind for a fee; the prostitution of the intellect for social status, social approval, security.

I cannot expect to be a busy practitioner unless I swallow the line that the lawyer's work is important and unless I take pride in doing it. Practicing law would require me to acknowledge the supremacy of the law. Clients acknowledge that, and it is for that reason they visit lawyers, who, supposedly, can offer their clients wisdom from the sanctified reservoir of law. Clients view lawyers as oracles; as representatives authorized to search the hidden secrets of the law's wisdom and then pronounce accordingly.

Days of 59

How could I ever have chosen a legal career—spent 25 years at the bar? I feel no kinship whatever with other lawyers. I prefer not to pass the time of day with them, even. In a way, I feel as though membership in the bar had been enveloped in a mist of sanctity and that the fog has been dissipated. The result is that I see lawyers as a bunch of cheap and shabby tricksters and shysters. The legal profession and I simply have come to a parting of the ways. I voluntarily foreswear further practice. Mine is the judgment.

I no longer have any respect for judges, lawyers, and all the retinue of flunkies. It irritates me to be approached as if I lacked the sense to be a man. It seems to me that a client in search of legal advice is treating me as a child and asking me what my father, the law, has to say about this or that. I bristle and send him away. I am not a child. I wish to be treated as a grown man and asked for my own opinion.

My own wish is to see what I see and to intone no creed which goes with a calling. The law concerns itself with behavior, which is to say with externals. I am primarily interested in the fundamental rather than the formal. The law disregards the spirit, the emotional, the internal, the fundamental, the important. It will blindly and blandly ignore A's extinction of B's spirit, but set its massive machinery of retaliation in motion if A should inflict so much as a trifling bodily injury on B.

I wish to see what goes on around me in my own way. To interpret everything legalistically seems absurd. To argue to judges and juries against other lawyers is like taking a nature walk blindfolded; it is like writing poetry in words of three letters—like skiing with one ski. In my philosophy, the litigant takes precedence over judge and advocates. Moreover, the problem rates above the solution. I seldom criticize a legal doctrine. It isn't worth it. If anything, I give an example of a contrary principle having equal validity. When I criticize, the object usually is an institution, a basic concept, a method of proceeding. Why bother with doctrines and principles; they are just a conglomeration of words. I want a bigger arena than a court; a less narrow audience than a judge; a more flexible, richer, more lyrical language than legal parlance; a better cause than another's plea for damages.

As time passes, it becomes more and more likely that I shall be forced to release my office space in the Majestic Building. This now begins to seem less of a horrendous admission of failure. Indeed, I feel a sneaking eagerness to let it go and to have done with this last vestige of law practice; and to shout praises to the lord for a definitive, complete, final, symbolic escape. So long as I keep the words "Law Offices" on my door, people will have an excuse for treating me as an infant. I could have those words removed, but the time is not ripe. If I come into a goodly sum of cash some way, I shall have the words obliterated. If I have no such good fortune, I shall be obliged to give up the space.

My strong impulse to relinquish my office and to get out of the practice of law is the wish to free myself from maternal leading strings. The conduct of a lawyer is more or less set by convention. He strives for respectability and for business. He bows before the majesty and wisdom of the law. Its rules are good; its minions wise, beneficent and just, at least generally; its procedures are conducive to sound results.

How will I explain to others my leaving the law? I can put on a bold front and say I have dared all. I can resort to metaphor and say it is for me to decide whether the Chinese coastal islands are useless for the defense of the USA. It is for me to make decisions about myself, not for you. You would hang onto useless islands, fearing, in your weakness, they might have value. I am strong enough to give up those islands, realizing they weaken rather than strengthen me. To announce to other attorneys and their families, the Garfields, the Switzers, the Halls, that I am turning my back on law would be pretty close to a downright snub. They stand firmly for middle-class respectability — grey hats, grey suits, grey personalities, regulated hours, actions, and outlets. The Garfields like to think they are arty, musical, enlightened; and listen to opera with libretto in hand. The *précieuses ridicules* are with us yet, but no Molière.

Suzanne asked me this evening when I would vacate my office. I told her that I must vacate as soon as possible; I cannot continue to maintain a law office. There was no regret mentioned. I am not reluctant. It is the thing to do. The only question is one of timing. In a way, perhaps a dim way, she senses that the move may symbolize something pretty significant for me. She even may sense what it symbolizes — the complete detachment from parental values, worldly values, the past.

Accordingly I moved out of the Majestic Building two days later. Tunnell and Goss came in to tell me they are overflowing into my space when I leave it. I told them I was glad. It is a nice office. It was not necessary to strain to welcome them, as it would have been if I had felt forced out of practice. I do not feel they are taking anything from me at all. I'll be darned if Tunnell's suite doesn't remind me of a cell block or, rather, of a rabbit hutch, each little office being a hole out of which a rabbit might pop.

Am I resigning from the practice of law in defeat? To an extent, that is so. Nonetheless, the words and tune of "happy days are here again" have possessed my mind lately. The idea of getting out of the legal profession has been accompanied with a feeling of being cleansed; "decontaminated," as the army used to say.

At the same time, I continue to work with unabated energy seeking other employment. I refuse to "put my tail between my legs." What work I shall do for a living—the question which most people settle early in life once and for all—remains to be seen. The answer lies in the womb of the future, perhaps, if I'm lucky, in the year 1960.

I went down to see Winkler & Winkler, employment agents, today, at Wendell Hogan's suggestion. I had an interview with a nameless young; man, 35-40. He also came close to being faceless. The guy wasn't bad looking in his standardized blue-grey suit. He had black hair which had receded on the sides. There was a certain vacuousness and fatuity in the face, plus grossness. He was a businessman without being a human being.

I felt humiliated. He is the type for which property values, name values, form values, count for everything. He said "You're an attorney," evidently expecting me to spread my tail feathers. He spoke of insurance adjusting and I compared that occupation with shoveling sheep manure, to the detriment of the former.

He expected me to wilt when I said I didn't own a house, but rented. He made a face to imply his surprise and re-evaluation of me. When I said I was divorced, he rephrased it: "You have no wife," as if he were subtracting an asset from a balance sheet. I don't know if humiliation is the right word. Maybe it would be closer to the fact to say that I felt nauseated after the interview."

****

By giving up his office, my father gave up his law practice. It was over, without ceremony, without regrets. With this decision, he must now move onto a new phase of life, find a new job, earn a living. Still under the pseudonym Jeremiah Jones, he elaborated on the diary's documentation of his decision to depart from the practice of law in an appendix to *The Days of 59*.

****

Appendix: Why I Quit the Practice of Law

If a guy told me that he had married a girl, had lived happily with her for twenty-five years, and then had fallen out with her completely, I should put it down as one of those curious things which undoubtedly do happen to people but which are quite beyond the comprehension of an ordinary citizen like myself. Yet something similar has befallen me. I do understand the mystery and would like to pass it along to others.

The law is a jealous mistress. I courted her through three years of law school. We were married more than twenty-five years ago: which is to say that I was admitted to the bar in that remote era of history known as the Great Depression.

My record at law school was outstanding. I was a conspicuous success. The law was for me. Despite the general bankruptcy of the early thirties, my services were in demand. In three years more I was a partner in a big-city firm which enjoyed an enviable reputation for conservatism, learning, and results.

It is possible that friction between me and my profession, my mistress, might have developed sooner had my career proceeded along the usual straight line. It didn't. I had friends outside the partnership (as well as within), and they pointed out opportunities in government and business which I could not resist. The war years meant change, distraction, and new honors as well as military service. In sum, the potential rift in the lute was hidden from sight while I prosecuted and threw stones at those accused of wrongdoing and sat in judgment on those less holy than myself.

Did I become dissatisfied with my mistress and quit her, or did she, rather, become weary of the effort of pretense and disguise and so permit me to see her as she is without the rouge, make-up, and theatrical smile which had enchanted me? Well, the process of disenchantment was slow; and many elements, not all personal with me, entered into the separation and divorce. Do not think the decision to turn my back on my chosen, previously profitable profession was a flippant one made in a moment of light-hearted abandon. It wasn't easy, but it was necessary.

It isn't easy, either, to single out this or that event or experience and cite it as the turning point in my relations with my work. Everything changed: all my attitudes; my entire outlook. Experiences buried beneath the thick dust of time were resurrected, brushed off, and seen in a strange and different light. I outgrew not only the practice of law and its hard, sharp, narrow viewpoints but much else besides.

One of my last clients was a woman in her seventies who wished me to draw up a trust agreement so she could turn the management of her property over to a bank. There was a good-sized estate. The woman, a spinster, had accumulated this wealth by her own efforts in business and as an investor. By concentrating on commerce and money matters she had been able to put various personal inadequacies and frustrations out of her mind. A heart attack and certain other signals of the failing health which go with age had caused her to review her assets as a general inspects his troops before a battle.

Years earlier the woman's wealth would have glamorized her for me. The knowledge that the tidy fortune had been earned, not inherited, would have been a comforting confirmation of the vaunted rewards at the beck and call of talent and enterprise. I would have exclaimed appreciatively to the client over her achievement. As a good lawyer I should have been thrilled at the chance of having a part in the disposition of so much of this world's goods. As it was, the flattering remarks died in my throat. No legal magic could dissipate the mist of pathos enveloping this woman and her future, no amount of money could substitute for what she had missed in the past.

But this is no time for homilies. A middle-aged, well-to-do businessman who owned an even half of the stock in a prospering operation came to me because the owner of the balance of the outstanding shares of the stock ignored him and had taken complete charge of corporate affairs. This is not a rare situation. There is considerable law on the subject. Lawyers like such cases. There are good fees to be collected, win or lose. At one time, I should have been delighted with the wind which blew this client my way. When the gentleman actually presented himself, however, my metamorphosis already was in process and I was terribly conscious that legal witchcraft was powerless to breathe courage into the guy's character or to stiffen his backbone so as to enable him to resist his opponent outside of court and to settle differences himself in a manly way.

A red-haired young woman came to see me early one morning. She threw a rolled paper on my desk with a challenging air and asked "What do I do with that?" I could be excused had I jumped to the conclusion that legal legerdemain would provide a solution. The client's visit was evidence that she thought so. Nevertheless, I had a premonition, before I unrolled the document, that the modern, civilized form of tribal voodooism known as law would be unequal to the girl's challenge.

The scroll was a marriage certificate. The client was an adopted daughter of a rancher in an adjoining state. She had come to the big city to work but didn't make friends easily and had been lonely. She met a man at a bar to which she had gone unaccompanied. He was fifteen years older than she, had been married and divorced, and had teenaged children. The night of their first meeting they drove to the girl's home state, had tests or physical examinations the next morning, and then, cold sober, were married. They lived together several weeks. She preferred an annulment to a divorce, she said, but either would do.

This last imbroglio is not extraordinary grist for the legal mill. My own experience includes a number of variations on the theme. I seldom use the formula "No, you see I don't handle divorce and annulment cases." In this instance I did resort to it. The law, so far as it has been revealed to me through study and immersion, cannot minister to a mind afflicted, nor pluck from the memory a rooted sorrow of the sort which propels a man and woman toward marital fiasco. True, all the girl wanted was a divorce or annulment, but a force superior to the worldly powers-that-be forbade my participation in such legal quackery.

This sort of a catalogue of cases could be expanded indefinitely, but there are other, different things to speak about, and I do not mean injustices. Not at all. My typewriter prefers to narrate personal incidents and miniature spotted actualities and to leave the Grand Theories, Brilliant Deductions, and Weighty Conclusions to the printing presses of colleges and foundations. It would be folly for me to argue with such a willful, ingenious and indispensable servant as my typewriter.

In the days preceding World War II, I read that a gifted lawyer in the high office of Attorney General gave a written, official opinion that a transfer of American destroyers to a foreign nation was within the power of the President without any special statute authorizing it. Maybe so. The official afterwards was promoted to still higher office. The governmental maneuvers to delay the sailing of the German steamer, Bremen, also appeared to me, in those days before Pearl Harbor, to rest on flimsy legal pretexts. Just the same, I did not go so far as to question whether the Government, which makes and insists upon respect for law, takes care to set a good example regardless of its own convenience under the circumstances. Now I feel free, nay bound, to question such unquestionable propositions.

Once upon a time, I assumed that anyone appointed or elected to a judgeship automatically increased in stature so as to possess the courage and intellect necessary to deserve the ceremonious respect wafted his way from all directions. I had too much faith in the magic of office and too little faith in the solid realities of human nature.

In recent years, I have noticed that men of less than average height and members of underprivileged, minority groups tend to seek seats on the Bench. I can understand their aim. It is nicer, doubtless to look down on others than to be looked down upon, and of course, neither a puny physique nor a felt inferiority of social status rules out keen intelligence and rare judicial courage. Still, does not the judging process seem less objective and Olympian—aye, even petty, mean and retaliatory—seen from this new viewpoint? I merely ask.

Men like Tom Dewey and Harold Stassen have spring-boarded to eminence from positions as prosecutors, and, so far as I know, the prosecution of one's fellows need leave no permanent, indelible stain on the soul. If it is otherwise, I am stigmatized as well as these estimable statesmen. The guy who has no claim check to respect, as I see it now, is the one who craves the job of stoning those who share his own inescapable guilt—but isn't the one who gets the assignment usually he who wants it badly enough to pursue it?

This personal valedictory is no place to rant about such abuses as may have been observed in the workings of the American legal system during the past quarter century. My disillusionment is with law at its commonplace best, whether American or foreign. I do not grieve over law gone wrong. Let him who will do that. Fate has decreed that I should graduate from the practice of law and leave it behind. That is why I have closed up the office which looked over tarred and sterile rooftops, narrow driveways, and a rabbit warren of intersecting streets.

There may be no green garden for me to cultivate, but at least, I hope so.

****

In these two chapters and the appendix from *The Days of 59*, my father, writing as Jeremiah Jones, casts aside two significant pillars of his post-war life: his psychiatrist and his profession as a practicing lawyer. Ostensibly, he has outgrown his need for psychiatric care and has made the conscious choice to discontinue his sessions with the psychiatrist. Significantly, he departs this relationship on good terms with Dr. Walker. In contrast, he has failed to establish a successful law practice and has made the inevitable decision to give up his office. He departs this relationship with the legal profession on bad terms.

My father summarized the appendix on his departure from the law in a brief diary entry. "I have just finished *Why I Quit the Practice of Law*. I lost faith in law. I lost faith in judges and the judging process. It is a story of lost faith in materialism. It barely can be called an inspirational story. It is, rather, a confessional type. I confess. Yet I confess to a conversion. I become Christian. I renounce a profitable racket. Yet I claim no credit. Fate decreed it."

Before reading the diary and *The Days of 59*, I knew about my father's departure from the practice of law, about his disenchantment with the profession. However, I didn't know how chilling the departure was. I was taken aback at the stark differences between my father the lawyer as a young bachelor in *The Eldon Jones Sextet* and a middle-aged divorcee in *The Days of 59*. How could a man change so much? As a lawyer, the younger Eldon Jones graduated from law school with honors (Order of the Coif), quaffed cocktails in pre-war Washington D.C. legal circles, and joined the JAG corps with alacrity. In contrast, an older Jeremiah Jones struggled to fit into Denver's legal community. As a scholar of the law, he was moderately successful, giving invited speeches at various legal forums and publishing articles in legal journals. But, as a practitioner of the law, he was unsuccessful. In frustration, bitterness, or jealousy, he seldom missed an opportunity to disparage fellow lawyers and judges. The struggle culminated with his resignation from the Bar, effectively renouncing his profession. The only memorable comment my father made to me about this departure is that "the law has no compassion." Oh yes; while I was a freshman in college, he advised me never to go into the law.

Once again, a question emerges: Why did the successful Eldon Jones transform into the unsuccessful Jeremiah Jones? I suspect that lingering mental illness tainted my father's practice of the law. His failure correlates with the rejection of his socially acceptable double, his transition from a dual to singular personality dominated by its a less socially acceptable bias against what he perceived as disingenuous, "herd-like" behavior. More bluntly, I suspect that other lawyers and potential clients felt uncomfortable in his presence and, therefore, spurned his practice. In that sense, they validated my father's latent concerns about his acceptance into the prevailing social order.

Thoughts of Death

The diary entries in *The Days of 59* were selected by my father. Presumably, he considered them representative of the thoughts and emotions expressed in the multitudinous, longer entries in the original diary. Most of the selected entries were fairly brief, sometimes no more than one or two sentences, whereas the complete entries often exceeded ten pages. I had mixed feelings about the brevity. On the one hand, it provided welcome relief from the tedium of reading long, repetitious discourses about my father's troubled childhood, his disaffection for standard social mores, his disdain of the legal profession. Of course, by nature, diaries constitute a private forum for expressing complaints and dislikes such as these. But, also by nature, I get tired of reading about these same dislikes and complaints time and again — even if they are my father's. On the other hand, the brevity sometimes truncated a thought or emotion that could potentially add insight into my father's state of mind, his mental health. In those cases, I found myself reverting to the original diary to read the complete entry, regardless of the length.

But, with time on his hands during this particularly momentous period in his life, my father wrote long and wearisome diary entries, often exhausting my patience. To bring them into the normal attention span, I decided to use his strategy in *The Days of 59* by extracting sections from various entries and organizing them into specific topics; by organizing his thoughts, I could organize my own thoughts. In that way, I hoped to assemble a clear image of my father at that time, uncluttered with distracting minutiae.

As I assembled extracts of several familiar topics—parents, Suzanne, doctors—I realized each of them referred to my father's own potential death in one way or another. Once again, I was shocked by this unexpected revelation that my father had seriously contemplated suicide. As I well knew from seeing him weekly, he was not dead but quite alive during that time; despite the temptations of death, he obviously chose life and all of its turbulence. Nonetheless, his frequent references to death sparked my interest. The references ranged from overt to barely liminal. And, they ranged between two emotional poles of thought. At one pole, when he discussed suicide, they manifested a decidedly morose component of my father's mental status. But, at the other pole, my father explicitly rejected suicide, expressing a hopeful, encouraging component of his mental status.

I set aside my extractions about parents, Suzanne, and doctors and prepared a single extract that concentrated on my father's thoughts of death. It began with a series of maudlin entries written in spring, 1959.

"An idea which crossed my mind is that the tempo of insanity in my everyday living is increasing. It is a real-life version of *La Danse Macabre*. I will quit my office this week. Suzanne will be around during my first week without an office. Then she will be gone for two weeks. The coming months will be a severe trial for me. Can I live as alone as I do? Have other writers known such aloneness as I shall be undergoing? Can I continue? Will insanity conquer me once again?

"Little by little, as time goes on, I shall see that there is no magical way for me to make a living. I cannot sell the produce of my pen. I shall have the greatest difficulty getting a job of any sort through an agency. The fact is that any number of local people may wish to come to my rescue, for no good reason at all. Maybe they just would feel better for being good Samaritans. It isn't so likely that anyone will exert himself especially, but given a person who knows of my plight and a job, why shouldn't he act?

"In reality, though, I have no true friends that care for me one way or the other. Those who claim to be friends will remain silent for long periods of time and then wonder if, by chance, I have muddled through in some surprising fashion. In a way, I threaten to disappear and thus to desert them. I wish to desert them but to have an excuse for doing so. Ah, you son-of-a-bitch, you would not lift a hand to help me when I was in need. For that reason, I deserted you. Or, how can you say I deserted you? You saw me drowning and would not lift a finger to save me. When I was at Perry Point, I thought my death by drowning was desired. I sought to please. Now it seems that I should like to drown, and to accuse these so-called friends of letting me drown, just as father died and thus left me, at nine years of age, to struggle in deep and dangerous currents.

"Did I survive? Well, I am still alive and kicking. But the memory of that awful struggle is a rooted sorrow. I regret that I did pull through. I should like to go back, re-enact the scene, and this time, die. So might I register my immeasurable anger at father for deserting me when in my tender years I needed help, companionship, example. Some people regret they were ever born. I suppose we all do. In addition, I regret I survived the days following father's death.

"Again and again in my stories, I cry out against the fall from paradise. I weep that I was ever born, and I sigh for what is not. When was this paradise which I have lost? Before my own birth? Before brother Dean's birth? Before father's death? Aye, quite likely the last guess is the right one. I keep seeking, seeking my lost father, but to deny him and to desert him. The concept of a God who might restore this lost paradise has never appealed to me. Perhaps I wanted Him, like everyone, but, after father's death, found it impossible to believe a God existed. If one existed, it would be to satisfy wants, but my own needs were too overwhelming to be met from afar. I wanted an immediate presence, my father. With father gone, God was impossible, could not be omnipotent. Perhaps I slew father and so slew God.

"Today I sent to five persons a notice of change of address consequent to my move out of the Majestic Building. I query whether it will seem to the recipients like a death notice. In truth, the card has a multiple aspect in the mind of the sender. It is a notice of the death of the sender, strangled to death by a constricting professional community. It is, in addition, an accusation of some neglect or wrongdoing on the part of the recipients. Finally, it is an odd paean of triumph and deliverance. The death notice also has a reproach that isn't a personal accusation. It gives notice not only of my professional demise but also of the unhealthy, noxious climate in which a law practice is carried on. There is no nurture in this stale and rancid soil for a healthy, strong, life-loving, incorruptible person.

"It may be that I have wanted to fail in order to level this terrible accusation at the profession. However, it has seemed to me lately that the profession is by nature a dismal, miasmic, malarial swamp. It cannot be drained. So why accuse it of anything? It is bound to be.

"Unfortunately, the alternative occupation as a writer which I have adopted also is a slough of despond. Suzanne may be right in insisting, as she does, that life has nothing to offer but comforts. For her, life is not a natural gift, but a social gift primarily. Even so, Suzanne seems to feel the force of my protest against society and its gift. I accept the natural gift but I reject the social gift and protest the pretentiousness of society. I abhor the culture which reduces living to a lockstep routine relieved by drunken orgies during the stop for the night. If that is the universe that I must live in, then I do not accept it.

"To say one does not accept the universe is polite phraseology for saying he wishes to die, to get rid of the too, too solid flesh, to escape from the pretended and the plausible. To die is preferable to life amidst the votaries of the false and the phony, the pretended, and the plausible. But then the wish to die even conforms to the prevailing pretensions. It is dressed up so we don't even realize that such rejection equates with a desire for death.

"Thus an attempt at suicide comes but once in each of ten who hate the world and life. One who attempts it may gloss over his own initiative by implying that he is passive, without a will. The attempt, he implies was forced on him by the temporary combination of adverse factors. Actually, the guy does have a will and his will is for death, an end. It is a matter of long duration, varying only in degree as circumstances vary.

"Gosh, the drift of my thought is toward the morose. One would think that I am witnessing and enjoying my own death even as Tom Sawyer was a spectator at his own funeral. Besides, Freud has spoken of a death instinct. The urge may be no more than the wish to repudiate an unhealthy environment: to extricate one's self by force and at all costs from a strangling social situation. At times, a violent, willful, do-or-die effort may be essential to life.

"Even so, I am enjoying my own death. In the sense that death is a prelude to life? No. It is the idea of going back to infancy and saying now what I wanted to say then: if this is life, keep it. Take it back. I don't want it. In a sense, I now engage in revolution whereas I formerly was a mere rebel. Now as before, I pass judgment on the strings that society has attached to natural life. But with the difference: now I maintain the strings have been torn off. It isn't the rebel's 'should be' that I shout but the revolutionary's 'have been.'"

Thoughts of death persisted in my father's mind. In a later entry, he referred to his departure from the practice of law as a manifestation of death. "My career as a lawyer is dead. By moving out of my office in the Majestic Building, I am enacting its death scene. I am cutting myself off from my past. For this suicidal submersion of myself, as for an enlistee in the military service, I understand that I was to receive the minimum essentials for subsistence. Coming to an end is this suicidal submersion. I shall emerge from this self-imposed confinement. Then we shall see what we shall see."

Occasionally, references to death would pop up as a sentence or two in the diary amidst some other topic, as a *non sequitur*. For example, my father abruptly inserted this short paragraph into a long discussion about fathers and sons: "Today I remembered the coffins sometimes used by the Nazis for the victims in extermination camps. Then my imagination added to the memory a realization of the similarity in shape of cradles and coffins! It was a macabre experience." When searching for an explanation of my father's mental turmoil, memories like that cannot be ignored.

Subsequent diary entries approach the concept of death in a more personal context. I found these entries about death particularly startling because of their blunt references to suicide. He spoke of real death, not symbolic death, starting with experiences during wartime and then abruptly shifting to early childhood.

"In my flight of ten years ago, insanity was intended to be but a way station on the way to death. I was trying my damndest to do what went against my grain — to value myself lower than the herd; to die.

"When I was first in the VA hospital at Perry Point, the suspicion that my death was earnestly desired and requested was strongest. The notion must have originated in my infancy, at home, by virtue of the conditions then and there existing. This much is certain: after leaving home, conditions have never been at odds with that presupposition. When we were all lined up to go to occupational therapy in the leather shop, I made my break for the bay with the intention of drowning. The people in the leather shop wished me to die by hanging; but as long as I was dead, they wouldn't be upset if I committed suicide by drowning.

"At Perry Point I supposed that my death by hanging was particularly desired, hanging by a collar like a dog or a horse, a snare or noose like a rabbit or other wild animal. My guess is that I equate domestication, as symbolized by a dog collar, a horse halter, or a man's cravat, with suicide or execution by hanging. The occupational therapy building where leather work was performed was barnlike. The horse harnesses which hung in the barn at Cozy Nook were of leather. There was a family story of a guy who made the rope with which he hanged himself. I knew the custom of German extermination camps of making the urn for one's own ashes. I thought I was to make the leather rope for hanging myself.

"My neck was awfully sore this morning. This has to do with the idea of death by hanging, no doubt. Is the pain in the neck merely disgust? 'You give me a pain in the neck' is an expression of disgust. Is it any wonder that I do not choose to go home on a vacation? Recently I have remembered the utter terror, the horror I used to feel when a pig had its throat cut in butchering. Its squeal for help, for release was ignored, and I understood I could expect as much sympathy. My turn might be next. Maybe the pain I have in my neck relates to the idea of having my throat cut.

"Today the two boys asked a few things about my war experiences. Had I been in the front lines? I told them I had been shelled, bombed, and strafed but never under rifle fire. I said 'I wasn't a hero, but I gave a good account of myself. I received a *Croix de Guerre* not for bravery under fire but for exceptional services in the liberation of France.'

"I told them of my broken back, of insulin treatment and of electric shock treatment. All-in-all, they probably heard of a strong man who does not need to boast or to exaggerate. Curtis asked 'Did anyone get hurt in the shelling?' At first, I couldn't remember. Then I told him of the deaths of the French prisoners of war who were on the way home.

"It is good for boys to know that their father has faced danger with fear or with intrepidity but faced it and lived through it. Dean surely knew that I had not demonstrated great heroism or personal bravery. Yet I had met whatever dangers came my way very calmly. I spoke of the automobile in which I rode being forced off the highway by a tank retriever and of my rejection of death in a stupid automobile accident. Death by enemy action, I said, was one thing, and death by accident another. In that same conversation, I said death when things are going as well as now would be most unwelcome, against my will.

"My telling the boys how insulin induces a coma, deep unconsciousness, probably led to the question whether I had been at the front. The first time I was given insulin, I resisted, and the attendants had to use force to tie me up. Much as I wanted to die I wanted to put up a show of resistance. I did not want to die that way. Besides, I wanted to test out how seriously the attendants and their bosses intended to inflict themselves upon me. Will they stop at nothing to reduce, abase, domesticate me?

"The boys speculated over my shock treatments. Dean said 'They wouldn't have done it if it didn't help.' I said 'It didn't make me well, but it started me on the road to recovery.' Here was a strange phenomenon: a terrific coma, strong shocks, a broken back, and all done for my own good! God moves in mysterious ways his wonders to perform. Yet, Dean's ready imputation of kindness to society was not convincing to me. It was a mental act, a characterization made by the mind. Faith in humanity, real faith, wells up from deeper springs. The mind may deny the spirit's doubts. The noteworthy thing is that I did not trust the people in charge of me at that time to act for my good. I suspected they would act rather to inflict harm on me, to see me dead.

"In my battles with society, as in the tussle with the attendants who wanted to make me ready for insulin, I probably have been halfhearted. I have expected defeat. The suicidal wish would then be granted without my encompassing my own end. Besides, I have been intelligent enough to appraise the forces arrayed against me as superior in strength to my own forces. Intelligence is a poor battle axe, though. It is easily convinced of futility. A suicidal wish can blunt it. Given a fighting faith, intelligence gives way; the battle is pressed and perhaps won."

Thus, my father traced suicidal thoughts back to early childhood, laying their genesis from his mother. "I rejected mother's teachings about the world. She indicated no place for the gospel of love, no room for the grace of acceptance. The world she presented preferred to sustain physical life and to starve the spiritual. Mother may have insisted upon tradition because otherwise her life was meaningless. In my book, love and acceptance were the supreme virtues. Were that not so, I probably should have committed suicide, for there was nothing about the world as she taught it that appealed to me. The only alternative mother gave me was the world she gave or none, or death. Ostensibly, but only ostensibly, I took her world. An outright, downright refusal to accept mother's world may have seemed to involve suicide. She would kill me. At the time, I was powerless to kill her and perhaps not so motivated. It was preferable to die than to kill. Even now, the preference for death has remained deeply concealed, hidden in the subconscious, buried.

Thoughts of Death

"Looking back at childhood, or trying to look back, I visualize the situation this way. I wished to die, to retreat whence I had come. That was impossible, but nevertheless desired. Mother painted the world as a horrible place. I could not accept such a foul habitation. The best I could do was pretend to accept. The pretense somehow kept alive the desire for death. Pretense meant guilt. Oddly, Mother may have painted the world of tradition, the territory beyond her orbit, as far more dreadful than it is. She always made a fuss about 'keeping the family together.' She feared the outside world. If we didn't, she would look ridiculous."

My father coupled these suicidal thoughts to his longing for acceptance by his parents as a child and by society in general as an adult. He pleaded time and time again for this acceptance, holding the potential for suicide as a remedy for failure to gain acceptance. "I try to gain a hearing for my message by striking a pose of humility. I get down on a knee and confess or, rather, I speak in terms of confidential friendship. I strike a note of great humility. I would be a gardener if I can. I want to work. I want a place. I have no place. This is to say: 'I have told you how I am. Let me come into your hearts.'

"What I have always wanted was love. Beware of substitutes: sex, money, reputation, market acceptance. Always I sing the old refrain 'I want to be loved — unconditionally, just as I am.' Some restaurants have a sign in their window: 'Come as you are.' I refuse to put on a disguise, even though I desperately crave an invitation. I want to be loved, appreciated, esteemed. No one loves a lawyer. I don't build up any degree of self-esteem insofar as I do legal chores. This is to say I don't feel worthy of love or respect. To feel loved, it is necessary first to feel worthy of love. To feel worthy of it, it is necessary to get rid of the guilt complex which permeates one who is in disguise; who is impersonating; who is acting or pretending.

"The world strikes me as a masked ball. I have been invited provided I come in costume. I want to attend the ball, but I do not care to go masked. I want to come as I am. Ah—I haven't been invited so much as ordered to attend in costume, a costume of my choice, perhaps, but in a costume.

"The chore I have been working on lately is that of expanding the element of choice in my life, beyond that of a mere costume. Up to now, the suicide wish has been a revolt against the order to live and to live thus and so. The suicide impulse was held in reserve. As a last resort, I can die. I can escape orders even if I dare not disobey them. When living and the manner of my living is based on choice, rather than compulsion, rather than submission to pressure, then the ace-in-the-hole of suicide is unnecessary. I suspect that my suicide wish has not been tantamount to a deep fascination for death, physical demise. It has represented an ace held in reserve against life. It was a sly triumph over life, by means of death. But, as Dr. Walker once said, what kind of adjustment to life is death?

"Looking back, as an adult I have been somewhat successful at choosing my own fate. The resignation from the government service was partly a matter of choice. I cut loose from a steady paycheck. My termination of my lease at the Majestic Building was a voluntary matter. I wasn't kicked out. I could have stayed longer. My virtual abandonment of my career at the bar was dictated by no one. My attempt to gain a foothold as a free-lance writer is entirely my own idea. I have persisted in it despite a succession of disappointments. For the most part, I have been confronted with choices, and I have chosen my preferred lot.

"Without the opportunity for choice, suicide becomes a sort of perverted posturing. 'Don't push me too far or I'll vanish.' This attitude sees nothing in people but a vicious compulsion and a vicious exploitation. The compulsion and the exploitation are overpowering and leave no room for choice. 'I have no choice but to kill myself.' What an awful situation. I at least have the choice of transcending the inacceptable by self-slaughter. In my case, the suicidal impulse may have been reinforced by a sense of the futility of effort. I want acceptance, to be loved; what more than anything else gives meaning and value to life than being loved? But love cannot be captured, coerced, attained by effort. One has it or he doesn't. One is blessed or he isn't. If I cannot accept that reality, I always have the choice of suicide.

"What triggered this morose line of thought? Yesterday, Suzanne was ill-tempered. She apparently sees our relation as one founded more or less on commercial principles of exchange. My purchase of certain foods for her to cook imposed a greater burden on her than I suffered in transporting her from office to home. I was making a cook of her. She saw her control of our relation broken if I should buy what I choose, should not transport her to market. If she loses control of our relation, then she will lose me as, in adolescence, she lost her father.

"For me, Suzanne's control of our relation is tantamount to death. For her, my control poses a threat to her security, which stirs up all her old fears of suffering a bereavement."

As I read this, my father's incidental comment about Suzanne's ill temper relieved the mounting gravity of his thoughts about death, suicide, extermination. In fact, it amused me. What triggered my father's morose thoughts? Jocularly put: Suzanne, of course. It was all her fault. In other contexts, this rebuke might portend a diatribe, but in this context, it provided relief. But the relief was only passing, for the next few paragraphs returned to gloom.

"As I came along Pearl Street from 9th Street, afoot, I saw two men approaching. The distance was not great. They looked like desperados. They were dressed in gray. I thought: perhaps they're prison escapees who will attack me. Their motive in doing so wasn't considered: presumably anger, hatred, sheer viciousness. I had no fear either. If 'twould be, 'twould be. I had a fantasy of being stuck by a knife till the blood flowed and of grabbing the knife from my wound, shoving it into my attacker, and twisting it around, thus killing my assailant.

"Then the two men were about to pass. Lo, one was my goofy neighbor in a checked, gray, shirt, looking rather tall. The other was an older man, bent, gray, respectably dressed with a coat on. To my neighbor, I spoke in a surprised greeting, so strong had been my fantasy of cruelly-disposed escapees.

"I wonder why I feared an assault by prison escapees. Because I am more fortunate. They are hunted, due to go back, ill-adjusted to freedom. I, on the contrary, have served my time, have no obligation to go back, am secure in my freedom. I do not belong in prison. That is an accepted fact. Escapees may attack me but not others. I expect attack; understand the hatred felt; will resist the furious onslaught and plunge the knife that let my blood into the heart of the assailant.

Thoughts of Death

"I'm not sure whether my fantasy of being attacked was a daydream wish to be killed and so have done with life. To be killed, and to inflict injury on the killer: that is a consummation devoutly to be desired. To find a quick way out of life and to wreak revenge—not for the benefit conferred, but for the hostile intent—that is good fortune heaped high. The infliction of harm on the killer also is a denial of a wish to leave. It must always be understood that one does not wish to die. No matter how cruel one's fate, one continues to sing hallelujahs to his Maker, the earthly paradise created by his ancestors and contemporaries, the heavenly company of his co-partners for the time being.

"I do not wish to go away. I want to climb above. I do not wish to admit the unchangeable, heaven-ordained perfection of what is. The extermination camp *leitmotif* is man-made. True, it is the handiwork of many; but what I wish to bring about will also be the product of many. I wish to plant new ideas; to impregnate the social will; to fertilize the social attitudes. I can't hum the social tune, but I can compose the tune; set it before the public; offer a superior theme song for public rendition. That is what I'm trying to do.

> "Ah! Up then from the ground sprang I
> And hailed the earth with such a cry
> As is not heard save from a man
> Who has been dead, and lives again.[10]

"Last night, I dreamt that I held something in my hand that was afire. I dropped it to the ground. Then I

---

[10] From: Edna St. Vincent Millay, *Renascence and Other Poems* (New York: Harper, 1917).

wanted to put it out with water. I took a copper container which resembled a cap with a handle to pump. I worked the handle but was unwilling to exert myself to get water. I kept thinking of a faucet which needs only to have a button pushed.

"The copper kettle? It reminds me of the red cap worn in the *Portrait of a Youth* by Botticelli that hangs in the National Gallery. A cap long has symbolized for me the containment of the head, the imprisonment of the mind, by the hateful doctrines of the multitude.

"The fiery object dropped to earth. I don't know what that symbolized. Maybe my life. It had low flames. Why not extinguish it, snuff out my life? But I don't choose to work at suicide. There ought to be an easier way: make someone kill me, assist me in my self-destruction. In the dream I won't work, labor, exert myself at self-destruction. If my death is desired, let those who desire it bring it about—or, at least make it easier for me to consummate."

And so my father recorded in the diary thoughts of his death as they continued to surface consciously and subconsciously. Time and again, he attributed them to childhood experiences. As I read these attributions, I found myself wondering if my father's childhood was really that deplorable. Yes, he experienced the trauma of his father's sudden death, but he didn't experience traumas of regular physical or sexual abuse, severe beatings, or other common precursors to PTSD-related suicidal thoughts and behavior. Wasn't there any sunshine, any happiness, in this world for him to enjoy as a child?

There must have been. How else could he (that is Ellis Worth) have written *The Legend of Drowsy Hollow*? With its descriptions of pleasant childhood memories in a bucolic setting, that autobiographical story contrasts with the analytical, oftentimes depressing, account of childhood characterized in the diary. In fact, it is quite disconnected from the emotional torment described in the autobiographical diary. Simply put, the benevolent memories of childhood in the Ellis Worth story do not conform to the malevolent memories of childhood in the diary, where my father wanted to resurrect and then punish his own father by abandoning him and to destroy his mother, where he wished for his own death. The plural autobiographic images portrayed by my father and by Ellis Worth do not align into a singular, well-focused image.

A plausible explanation for the disconnect between story and diary occurred to me: the memories documented by Ellis Worth, the story teller, and Everett Smith, the diarist, describe two different epochs in my father's childhood. I hypothesized that the benevolent memories described by Ellis Worth were formed before my father lost his father, whereas the malevolent memories described in the diary were formed after my father lost his father. Thus, the misalignment is a function of time. This hypothesis seemed reasonable but only marginally convincing because some of my father's malevolent memories preceded his father's death.

A second explanation crossed my mind. I hypothesized that the misalignment is by-product of artistic genre. Ellis Worth wrote fiction whereas Everett Smith wrote fact. Therefore, Ellis Worth could describe memories however he wanted them to be, fantasy or not, with no obligation to align them with fact represented in the diary. In other words, the misalignment isn't real. I could not refute this hypothesis, so I accepted it as a reasonable explanation of the discrepancy between story and diary.

But, this explanation prompted a third, heretical explanation that I had raised previously in a different context: I questioned the legitimacy of my father's agonizing ruminations about desertion and abandonment by his father and mother. I hypothesized that they were inadvertent by-products of misdirected psychoanalytic therapy. During therapy, Dr. Walker searched for the cause of my father's mental illness, but he could not possibly detect the real cause, wartime experiences, because shock treatment had expunged those traumatic memories. Consequently, adhering to classical psychoanalytic theory, Dr. Walker focused on what he could detect: tractable childhood experiences. Accordingly, during talk therapy sessions, he coaxed my father into introspective analysis of his childhood that resulted in poisonous interpretations of non-poisonous memories. Dutiful to his therapy, my father recorded these interpretations in his diary. But, unbound by therapeutic duty, Ellis Worth wrote about the harmless memories, not poisoned by interpretation. This explanation blurs the line between fact and fiction. I could neither prove nor disprove it, so, I discontinued this heretical line of reasoning.

As an afterthought, I wondered how often Everett Smith strayed across the boundary separating fact and fiction in the diary. I had assumed all along that the diary represented fact, only fact, non-fiction. Perhaps I erred in that assumption. With this unsettling afterthought, I had reached an impasse in my efforts to resolve the misalignment. Maybe one of my hypothetical explanations is correct; maybe all of them are partially correct. At this point in my exploration, I certainly don't know.

Before concluding this chapter on my father's suicidal thoughts about his death, I must confess to my own wishes for his death as a young boy. Alas, I remember occasions when I hoped that he would fall to his death while we were hiking on a mountainous trail with a steep drop off. I made no physical effort to hasten his demise, but I recall the longing shamefully.

Of course, I have wondered what could have triggered this destructive line of thought. Probably, it was normal psychologically for a boy my age. I was about eight years old at the time, in the upper range of the classic Oedipus complex. Retrospectively, I suspect also that I was reacting to my mother's harsh invectives against my father. She was still quite frightened of him and uneasy about my brother and me spending all day Saturday with him, often reminding us of his earlier threats on our lives, threats made at the nadir of his mental illness. With no superior understanding of a young boy's expected behavior in these circumstances, I surmise that my reaction was protective of my mother: kill the man, my father, the monster who made her so unhappy.

Fortunately, this episode in my life came and went within about a year. Quite likely, I outgrew normal Oedipal feelings. I may also have matured sufficiently to understand my mother's fear or she became less hostile towards him in my presence. Regardless, these are embarrassing and painful memories from my youth. My father deserved better from his son.

Transitions

As the years passed by, my father's life, that is, the life of the father that I didn't know, transitioned for the better. Time alone may have healed some wounds. Perhaps, too, the transition marked emergence from a "mid-life crisis" — he was, after all, nearly fifty years old. Then again, perhaps transitions were an inevitable consequence of financial stress: the need to change life style or face bankruptcy. Regardless of their root cause, changes occurred and, for the next four years, 1960 to 1964, the diary entries and short stories chronicled the transitions.

At the outset, 1960, two significant transitions occurred: my father took a new job in Colorado Springs, which altered his relationship with Suzanne; and he discontinued therapy sessions with Dr. Walker. The wounds of early childhood persisted, as the diary continued to tell of partially healed open sores from the loss of his father, an inattentive mother (the widow with five children), and pre-mature entry into the adult world. But, they were mentioned less and less often with time, overshadowed by more eventful transitions.

A third transition was occurring as well. I exited puberty into the realm of a budding adult. This transition occurred without any serious complications. Of course, my body changed, but I adapted to that with little effort. I was quite attracted to girls and got along well with them. With my new voice, I sang tenor with ease. More significantly, my intellectual interests changed. Instead of reading books about ice hockey players, race horses, Antarctic explorers, and the like, I now sought books about more academic topics, such as the cosmos, neurochemistry, psychotherapy, and world history. And, I developed a corps of like-minded friends. Despite our intellectual interests, we were active outdoors: skiing, fishing, spelunking, mountain climbing, et cetera. I coached little league baseball teams during several summers. And, my mother took my brother and me on several fishing and camping trips each summer during these formative years.

Curiously, it was on these fishing trips with my mother that I decided to go to Harvard. Her favorite fishing spot in Colorado was along Chalk Creek, which runs along the southeast side of Mt. Princeton. In my young eyes, Mt. Princeton was the most beautiful mountain in the entire state. "It's part of the Ivy League Range, along with Mt. Harvard and Mt. Yale," explained my mother. "Then I'm going to Princeton," I declared. And, so it was decided. Until I learned that Mt. Harvard is 217 feet higher than Mt. Princeton, that is. I changed my mind; I would go to Harvard, instead. My future was determined by that simple fact of geography when I was in the seventh or eighth grade. My mother smiled when I told her of this decision, but my father simply stared straight ahead, without comment. I sensed his disapproval.

Meanwhile, during the transitional period, my father continued to wrestle with rejection and acceptance. After rejecting his double, my father unmasked his core personality, characterized by raw intolerance of other people's doubles, their false fronts, their facades, but forgiving tolerance of their fundamental qualities, their love, their generosity. For good reason, he questioned how well this unmasked core personality would be accepted in his new, post-transitional settings, expressing anxiety directly in the diary and indirectly in Ellis Worth stories. Indeed, rejection and acceptance became a dominant theme in both the diary and the stories of this period.

A short diary excerpt (July 20, 1960) relates my father's anxiety about acceptance. "What I am trying to do now is the most important thing I have ever tried to do—that anyone ever tries to do. I am trying to force the world to take me at my own valuation—not my own valuation in dollars and cents only—not just at a high salary—but as a guy with a message of importance—a guy with strong feelings and keen insight."

Ellis Worth explored these feelings of rejection and acceptance in a quirky fantasy tale, *The Last Frontier*[11], written about this time.

****

The Last Frontier

It looked like a remnant of the wilderness of his forefathers as he stood there at its edge. It wasn't vast, but it was thick and green. Beyond its shadows, the sun beat down fiercely, so far as the eye could see, on fallowed fields. Even weeds had to fight desperately for a toehold on those sizzling arid stretches.

His name was Slim Tandy. He proposed to make a journey into the forest. His reasons were not clear. He was prodded by instinct. If he had anything in mind at all, it was exploration, not exploitation. He paused now,

---

[11] Ellis Worth, *The Sonora Springs Tales: A Collection of Ellis Worth Short Stories* (Spokane, WA: Annandale Press, 2021). Pp. 126-129.

gathering strength before he plunged forward. He removed his hat.

A nutshell fell on his head. He felt something hit, and he saw a shell tumble on the ground. It was midsummer, not fall. It was not yet the season of harvests, mists and mellow fruitfulness. He picked up the evidence at his feet and examined it. It was a shell, but he was unable to assimilate it to any variety of nut known to his experience.

Another tidbit made itself felt through the thickness of hat and hair. He didn't see where it landed. He looked up. He saw nothing and heard nothing except the movement of the branches and their soughing sound in the breeze. A tiny hailstorm of shells pelted around him. "What ho," he said, "am I not welcome here where I stand — or, maybe, not wanted at all in these parts?" Some more refuse dripped from above.

He walked along the border of the woodland, keeping in its shade. "I might have been so close to a nest of young squirrels," he said to himself, "as to worry the parents." He paused, still bracing himself for his trip into the shadowed recesses of the giant grove. This time, a shower of shells slapped his face and cuffed his ears. He decided to look into the matter.

In his youth, Slim had bought peanuts to feed to the squirrels that fattened in the parks of his hometown. He knew their cleverness, their timidity, their greed; but insolence was something else again — at least this kind of impudence. Red squirrels, of course, will scold like a jay, vociferously and at length, but they aren't sly and covert and — let's face it — they aren't intelligent.

Without losing sight of the blazing light which held the fields in thrall, he stepped off, experimentally, a short distance into the forest. He surveyed, as well as he could, the tops of the circumambient trees, hardwoods of various species. While he was looking up, a shell conked him in the eye before he could turn away. The speed of its descent exceeded that of gravity. It was as if it had been thrown by an invisible monkey. If this stoning were the work of squirrels, the creatures were either numerous or well-organized; or both.

He wasn't by any means, panic-stricken, or even especially fearful. He had faced real dangers with courage and could do it again. The point was that he had been challenged at the very outset of his mission into the interior. He had to meet that challenge before he did another thing. The threat to his safety might be negligible or nonexistent, but he needed information so that he could evaluate the situation. Reconnaissance was called for.

He gathered together a few stumps which he managed to kick out of the earth. Then he took up a position beneath a huge maple in a cluster of maples. He tossed his heavy missiles on the far side of neighboring trees while he scanned about him for the quick motions of squirrels in the process of putting a trunk or a limb between themselves and the noise of the thrown stumps. It was like a mass movement. The woods were alive with squirrels! He was reminded of the current war and its tides of displaced persons. Only that is pathetic; and in this swift, silent re-arrangement there was a suggestion of the sinister and ill-disposed.

He half-expected a volley of shells to sprinkle on him and around him. Instead, he received a single, bouncing blow which served notice with rude emphasis that the previous use of bits of shells had been dictated, partly at least, by a desire to conserve ammunition. He glanced at the latest pellet as it rolled into the dark, earthy leaf-mold. It resembled, in its color and its corrugations, a black walnut—perhaps one which was so thick-skulled as to have no room for a meat inside. Still, he couldn't swear it was a black walnut—only that a resemblance existed.

Now he saw that the strangers were emboldened. There were dozens visible on the near side of the trunks, heads down but thrust away from the tree so as to mark him and measure him better. They were gray, mostly—but wait! What a tail! There were a few tan or tawny hairs in head and body, but the tails were golden. Even in the dim rays of sunlight which managed to penetrate the dense foliage, these tails shone like spun gold. And they thrust stiffly outward from the squirrels' posteriors, outward and downward toward the head, for all the world like so many deadly arrows, down-turned thumbs, or inverted phallic symbols.

To see these curious creatures poised so, in the stereotyped alertness of a military formation, was enough to make Slim hesitate. These were the familiar gray squirrels in a familiar pose, but there was a difference which he needed time to reflect upon. The squirrels he had known had been acquisitive and conservative, but not organized, aggressive, and unfriendly. They had treasuries, not armories. Those bushy, golden tails were more expressive than anything else, but of what? Some pitiful regression—some rabid possession within? The whole spectacle, indeed, was more disgusting, somehow, than frightening; more vaguely disturbing than disgusting.

He might still go forward as he had planned; he might well do so. The forest was big enough for both himself and its oddly hellish denizens. Coexistence was one of the alternatives, certainly; but he had anticipated something different—if not friendship, at least a benevolent neutrality or indifference. He had some thinking to do. For the time being, he would just withdraw. The squirrels proceeded to do likewise, vanishing instantly. Slim's retreating steps made no visible or audible impression on the soft, moist, cushioning, forest floor. Not an owl blinked to see him go. Not a canary chirped to call him back. The sustained hush left the next move squarely up to the departing man.

****

Once again, I learned more about what my father really intended to say in the diary than in the stories themselves. In fact, many of the stories made little sense without the explanations in the diary. The *Last Frontier* is a prime example. The story itself is undeniably bizarre and probably for most (if not all) magazine editors unacceptable for publication. However, in his diary, my father expands on the simple story, revealing his struggle with acceptance and rejection by his colleagues, by individuals with a different perception of the world. Allegorically, he associates them to squirrels. They reject him, a man, accepting into their community only creatures sharing their perception of the world. In the story, the man (Slim) retreats, counter-rejecting the squirrels. But in the diary, my father advances, seeking acceptance by acknowledging the squirrels' perception of the world, a perception quite different from his own.

"I hate squirrels. I see them in the parks, but I don't try to make men of them. I don't feed them. I leave them alone. Let's not strike a pose of righteousness in trying to improve the lot of the lowly creatures. They are squirrels. I'm a man. Never the twain shall meet. It is the ordinance of heaven. Let it stand. Respect the status quo.

"But, in *Last Frontier*, I discover that I live in a world of squirrels. The discovery doesn't generate a consuming anger. It isn't a sudden and mistaken discovery. It rests on scientific experimentation and a judicial examination of evidence. There isn't any question about the man becoming a squirrel. Squirrels are squirrels and are happily squirrels. They have no sense of higher potential, no disappointment in being grubbily greedy. They don't pursue people, nor does fear induce flight from man. They don't, however, welcome people into their ranks. They are exclusive. They reject man. They reject me. If they are happy so, why interfere? For their benefit? No. For my own to banish the specter of separation? Ah, very well. The thing is, however, that I don't belong to the squirrels' community. I am separated from it and can only belong to it by becoming a gamekeeper, by feeding the gang peanuts.

"I accept the distinction between me, a man, and the squirrels, and I accept the tragedy of separation between us. Still, my acceptance of squirrels is grudging; there is anger and disquiet mixed with the acceptance. A vision of my fellows as squirrels represents a degree of rapprochement, even though I hate squirrels. They have a definite place in nature, and I accept nature. Squirrels cannot escape their ingrained instinctual way of life just as the rank and file of mankind is similarly enthralled with a comparable way of life. Squirrels have their way, I have mine. I respect the status quo, the world as it is. It isn't for me to change my portrayal of it. Let others do the judging. If others agree with my portrayal of man and squirrels, then the separation is less frightful. My demon doesn't insist that I turn upside down the world as it is. He insists that I portray what I see and derive my pleasure and satisfaction in knowing that others see the same thing. But others, the squirrels, don't see the world as I do. So be it. I am trying to achieve communication, to exorcise the haunting horror of separation of living in a world of my own, without company.

"Deep under the story's surface, I justify my withdrawal from the world of the common man, the common gray squirrel. I justify my action by portraying the world as degenerate, regressive, diseased. If I must be separate, alone, withdrawing, I at least want understanding — union enough for me. It gets down to this: I want people to understand me. All I want is understanding and compassion, but I feel that in order to achieve that, I must change the accepted vision of the world. I must change the way others see the world to the way I see it. I keep screaming for some similarity in vision; I want some understanding of my disagreement with the official version.

"I am beginning to realize that to compel acceptance by inducing others to share my vision of reality is a cock-eyed, mixed-up procedure. I can't wheedle anyone to see things as I do, and I can't compel anyone, certainly not the squirrels, to accept me for what I am. But perhaps a shared vision of reality is not required for acceptance. Perhaps I have been so desperate for genuine acceptance, indifferent to all visions of reality save my own, that I have overlooked this possibility.

"Seemingly, it has never occurred to me that people might understand me without just sharing my vision of reality. The power of love, the possibility of others giving freely and voluntarily, has not figured in my dreams and yearnings, in my dreams and drives. People would understand me, I have assumed, only if they shared my vision of the world and so were obliged to understand me. The idea of others voluntarily seeking to understand me, to love, to sympathize, and to cherish did not occur to me because such seeking was foreign to my experience. Given such seeking for me on the part of others, I need not seek to change the world in order to gain a modicum of diluted acceptance and understanding. That realization has been missing from my thinking.

"Now that I realize what was missing, I feel like some watcher of the skies when a new world swims into his ken—a world where squirrels live their life, and I live mine in harmony. To recognize what has been missing is at least a step towards a realization of what can be present.

"When I had a law office, I didn't seek acceptance as an ordinary, client-property-worshipping, dollars-obsessed lawyer. I didn't stick closely in line and proclaim 'See how I hew the line.' Instead, I wrote articles, delivered speeches, avoided shop talk, and called attention to my differentness. I didn't consider the group-ordained standards of mediocrity as glorifying. I didn't seek glory by the well-trodden path of sameness. I criticized the customary courses.

"As a writer, I have sought acceptance from strangers, from those qualified to speak authoritatively. I haven't waged a campaign for acceptance as a friend, a comrade, a confidant, a frequent guest locally. I have been a maverick. My stories are different. In effect, I have sought to establish new standards for story telling as well as a new vision of existing reality and a new glimpse of what ought to be. I have sought acceptance for myself, yes—and to that extent have been selfish—but I have sought first to establish a basis on which acceptability would be available to all. Given recognition as a writer, my cup would runneth over. On that basis I have lived lately.

"There is no doubt that *Last Frontier* is shaggy and wacky superficially. Yet, it is obviously serious below the surface." Wacky, indeed. As a story, *Last Frontier* is more suitable to cocktail-party or barroom tales than to publication in a literary magazine. But as a fable, this wacky story and its attendant diary entry highlight a significant transition in my father's mental outlook, a transition for the better in his recovery from mental illness.

The transition occurred as my father realized that others might accept him without adopting his world view, his vision. The significance of that transition traces back to my father's rejection of his double and assertion of his singular personality, a narcissistic personality intolerant of attitudes and values different from his, intolerant of a world vision different from his. As a consequence, he anticipated rejection by squirrels: that is, by professional colleagues, personal friends, even Suzanne on occasion. But, he came to a striking realization that acceptance does not require others to adopt his world vision. Acceptance is not conditional upon a shared point of view. He and they could differ. This epiphany marked a milestone in the pathway to mental health.

As I read about his tussle with acceptance and rejection, I felt uneasy. Like so many other things, it simply did not conform to my teen-aged concept of him as a stable father, an icon of stability. And even today, as an older man, I puzzle over the timing. After his discharge from the Army, my father was accepted as a war hero (*Croix du Guerre*, et cetera), offered a prestigious position at the National Gallery of Art, invited to speak at law conferences, and so forth. Why, then, did this struggle documented in the diary emerge ten years later? Although I could easily postulate reasons, none of them proved satisfying.

Another question puzzled me: were my father's concerns about acceptance—those expressed in the diary—really different from anybody else's? In the abstract, no, but in the details and the timing, perhaps yes. Certainly, as a teenaged son, I, too, was concerned about acceptance and rejection but of an entirely different nature. I had typical adolescent concerns: how to dress, dance, behave with members of the opposite sex, and so forth. And as an adult, I wanted acceptance by my peers, professional and social. In retrospect, these concerns were just as critical to my comfort in society as were my father's concerns to his comfort in society. Furthermore, I presume that most members of society, at any age, have comparable concerns about acceptance and rejection by their parents, family, and peers. The major difference lies in the rigor, the depth of my father's analysis of his quest for acceptance. In that regard, the diary opened a window of retrospection into my own anxieties about peer approval at various stages of life.

Setting aside this somewhat inane discussion of man and squirrels and these questions of acceptance and rejection, trouble of a more mundane nature lay ahead: the need for money. My father's defunct law practice had not generated significant income, nor had his part-time job as a proxy agent for Georgeson. And his writing—a pittance. For nearly ten years, his primary source of income had been proceeds from the sale of his house in the Washington D.C. area, and that source was now approaching exhaustion. Thus, my father reluctantly resigned himself to looking actively for a job. "What else can I do? Take a senseless, imprisoning job and drive to and from a factory each day? Forbid it, Almighty God.

Forbid it. Forbid it. Yet I feel impelled to find and take a job of some sort. It is virtually impossible for me to keep going as I am."

Despite his pecuniary difficulties, my father continually honored a child-support clause in his divorce settlement: $75 per month to my mother. He reminded us periodically about these payments. When the topic came up with our mother, she complained that this was now inadequate: the cost of living had gone up, older boys were more expensive to feed and clothe, and so forth. To compensate for this inadequacy, my mother urged my brother and me to take as much as we could from our father. He quite willingly paid for our haircuts, Saturday lunches and entertainment expenses (movies, bowling, swimming, et cetera). But our mother insisted that we take more, mainly more expensive objects such as baseball gloves, skis, boots, camera film, and so forth. Her insistence led us to expect, to demand from our father some new object every Saturday. Occasionally he grumbled about our neediness, but more often he quietly parted with the money to satisfy our wants. These $75 support payments to our mother continued until midway through my brother's freshman year at college. Then, the payments stopped altogether.

Confronted with the necessity to earn an income, my father ruminated about various corollaries of a new job. "Last night, I had fantasies of getting a job at a decent salary, of marrying Suzanne, of moving to a new place to live. Is this a case of accepting defeat in what others consider victory and making the most of it? Is it, on the contrary, an acceptance of society? It is, surely, a case of making peace, of giving up my effort to conquer society and to administer the *coup de grace*.

"If I could do all the things I fantasied, I would perhaps be able to do those things which make me happy. A dumb job would take a minimum out of me. It would give me no satisfaction, but it would give me the funds with which to finance enterprises that are inspirational: contact with nature; a chance to write; more time with the boys at a fairly crucial period. My life with Suzanne might be agreeable. We have gotten along fairly well up to now. I would perhaps make Suzanne happy. A move to Colorado Springs, for example, would be a step in the right direction. The cultural advantages of a big city would be available as now: concerts, theaters, etc. And we would be closer to the mountains.

"The idea of finding fulfillment and satisfaction in a job is a delusion. I certainly tried that as a lawyer in private practice and as an agent for Georgeson. There is no satisfaction if no financial security, and if there is no financial security, the job is a meaningless one which fits with the nonsensical culture. I have come around to the disagreeable fact that one must work for money and, when the work is done, find such satisfaction as is possible in the present-day life situation.

"Now that I accept work as drudgery, can I connect with a job which will compensate me well for drudgery without forcing me to pretend that I am carried away by the importance of what I am doing? Shepard's is looking for editors in their main national office in Colorado Springs. I'll get a letter off to them. Stanley Aviation is looking for a contract administrator here in Denver. What is a contract administrator? If it involves dealing with the military, I'll do all right. I'll go out to Stanley's. Perhaps it would be a good idea to call their personnel office tomorrow. Or should I drive out without an appointment? Go early? How should I dress? In a white shirt? Yes, by all means.

"It is odd how closely opposites approach each other. Thus, I have to ask whether my present attitude represents an acceptance of defeat or, on the contrary, an acceptance of life. Or is an acceptance of life bound to be an acceptance of the limited possibilities? One has to settle for consolation prizes: dull jobs, brief respites from battle, few friendships, uninspired if not actually hostile companionship. In any event, I shall have to fight fiercely now — or I miss my guess — for a paltry position as a so-called editor or as a contract administrator."

Thus, in the summer of 1960, nearing bankruptcy my father started to hunt for a job. His first foray into the employment market was a visit to a local maker of airplane parts, Stanley Aviation.

"I went to the Stanley Aviation employment office today. The receptionist took one look at me and genuflected, did a curtsey. There was something about me that she was accustomed to defer to. Having saluted me thus with her eyes, she became business-like again. She said 'Do you have the qualifications for the job?' I said 'I think so, yes.' As if that would be easy for me.

"I took out an application form and gave it to the receptionist. She scanned it quickly, nodding here and there with approval and then took it into one of the interviewers in the adjoining office. Later she came back with the form in her hand. She huddled toward me and said: 'There's an offer out for the job as contract administrator.' She looked up at me to see how I would take that. I looked down at her, but I was only half seeing her because I was looking inside myself for prompting at what was meant.

"I got this idea anyway: that I was being given the brush off. I may have been quite debonair after the first shock. I may have been glad to learn that I could dismiss Stanley Aviation as twerps—rejects. I may have implied to the woman that I wasn't disappointed, that my inclination to dismiss Stanley, to reject them, had antedated their rejection of me. She tried to smooth it all over, to establish a personal contact with me. She wanted to escape my rejection of Stanley by stepping aside to deal with me directly. I did not encourage that.

"My quick interpretation of the affair was that a personal rejection of me was involved. I didn't fasten onto any ground for the rejection right away. Then I said 'Oh, oh. I know. Nervous breakdown…security risk. That's it.'

"I called before I went out to Stanley and made it plain that I was calling about the job of contract administrator. It could be that it was apparent from the form that I lacked the requisite technical qualifications. It may have been simply that I was too late, as I was told. Somehow, however, the receptionist did not inspire confidence in the excuse she gave.

"I suspect that the woman understood that I felt that I was being given the old heave-ho and that I was responding by a counter rejection. An interesting thing, I suppose, is that the woman was willing to prefer me to her employers. That was her quick emotional response. I rejected her, however, by shaking off the personal connection she tried to make with me. I wanted a job, not a woman. Ah, she was trying to connect with me by being an intermediary with the powers that be and therefore as more powerful than me. I gave her to understand I could get along without her and without the powers that be."

In this entry, I realized how my father still bore the stigma of mental illness. Faced with rejection, he blurted: "Nervous breakdown...security risk." Ostensibly, the employer discriminated against him because of his history of mental illness, which my father may have mentioned in his curriculum vitae. Discrimination may or may not have actually happened, but in my father's mind it did. Moreover, I could easily imagine in those days an employer's hesitation to hire somebody who required hospitalization for a nervous breakdown — even though it occurred ten years earlier.

Of course, nowadays The Americans with Disabilities Act (ADA) prohibits employers from discriminating against employees or applicants with disabilities in all aspects of employment, including hiring, pay, promotion, firing, and more, as long as it does not interfere with job performance. But in that era, thirty years before the ADA, there was no legal protection against discrimination based on disability. For my father, his hospitalization for mental illness thirteen years earlier served as a persistent warning flag, an albatross hung around his neck for potential employers to see.

Incidentally, the stigma of his mental illness transferred to subsequent generations. As his son, I bore the humiliation of my father's history of mental illness. Family, neighbors, and friends occasionally provoked shame, intentionally or unintentionally. For example, elderly neighbors pejoratively raised the subject of his "illness" now and then in various contexts, out of fealty to our mother, who had known them closely since early childhood. I suspected that every member of the neighborhood knew that the "illness" referred to "mental illness." Moreover, my mother raised the subject of "your father's illness" now and then to denigrate him in one context or another, often out of concern that he might try to wrest custody of my brother and me. (He never expressed that possibility to us.)

The stigma of my father's mental illness transferred generationally even further. His grandchildren and great-grandchildren, my sons and their children, bore it as well. At one time or another, they queried me whether episodes of mental unsteadiness (such as depression) in one of their family members could be traced back to my father. When asked, I explained that his illness was attributable to trauma and, therefore, is most probably not heritable genetically. Nonetheless, in this way, the non-biological correlate of his mental illness, the stigma, passed onto subsequent generations.

Rebuffed by Stanley Aviation for whatever reason, my father shifted to musing about a job at Shepard's Citations in Colorado Springs. When my father first alluded to the possibility of working at Shepard's, I knew very little about the company or what the job would entail. In fact, to my knowledge at the time, Shepard's Citations was simply the name in large red letters on a sterile-looking, cube-shaped concrete building on Cascade Avenue, not far from the Colorado College campus. I drove past it on many occasions; indeed, it was on the main route from my home to high school. But I knew nothing about what went on inside the building. When I asked my father about the company, what it did, he explained that it published law books called *Shepard's Citations*. He continued to explain that lawyers often need to determine the history of a legal decision when developing a case. Accordingly, they turn to citators, like *Shepard's*, that document the history of a judicial decision: what other court decisions have cited it, critically or approvingly, and what cases have been overturned or modified by subsequent cases.

In that pre-digital era, to produce these citators Shepard's staff of lawyers, known as editors, assiduously pored through decision after decision, noting what other decisions they cite and, ultimately, compiling their notations in reference law books, the *Shepard's Citations*. Conversely, in that pre-digital era, every law library had an ever-growing collection of *Shepard's Citations* utilized by an ever-busy corps of lawyers as they "Shepardized" their cases. In the diary, my father writes gleefully about his potential contribution as a Shepard's editor to the ever-expanding mountain of data to be mined, picked through hour after hour by lawyers practicing their trade. This mind-numbing tedium would be his revenge on the profession that rejected him.

"To work at Shepard's would mean that I return to law, but as its master, not its slave. I would record its doctrines as a warning to others without having any real respect for the fine print myself. I am pandering to the ignorance of the legal profession—making the bastards pay for their liquor, as it were. I would handle the law as a commodity; sell it to the simple-minded lawyers. It is a case of preying on the predatory. It is a case of shoveling shit onto others instead of having theirs shoveled onto me. This type of work with law is less disagreeable to me than other types. I know law. I might as well be paid for knowing it. I might as well make my anger pay off. Of course, I would rather get rid of my anger than be paid for it, but....

"I want a predatory position such as this. Or should I say parasitic? I want to prey on the parasitic profession of law. I want to make the bastards pay with blood for the evil religion to which they salaam. Here are the priests and the elders, the promoters, the medicine men of the barbaric legal cult. I will supply them with props for their séances, at a price. To fight wicked witchcraft, to expose it as humbug is a losing proposition. It will put me in the poorhouse. To service it by working at Shepard's puts my anger to work at a profit.

"The handling of the law as an editor for Shepard's is a case of handling the law from which all sanctity has gone—all sanctity, authority and life. It is like a son viewing his father's lifeless body—a Christian partaking of the Eucharist—a son handling, touching the dead king. The once-living cells of the father's—the king's—body are now just so much inert matter. I accept the father's death—accept it to the point of savoring it. The king is dead. Feel his skeleton.

"Shepard's represents a chance for me to trample over the law, the practicing portion of the legal profession. Though a stooge in a cubicle, I will grind ever finer and finer the materials with which the local yokels and the domesticated legalized eunuchs must work. While I bend my back to the whip of my employer, I will at the same time be scourging the little fellows all over the country who pride themselves on their being progressive practitioners—scourging them by forever adding new refinements to the legal nonsense already in existence.

"To read case after case and to note point after point and citation after citation will be terribly routine, dull, and boring. But the emotional satisfaction of sucking blood out of the vampires will equal the satisfaction of writing a story which won't sell. And I'll be well paid.

"No. It's settled. If Shepard's offers me a job paying $400 or more, I'll take it, traveling sales jobs excepted. Of course, I'd prefer a plain old dumb factory job which leaves my evenings free and my weekends untouched by solemn thought.

"My willingness to embrace a dumb job at Shepard is a willingness to compromise. I prefer to write, but I need to have firm financial backing while I continue to work at launching my writings. The truth is that I see very little prospect of a job which would pay me as well as at Shepard's. Besides, I have an idea I could do a job at Shepard's with my eyes closed and so have a fairly fresh mind when I get home. I suspect as well that I would experience the suffocating imprisonment of dull work and look for a counter-balancing release in Suzanne's company.

"For that reason, Suzanne fits into the pattern of my going to Shepard's. She fits. I feel that I would want her. Should I take a dumb job, she would soften the blow. I want Suzanne to help me adjust to a terribly routine job. Yes, and to the loneliness of new surroundings. Would she be able to rise to the occasion or would she seek to draw the spotlight onto herself? For her there would be changes, too—many of them.

"Suzanne has pretended for a long time to be anxious for marriage. Actually, she isn't ready, never was, and maybe never will be. Maybe she wishes to see the old experience of her father's death repeated, wants to be once more deserted, left in the lurch. That would be a masochistic wish.

"To move to Colorado Springs, to take a routine job, to take a wife would be compounding change upon change. I did something like that in the army. Having changed from civilian to soldier, I changed from single to married. I wanted a wife to help me meet the challenge of the strange life.

"But what I find difficult to fathom is this sudden new attitude toward marriage. For long, I refused to consider it. I repelled any thought of it as inapplicable to me. For that matter, Colorado Springs seldom figured in my mind as a possible home. Now I am quite willing to consider it. I wonder just what part of the move would be best: the new job, marriage to Suzanne, a new hometown. That is getting down to brass tacks."

Page after page, my father wrote enthusiastically about the opportunity to work at Shepard's. He felt exalted by "this fierce joy, this wondering exhilaration at reading a legal case, knowing it is no more important than a grain of sand sifted through the fingers." Admittedly, I enjoyed his enthusiastic *Schadenfreude* when he wrote about his potential contribution to the practicing lawyer's mind-numbing task of Shepardizing cases.

Oddly, however, my father seldom, if ever, spoke to me so enthusiastically about a position at Shepard's as he wrote in his diary. Indeed, I still remember his lack of enthusiasm for the job when he described it at the time. Pejoratively, he called it "terribly routine." And that was about all he said. I understood the basis for that assessment. But in the diary, he wrote a different assessment, about benefits that outweigh the routine: money; leisure time; a sense of freedom and power "with each perusal of a legal decision binding on others but powerless to affect me."

As the likelihood of a job offer from Shepard's increased, however, this initial enthusiasm for a job at Shepard's began to wear off. My father no longer expressed maniacal satisfaction in preying on parasitical lawyers. Instead, he expressed defeat as the context of the move settled into his consciousness: defeat that accompanies failure to achieve personal goals. Nonetheless, my father rationalized the pursuit of a job at Shepards, analyzing positive aspects of his decision: he would be more accessible to his growing sons; he would use the move as an opportunity to marry Suzanne; he would, essentially, start a life anew. It was not all doom and gloom.

"It is, I think, probable that Shepard's will make me a job offer that I can and will accept. Of course, there is no certainty, whatever, that I will be offered a job I can accept, any more than a sale of a manuscript to Harper's is a forgone conclusion. Still, I surmise that Shepard's is impressed by my past record. I appear capable of acquiring skill. It is likely that I will remain for years whereas a young man is likely to move onto greener pastures before long. I may be an example and an influence on the other employees.

"What does employment by Shepard's mean to me? It is factory work. It is a retreat into the suicidal cave of routine work. It is at the opposite extreme from my present setup of freedom, speculation, production. It is a dramatization of the blighting, stultifying, destroying effects of the current culture. I suppose my willingness to go to work for Shepard's is that I can offer it as proof of my contention that our society is an evil, wicked one. See how it forces one of the giant creative spirits of the age into chains. In a sense, financial pressure is driving me out of my present setup. Suicide may be involved, but it won't be a wholly voluntary proposition.

"In that respect, I am defeated. Many people look upon a steady job with a regular salary as the *summum bonum* of human existence. I regard it as a defeat. My apparent, observable defeat will be a reproach to the society which forced so talented a creator to work under handicaps. It will fortify my conviction that I live in a wicked world.

"However, if I go to work for Shepard's, there will be a considerable element of choice in my doing so. It is one way to earn a living, a way which is less repulsive than such others as are in evidence. I won't hold an especially honored place in the community as a successful practicing lawyer does, but neither will I have to suffer having my tail cut off as the lawyer does. The fact is, I guess, that I prefer the visible clear-cut defeat of Shepard's to the blurred, dusted-over, defeat of private practice. But even as I fall a victim to the fire of the hunter, I weave plans to escape the full impact of the numbing deep freeze of routine, regularized mumbo-jumbo.

"I think I will be able to bear up all right beneath the burden of routine, be able to maintain good cheer in spite of the blank-faced or insolent morons who will endeavor to engage me in conversation to prove I'm wrong, prejudiced, senile. The whole staff probably — the males anyway, the lawyers — will consist of failures who know they are failures and refuse to admit it while trying to get their fellow workers to admit it. I suppose that most of them despise their work, despise the law. I suppose that work at Shepard's would be tolerable partly because I could despise it too. I despise what has encompassed my defeat, the cause of my undoing. My main consolation lies in the opportunity to inflict defeat on others.

"For my father, society was a work environment. One worked with others. When one was not working with others, one planned for work, discussed it, reflected on it. My plan to go to Colorado Springs to become a slave to routine work at a publishing plant takes a leaf from father's book. Father had mother to soften the rigors of well-nigh constant work. Why should I not have Suzanne in lieu of mother?

"I won't leave many friends behind. Whether I take Suzanne with me or leave her, I haven't decided. Many persons would, of course, use the move to Colorado Springs as an occasion for a big party and an announcement of the news. I'm not so inclined at all. The transfer isn't necessarily good news, not exactly a victory. But, aside from that, I don't have complete faith in the goodwill of those who purport to be friends. Finally, I can ill afford to pour free liquor for the multitude of free-loaders.

"Strangely, the notion of simply pulling out of town without notice to anyone has a certain fascination for me. I would, I guess, take that way of bawling out people for neglecting me. By slipping away unannounced, I would serve notice, as it were, that I feel neglected. My inclination is to give no notice of my relocation to any of my old friends. Actually, I would simply sever relationships, part company. When they should chance to look for me, I would be gone, gone: sunk without a trace, as if dead. Or should I say, as if permitted to die.

"I wish to die and be born again with a wife to serve as a better mother than the original and only. I wish to restate the terms and conditions of living. Being a soldier in the ranks and being just another lawyer among dozens is to be—if not dead—one of the untold millions of the not yet born. I wish to be born, to be recognized as unique; to have a new mother; to gain identity and status and importance; to repeat the life cycle, ever repeating it to gain finally birth under favorable circumstances.

"As I contemplate moving to Colorado Springs, I sense some dusky mysterious impulse to get closer to nature, to fields, to streams, to horses, to start life anew. I have an odd, vague notion that I shall do what my father did not do. I shall return to my children, to be near, handy, readily available whenever they need me. I shall put myself in father's place fifty years ago. And in doing so, play his role as I thought, as a child, it should be played. He left, died, deserted, and, of course, did not return. I see myself as father. I am at a distance from my children. I would return to them, as father should have done to us. Thus do I correct father, set a better example, give expression, even, to a better culture. Here is a reunion—a union of father and child. We shall go to hockey games, go skiing, go fishing, swimming, skating.

"It is as if I were rewriting life. I am father, and I will return. I set my own ideas and values above those of father. I set myself above father but I am father. He and I are one and the same. I rewrite the script as each new age rewrites Christianity and as the varying Supreme Courts rewrite the federal constitution. On the eve of my departure from Camp Carson for Texas in 1943, I proposed to Margie. I wanted to take her with me. Now, in anticipation of a move to Colorado Springs, I have considered proposing to Suzanne in order to take her along. These two parallels raise a question concerning an earlier one. Did I, as a child, have the unconscious wish to run away from father and to take mother with me?"

Several days later, my father's future was decided. On that fateful day, August 11, 1960, three days before his 49th birthday, my father got a job offer from Shepard's. "When Shepard's asked me if I wanted time to think over the job, I didn't say 'yes.' I made it plain that I wanted the job without ifs, ands, or buts. That has remained my attitude." More to the point, my father accepted the job offer without hesitation.

That evening, he took Suzanne to "a nice lobster dinner" and told her about his job offer and impending move to Colorado Springs. Significantly, he asked Suzanne if she would move down to the [Colorado] Springs to be with him. In other words, explicitly or implicitly, he asked her to marry him. She said "no," and "explained to me that she already had a better setup than I was going to get. I took the answer as a reasonable one and as a justifiable one within the economic, rational framework from which it emanated. I didn't argue.

"My abstention from arguing with Suzanne whether she should come with me to the Springs was based on the recognition that my request and her refusal proceeded from two different frameworks. The request was emotional and was indifferent to profit, gain, security. Her refusal came from a rational, thrifty frame of thought.

"In a way, the request challenged Suzanne's regular, customary, ingrained orientation. Indeed, the challenge also is to the whole cultural framework. Suzanne is well adjusted, knows where she stands in the familiar framework of money, jobs, speech, daily concerns. I don't challenge her orientation to all of that so much as I challenge the framework's right to preempt the field of the individual's orientation, vision, concern. Perhaps I intended to present Suzanne with such a challenge. Perhaps she would be happier in familiar surroundings. She is beginning to realize I may have her in a pretty lonely situation.

"After we got home, I aired some of the things I wanted to say but not in the restaurant. I especially tried to clarify for her that I am not leaving her, any more than she is electing to stay behind. She figures she has good and cogent reasons for staying behind, and I enumerated those without disparaging their importance. She spoke of her getting a job in the Springs as a well-nigh impossible task. I added 'Besides, you have a cozy, comfortable apartment and such a place might be hard to duplicate in the Springs.' She countered 'Oh, that's not important.' I replied 'Oh, yes, it is important, decidedly so.'

"Suzanne referred to my escape. I said 'What escape?' She said 'From reality.' I replied 'I am facing a very real financial situation.' It may be that Suzanne senses that I am escaping from something unrealistic, an unrealistic attitude of dependence on her, an unrealistic submission to cultural shibboleths.

"It is good for both of us to have our imminent separation discussed without rancorous bickering. I feel better about the whole situation after this evening's parley, and I suspect Suzanne does too. She looked a bit beaten up when I first arrived.

"Well, we'll get along, no matter how, no matter what."

As a rejected suitor, my father was undoubtedly stunned, bruised emotionally. However, he certainly concealed any pain from my brother and me. Since we had scant knowledge about Suzanne, my father had no reason to share his disappointment with us; we could not have offered much consolation. In fact, I doubt that he had any confidantes to share his disappointment with. Thus, he turned to the diary as an outlet. And, he wrote effusively about this rejection over the next several days probing for ways to soften the blow.

"Suzanne has been willing to see my confidence shaken. Apparently we are parting quite definitely. Maybe Suzanne is fairly well satisfied with that. It could be that she would have been pleased to see our relationship legalized as an engagement, but, contrary to my supposition heretofore, lacked interest in marriage. In any event, my suggestion that she accompany me to the Springs gave her confidence, a shot in the arm. The young man was willing to marry her. The young man considered her desirable. Maybe this recognition of the desirability of Suzanne was a good thing for me, too. At least, it created a good atmosphere on which to part.

"Actually, Suzanne probably will be delighted to share my fate if I keep the question open, if I show I am serious about it and if I use the right approach. I told her 'like Churchill, I have nothing to offer you but blood, sweat, and tears.' With Suzanne, a tug of war may be involved. Who is more important? Who is dominant? Who leads whom? I made it clear that I regard myself as the leader. I even made it appear that following me is a test of strength. Remaining behind is the easy, weak, comfortable way.

"In all of this, Suzanne is showing so plainly her lack of faith in me. She still hasn't withheld a sneer at my 'literary career,' but her occasional disparagements do not cause me any concern. She has reasons for fearing to concede my value. Her own value depends on the non-recognition of me and on constant reiteration of her own greatness. It isn't terribly important for me to reproach her for her lack of faith in me. I have confidence in myself. Having faith in myself, what care I whether she shares that faith or doesn't? If she goes her way, I'll get somebody else who isn't disqualified from recognizing the merit of others generally and my merit in particular. In any event, I should like just as plainly to prove her to be wrong. I would like to be able to bombard her with copies of my published manuscripts showing how others accept me, have faith in me, value me. The chances are, however, that I shall not even keep Suzanne *au courant*. I may create a literary career for myself, while to outward appearance, I am merely a poorly-paid salaried flunky of Shepard's Citations. For that matter, do I want to bombard members of the bar here, or members of the press with copies of my published pieces? No, I don't give a damn what the local yokels or Suzanne think about me, about things.

"I would like to locate a woman who will share my ambition as worthy and will think I am worthy of pursuing that will-o'-the wisp as a literary reputation. I simply want to have my stories published. I think that this ambition to be a writer is a worthy one. I hope to have more influence on my contemporaries and on succeeding generations than presidents, senators, and ambassadors — influence for the good. The great evils of the day are beyond political correction but not beyond effective literary treatment. Notably, my ambition has little to do with the job at Shepard's."

Thus came a transition point in my father's life: a new job, a move from his home in Denver to Colorado Springs, an inflection in his relationship with Suzanne. Surely, all of these changes must have been exhilarating. Indeed, he took Suzanne out for a celebratory lobster dinner.

The decision to accept a job at Shepard's would most probably test my father's mental health, and the outcome was not a foregone conclusion. The job at the National Gallery of Art tested him after returning from the war, and he failed the test, ending up in a mental hospital. This decision initiated a fateful iteration of that kind of test. At Shepard's, his mental well-being will be tested as he seeks acceptance in his new environment:

accommodating new colleagues, performing assigned routine tasks at work. Furthermore, he will see Suzanne, a provider of emotional support, much less frequently. As he stated in his diary "My final recovery from the illness which has plagued me for so long depends on the study of peculiarities and intensities which dictate my behavior in crises."

Notably, with the move, came another change, another test: my father finally bid a final *adieu* to his psychiatrist, Dr. Walker. Gradually, during the past year or two, he had been reducing the number of visits, from regularly scheduled appointments to ad hoc visits when he felt the need for psychiatric counseling. The relocation in Colorado Springs provided a convenient stopping point. I cannot pinpoint when—or, for that matter, whether—my father saw Dr. Walker for the last time in Denver. On rare occasions, he alluded to Dr. Walker, but he never spoke about appointments or what was discussed. However, the diary does not mention any further visits after the move to Colorado Springs.

The only comment on the significance of his last visit is a diary entry on July 27, 1960. "Dr. Walker doubtless saw that much remained to be straightened out when I ceased to be a patient. He doubtless knew, as well, that it would be best for me to finish the job; that only I could finish it and that I would work at it. I trust what I dredge up and I distrust what others tell me." My father is on his own.

The Springs

Admittedly, my father began his employment at Shepard's Citations with a sullen attitude. In numerous diary entries leading up to the move, he wrote explicitly about his disdain for the company and the job. The company served the profession that he had repudiated, namely the law, and the job entailed pedestrian transcription of legal citations.

From what my father told me, I knew a few facts about the job. His starting salary was $5,200 per year. With adjustments for inflation, that corresponds nowadays (2023) to about $55,000 per year, enough to live in frugal comfort. And, I knew that his title was "editor." As I understand the job, editors were assigned a passel of recent court cases for a particular jurisdiction (for example, a region of the country). Then, they documented every case cited by each of these recent cases onto slips of paper, one slip per citation. The citations were sorted, tabulated, and printed in books, the *Shepard's Citations*, where lawyers could look up the various citations to document precedence when preparing their court cases. Looking forward, these tasks were ideally suited for automated digital technologies. But at the time, they were performed by scores of lawyers (editors) and support staff.

He told me a bit about the workplace as well. The editors' desks were arranged in a large room, with no privacy. The boss, the editor-in-chief, had an office where he could see all of the editors' desks. Under his watchful eye, there was little fraternizing among the editors except during regularly scheduled coffee and lunch breaks. As my father puts it in his diary: "At Shepard's, the setup denies the least privacy, except for the upper echelon officials. A sneeze or a fart, a smile or a smirk takes place within the hearing and observation of many. It's as though private life is non-existent. Abandon individuality, all ye who enter into employment here." Moreover, according to my father, the entire operation was very cost-conscious. For example, to minimize waste and pilferage, editors were required to turn in their worn-out pencil stubs when requesting a new one from the women who circulated with a tray of office supplies. Every pencil must be accounted for. It's not hard to imagine why my father considered the work tedious, disdainful, Dickensian.

Only three factors provided my father any consolation. First, he would be earning a regular salary sufficient to stave off bankruptcy. That, of course, was important—indeed, critical. Second, during evenings and weekends, he would be free from work obligations that might limit his opportunities to write and to visit Suzanne in Denver. That, too, was important. Third, my father would be adding more and more minutiae to the expanding documentation of legal precedents, thus compounding the workload for practicing lawyers. Repeating what he wrote in his diary: "Though a stooge in a cubicle, I grind ever finer and finer the materials with which the local yokels and the domesticated legalized eunuchs must work. While I bend my back to the whip of my employer, I will at the same time be scourging the little fellows all over the country who pride themselves on their being progressive practitioners—scourging them by forever adding new refinements to the legal nonsense already in existence." I must confess that the perversity of this consoling factor causes me to smile. Nonetheless, it seemed quite important to my father, for it constituted revenge on the profession that had denied him a living: "payback," so to speak.

With such a sullen attitude a priori, it is hard to imagine a graceful transition from Denver to Colorado Springs and into the workforce at Shepard's. Unfortunately, the only recourse is just that: to imagine, because during this period, there is a 105-day hiatus in the diary. I know from estate tax forms that my father began work on September 1, 1960. But the diary has no entries between August 19 and December 2. It resumes three months after my father had relocated in Colorado Springs and started the job. The hiatus is particularly frustrating, because I don't have any record of the move, its challenges, its frustrations.

Only recently, as I was curating the diary notebooks, did I learn what happened to the missing entries. They were the victim of bugs. Yes, insects. According to my brother, many years ago when he was moving from one house to another, he noticed that one of the boxes containing the diary notebooks was infested with some kind of insect. Inside this box, several of the notebooks were being consumed by these vermin, with many pages eaten nearly to the metal spiral binding. Understandably, my brother could not tolerate those insects infesting other items in his house, so he discarded the damaged notebooks; he doesn't remember how many but estimated three or four volumes. In any case, the hiatus is an unrecoverable loss. Of course, I wanted to ask Suzanne about the transition, but that is out of the realm of possibility. So, like many Ellis Worth short stories, the diary does not tell the whole tale. It requires readers to infer, to imagine what happened during this hiatus.

I was particularly concerned about Suzanne during this period of time. How did she and my father part? How did they get through this transition? I imagine that they had a two- or three-month period of adjustment after the move. For about eight years in Denver, they had shared meals, social outings, sexual intimacy, and comforting companionship on almost a daily basis, even on Saturdays after my father drove back from spending the day with us in Colorado Springs. The move disrupted the comfort and familiarity of that life style. In a sense, it reversed my father's routine. Now, he drove from Colorado Springs to Denver, the opposite route, every Sunday and sometimes on Saturdays as well to spend time with Suzanne. But it wasn't the same. They no longer shared their lives so closely.

I imagine that Suzanne helped my father with the move. Although my brother and I knew that our father planned to move to Colorado Springs, he provided no details at the time. Nor did he ask for any help with the move, although we were 14 and 16 years old at the time, certainly big enough to help carry boxes and furniture. If he left Denver without fanfare, he certainly entered Colorado Springs in the same reticent way. Suddenly, our father just lived in Colorado Springs.

I imagine that my father had little difficulty finding a convenient apartment. Shepard's is located in an old, established neighborhood with large, stately mansions built to accommodate large families along with household staff, such as maids, nannies, au pair girls, and other domestic help. As these large families went out of style, several of these mansions were converted into apartment buildings. My father rented a spacious apartment in one of these converted mansions, located about a mile from the Shepard's plant. He gave us each a key and invited us to enter the apartment whenever we chose.

Because the apartment was on my driving route home from school, once or twice a week I used the key to let myself in, where I had something to drink and went to the bathroom. Jokingly, he once said that I used his bathroom to rid myself of all the crap that I had ingested at school. I smiled, knowing that this comment wasn't entirely said in jest; he had little respect for formal education. Usually, I stuck around until my father arrived, when he often would ask me to read his latest story, a task for which I had negligible enthusiasm. These after-school visits replaced my regular Saturday visits with him, except for occasional excursions together into the mountains for a day of fishing or ice skating on a frozen beaver pond.

I imagine that my father settled into the job at Shepard's with controlled anxiety. As the "new man," he was the center of attention for a week or two. Presumably, fellow male editors probed for background information about his past experiences, interests, and family life, with the usual trace of competition. Females sized him up as a potential source of responsiveness, with the usual trace of sexual tension. The editor-in-chief, George Wilcox, made his job-performance expectations clear with the usual trace of menace characteristic of most bosses. And, the company's owner, William Packard, known by the editors as "old man Packard," showed up now and then, with the usual trace of indifference to the editors and other lower-level staff members. In other words, the first several weeks for my father were probably about the same as they would be for any other new employee in an organization of this size.

If my father, in fact, kept current in his diary during this transition, I imagine that he recorded initial impressions about his job: the company "atmosphere," workload assignments, colleagues' personality traits, and so forth. Likewise, he most likely commented on Suzanne's, my brother's, and my initial adjustments to the move. And, he most likely told about any of his nighttime dreams and their presumptive meaning. All of this can be deduced with near certainty because he wrote effusively about these topics in the extant diary after the hiatus. It remains less certain whether he wrote any new stories during this period. I suspect that he did, but he seldom affixed a date on his manuscripts, so I had no way of knowing when he wrote manuscripts not mentioned in the diary.

However, Ellis Worth wrote one story, *The New Man*,[12] that I infer had been inspired by the first day of work at Shepard's. Uncharacteristically, the extant diary makes no mention of this story. Presumably, it was written during the hiatus. I imagine that, characteristically, my father had much to say about the story in the diary, but any clarifying comments about the theme, the characters, the setting are lost. The story must stand on its own as a chronicle of my father's introduction to Shepard's.

****

The New Man

One couldn't blame Maury Sogard for taking the first job that came along. He had been out of work for

---

[12] Worth, *The Sonora Springs Tales: A Collection of Ellis Worth Short Stories*. Pp. 206-212.

months when he received a telephone call from Mr. Gast at the Micromatic Division. There was very little industry in the mountain town of Sonora City, and, the situation being what it was, a guy couldn't afford to pass up anything at all. Micromatic's wages were minimal, but there were fringe benefits: grocery checkers who got to know one's employer unconsciously forgot to add in certain charges, such as bottle deposits; laundry clerks saw to it that elbow holes were sewn-up free; things like that.

As a Hollis-Henlein Company, Micromatic had been going downhill fast. Then, the Rudy Robot Stoker Company, which wanted to diversify its manufacturing and take on a few products with a different market from that for coal-stokers for home furnaces, had decided to take over Hollis-Henlein and its government contracts and operate the business in Sonora City as a division of Rudy Robot Stoker. This merger of Hollis-Henlein into the bigger Milwaukee outfit gave the Sonora City satellite a financial shot in the arm, and, as it turned out, gave Maury Sogard a job.

Mr. Gast introduced Maury to Mr. Wilcox, who was the foreman in charge of "civilian commercial production," a minor phase of Micromatic's "output" or "product line," as they called it. "You got pretty good eyes, I guess?" Mr. Wilcox asked.

"I guess," Maury said. "I passed the test."

"Well, come with me, then. You can work here at this bench. Remember, your number is 27, right between Mr. Slocum and Mr. Carver." Bringing Mr. Slocum into the conversation now, Mr. Wilcox said, "Frank, this is one of our new men. Will you see that he gets what he needs and keep an eye on his work till he gets the hang of it?"

"Sure will, Oscar."

"OK. Introduce him around a little. Get Earl to help you with instruction if necessary."

"Sure thing, Oscar," Frank chirped to the chief who was now going back to his battered desk in the corner of the plant.

Turning to Maury as if the two, being alone, could slough off pretense and talk sense, Frank said, "How much did Willie tell you?"

"Willie?"

"Yeah, Wilcox."

"Oh. Oh, nothing at all."

"Well, then I might as well begin anywhere. Here are some time cards. The company keeps a strict count on how much you do in a day, a week, a month, but that will come later, when you're 'on production.' In the meantime, you can just disregard this column, number of units, and write in there 'Training'."

At this point, Maury's attention was distracted by the sight of Wilcox "barreling" down the aisle between the workbenches at a terrific speed. His head was thrust forward so as to add to the momentum achieved by his pistoning feet. Every soft, bulging, muscle on the foreman's body seemed to ripple and bounce and quiver with effort. His face was flushed to an apoplectic red and managed, somehow, to suggest all the timeless, tragic, woes and miseries of the world. In his hands the frenzied foreman clutched a bundle of papers, some white, some yellow, some blue, some pink. Whatever the papers were—letters, orders, contracts, time cards, blank forms—they were held high on the chest, tightly, to signify the great value the holder attached to them.

The two watched the guy disappear into a cubbyhole office at the far end of the shop. Then Frank explained: "You'll get used to that. That's just Willie training for a heart attack. You'll see that performance twenty times a day, every day. That office down there is Mr. Carr's. We call him Jitney. He's the vice-president in charge of production. When he crooks his little finger, Willie starts running. There's no intercom system between the two offices. Willie knows by instinct when he has to start sprinting for Jitney's office. You can pity the poor fellow, if you want to. At home his wife uses him as a door mat. But he's the guy we get our orders from, and that's that. Maybe he's heard the crack of the starting gun again." They watched Willie race off in another direction.

"Looks like he's suffering from the GIs, a bit," Maury commented. "Yeah. As I said, you'll get used to that. Willie's not a bad sort, really—only got no backbone. He's been with the company, though, for years and got seniority galore. The company sent him out here from Milwaukee. He's a real company man. He'll never retire. He'll die on the job, have a heart attack right here one of these days, right in this very aisle. Some of us will carry him out.

"You know what the company's retirement plan is?"

"No. Mr. Cast didn't say. Said something about insurance after being here long enough."

"They got a plan: those steps right out in front. The guys all call those our planned retirement. At this altitude, climbing those steps is sure to get you in the long run. Then your beneficiaries will collect the insurance. Ha ha!" He seemed to think it was one whale of a joke.

"Won't you run behind with your work if you don't finish explaining what I'm to do and get back to your own bench?" Maury asked.

"Not that I don't enjoy talking, but I'm just wondering."

"Don't worry about me, Fella. What's your name, again? Well, don't worry about me, Maury. I can take credit for training on my time card, too. This is a gravy assignment for us both, trainer and trainee, while it lasts, and we'd better make the most of it. We'll be on production soon enough, and then there's no rest for the wicked."

"Tell me: Does our pay depend on results? I mean, on how much we turn out in a day?"

"Listen. How many units did they tell you they expected? Did they say?"

"I'm not sure. I think Mr. Gast said something about fifteen an hour."

"Fifteen an hour! You do fifteen an hour, and they'll want twenty; do twenty, and they'll come at you because you're not doing twenty-five. I actually think they'd ride you to do more if your rate of production was a hundred an hour. Your best bet is to keep 'em complaining. You're a fool to be over-conscientious. You know that, I guess. You weren't born yesterday. I'm only telling you because you're a new man."

As Frank talked, he had been giving Maury a demonstration of the work to be done: slip the little mica disc into the slotted shell this way, then hold the hairspring taut and insert the set screw, so. Maury, in turn, had started to copy the technique of his instructor.

"That's good, Maury. That's it, exactly. Your fingers are naturally nimble; and you have no idea how they'll improve as you go along. Just spare your eyes.

The Springs

Make as much use of that glass there as you can. When you've really got the knack of it, you'll be able to recite the box score of the last game of every team in the major leagues as you go along; and you'd better talk it up or you'll go mad, stark-raving mad. Why does a hockey goalie talk it up during a close game? Same principle.

"Another thing. You'll never do more than a part of a part, but don't let that get you down. The company itself simply makes a sub-assembly of a sub-assembly of a sub-assembly. Get it?"

Earl Carver had come over from his bench to look on. "I'd say he's well on his way to micromagnetic migraine, wouldn't you, Earl?"

"Gosh, yes. I've never seen any guy pick it up as fast as you have, uh, uh...."

"Maury Sogard."

"You carry on with him, Earl," Frank said. "I gotta go you know where."

"Maury's for Maurice, I suppose," Earl said. Maury nodded. "The other guy that began this morning was late the very first day," Earl went on genially apropos of nothing in particular. "You ever been analyzed, Maury?"

"No. Do you mean circumcised?"

"No. Analyzed, psychoanalyzed?"

"For crying out loud, whatever gave you such an idea?"

"Oh, I don't know. I gotta nephew, says it's wonderful; thought you might have tried it, being as you're a young man. Got a family?"

"Gotta wife and two kids. They're both in school. Wife works at the Moonbeam Film Company. Secretary to one of the big shots."

The Man I Didn't Know

"I wouldn't have thought you were old enough to have kids in school."

"Oldest will be in junior high next year. With a little luck, we'll see him educated. There's nothing like an education for the young people."

"Yeah? Some say that, all right."

"It's taken some doing, I'll tell you."

"I'll bet."

"You ain't seen the boss yet, I guess. The big boss? He's just back from Arizona; spends the winter there; comes back here in the spring when it gets too hot for him there. The company's got a division down there, too."

"You mean the vice president in charge of production, Mr. Carr?"

"No. I mean Mr. Stamwhite, the big boss from Milwaukee; originally from Milwaukee. You'll see him around if you stay here long enough. He doesn't come into the shop very often. He has more allergies than he has dough. We've got a saying that the reason he visits the shop is to check and see if the exit lights are on. You like it OK?"

"Of course, I like it. I need a job. Maybe my wife can quit after a while."

"That would be nice, wouldn't it? By the way, have you been saved?"

"You mean at church?"

Earl was reaching into the pocket of his plaid western sport shirt, fumbling to get his fingers on something and twisting his whole body around like a corkscrew to help his fingers. He brought forth a circular—blue printing on cream-colored paper. "Read that," he said, as he unfolded the tract and put it before Maury.

The Springs

As Maury took it, he saw the warning in bold letters at the top: "Unless ye be born again…."

"Thank you," he said. "I'll read it tonight at home. Do you want it back?"

"I can get more," Earl said, "at the Blessed Fury Tabernacle. That's my church."

"I'll take it home with me," Maury repeated.

When things had quieted down that evening — dinner over, dishes washed, kids at their homework — Maury's wife asked, "Did it really go all right today, Maury?"

"Why, certainly, Sue, Sweet. It's a great place. I feel like an old man."

"You said 'old man,' darling."

"Did I? I was absent-minded, I guess. I mean I feel like a new man. New faces, new opportunities, new products, and the same little woman, which counts most of all." He went over, put his arm firmly around her, and, with his eyes closed, gave her a lingering kiss low on the cheek. She yielded, partly automatically, to the embrace, but with her eyes meanwhile staring over her husband's shoulder into space. Then she, too, closed her eyes, put a hand on his shoulder and cuddled to him. There they were standing, silently, when Dennis and little Arleta looked up from their books in wonder at the complete hush which had come over the household.

****

When I first read this story, the ending warmed me. I assumed that in this allegory the main character, Maury, represents my father; the wife, Sue, represents Suzanne; and Micromatic represents Shepard's. Thus, I imagined that my father had found comfort with Suzanne as he began working at Shepard's. Stating this differently, Suzanne had comforted and supported my father as he launched this new phase of his life. My father dreamed of, longed for a woman's comfort in times like this. I was happy imagining that this particular dream came true, that he got what he longed for. Did this story herald loosening the chains of mental illness?

However, as I thought in more depth about *The New Man* and its warm ending, I began to question whether my imagination had gotten the better of me. Could this ending signal a pleading call for the comfort he missed so terribly as a child? Or the comfort he now misses with Suzanne staying in Denver? Surely, my father would have answered these questions in the diary. Unfortunately, because of the hiatus, once again I was left with the ambiguities, dependent on my own imagination.

Fortunately, imagination is swept brusquely aside when the diary resumes on December 2, 1960. My father's attitude towards his new employer had not improved during the hiatus. Indeed, it can be described in one word: bad. "The notion that one's own employer is awful, a stinker, is decidedly noxious. Wages and salaries are low. The boss shows contempt for his employees, evidenced by his cavalier dismissals without warning and by the police-state discipline which pervades the organization. There is a degree of humiliation, mortification in working for a miserable outfit, and there is extra mortification in working with employees who weep and wail in helpless anguish, grief, and protestation. There is scarcely an editor who has the slightest pride in his work. Why not walk out *en masse*? Why not fight back by giving the story to one of the newspapers (not very effective, I suppose). Why not leave?"

The next day: "Personnel did a 'close check' job on me today, but I think they gave me a pretty clean bill of health. It could be that my eligibility for a Christmas bonus may be involved. I surmise that my rate of production has few if any equals. If I am as accurate as I am fast, the theory may run, I deserve a pretty good bonus. I hope to get Personnel off my neck by establishing a reputation beyond the purlieus of the plant, with the local press, et cetera, which will make me, and not just my work, an asset. Right at present, their tactics strike me as blows to break my spirit, to soften my backbone, to ruin my independence. I take them as a way of fighting back. I am not just fighting to keep a job but fighting to keep it and still remain a man. Those in charge at Shepard's quite likely are terrifically impressed by the various symbols of value at which I can point: honor societies at college; professional, military, and business titles; scholarly articles. However, were I to rely on those factors, my colleagues would denigrate the importance of them. They would say 'Here, what counts is performance, salary, seniority, and they don't count much.' What baffles everyone at the office is that I don't show any disposition to claim importance either on the basis of my record or on the basis of my current performance. I imply 'Value is an inherent attribute. I have it and, therefore, feel no need to claim it.'

"My work habits at Shepard's are such as to raise the question whether a good day's work isn't a matter of conscience with me rather than a truckling to the employer's whip hand. That is to say, I may want to do a good job, irrespective of their insistence, and my conscientious concern for results may mean more than the stern whip cracking of the official flunkies.

"What may cause confusion at the office is the question why I should consider working for so low a salary. Why do I show so little interest in acquiring money? Understandably, it is puzzling to the Shepard's people that I do their work better than others and yet make no claims based on that superiority. Instead, I seem to say that the better one is in such trifling matters the more he is to be pitied. To be good at the nonsensical affairs of business, schools, governments, is a curse, a cross. Furthermore, why do I complain so little of the pettiness of spirit and coldness of character in the management team? The limitedness of my demands on Shepard's is wondered at. Can it be true? How long will the guy stay? I show little interest in my own predecessors. Their merit is not essential to my own. Is he willing to work here only for his salary with little hope of ever doing much better? Is this man of intelligence, industry, culture, sense of destiny, willing to associate for any length of time with so many little minds?

"There is and there will be some animosity toward me on the part of those who fear that my work will make theirs look bad, that I will jeopardize their jobs and, at the least, will put them under pressure to work hard, labor mightily, strive ceaselessly. Before I came, the job was a relative sinecure. Now it is a rat race with no prospect of letup. For example, Hank spoke to me today for a few minutes about my practice before coming to Shepard's. He was, in truth, seeking, as an enemy, for some soft spot in my armor. Had I really been a tax practitioner? Did I have something to conceal, some chink in my armor, some weakness of character, some fearful recollection?

"I tensed up as he questioned me. The pretense of friendly inquiry was so thin that it hardly could have fooled anyone—him, me, those around, who were all listening. I felt like throwing off my own pretense of friendly patience and tolerance. Or, I felt as if he were a

The Springs

pesky cur whom I might kick in the ass or pick up by the collar and fling away from me.

"My answers were so designed as to accentuate the difference between us. They were such as to portray Hank as a churlish, lonely nuisance and myself as a paragon of intelligence and a favorite of fortune. I overstated my case, to be sure, but I did so in response to a prying, ill-mannered, cross examination. I don't go about bragging.

"One of the protective devices which the various people at Shepard's may bring into use against me is the assumption I have something to hide. Various things which have been said bespeak a probing campaign. Does he drink to excess? Has he embezzled funds from a client? Why does he show no interest in forming friendships? Et cetera. Maybe I'm mistaken, but I wondered at Walt's reference to McDougal's membership in Alcoholics Anonymous. I wondered at Hank's reference to his ex-partner's conviction of gambling. Ah, I may be quite wrong. Those may have been quite innocent references. Anyhow, I haven't anything to hide.

"The more I see of Wilcox, the more contemptible he seems. His greeting when I come up for a new assignment is 'Need a job?' He wants to wring an admission of need from me, probably from each employee subordinate to him, at every opportunity. Yet, insofar as he acts upon the other's need, he does it grudgingly, as if he were scourged. I suspect him of promoting rumors which will render the work-force less secure about their jobs. The less secure the employees are, the more tractable will they be in deportment. This is to say, his leadership is perverse, if not perverted.

"Wilcox, who has a fanatic desire to load his subordinates with work against their wishes, who takes a sadistic pleasure in thrusting work upon employees, is puzzled. I ask for work as though I took a fanatic delight in doing it, as though I were taking something from him, draining his resources, leaving him short. Several of his assignments have been relatively grudging.

"He asked me today what my rate of production is. I replied 'I don't know.' I added 'exactly.' He said 'I'll take a look.' He went to his office to pull out a chart. He showed me the figure 18 per hour. He said 'I don't want to rush you just now, but your average ought to be 20 or 21.' I said gently, so gently 'I am surprised. I'll keep at it.' I take it I was asking him to accept my setting my own pace so long as I wasn't dawdling, wasting time on gabbing. The quality of my work was taken for granted on both sides. I was asking. I wasn't demanding, arguing, or striking a pose. What Wilcox may have wanted to impress on me with his table of production ratings was that I was nothing to him but a statistic, just one of a crew of no accounts, a guy who could be summed up in a figure on a piece of paper and waved around at will.

"It may well be that some of the deep-down competitiveness I felt toward father is operative. I want to defeat, to overcome, vanquish this giant bastard Wilcox in some underhanded, secret, sinister, malevolent manner which is stronger and more furious and more virulent and all-encompassing than the hate and passion with which he hands out his whiplashes of slips, of work. I will undercut you, you dirty bastard. I will get around you, and from the back when you aren't looking I will crack your skull with a hammer. I put my masochism against his sadism, as it were. Yes, you viper, you evil, loathsome, cancerous condition, I will get even. I will cement you up in an underground cavern as did the hero to the victim in Poe's *Cask of Amontillado*.

"When I was at the Shepherd-Pratt hospital, I read Poe's *Cask of Amontillado* for the first time. I thought that I was being accused of being so filled with anger that I would like to bury somebody alive, presumably father and, by extension, many, many others—all oppressors, tyrants, bosses, authoritarians. Now I see that I did have as much anger as, in my fevered imagination, I was accused of having.

"A day like today exhausts me."

My father had been on the job at Shepard's for three months during the hiatus and had established a routine going to work at the office and in his home life. My brother and I became comfortable with this aspect of our father's life; he was predictable. But, unknown to us, he was still adjusting to his new work environment, establishing and refining opinions about his co-workers, jousting with his colleagues, including his boss. That is, he jousted mentally in the diary, often perceiving colleagues' words and actions as threats that he must thwart. Initially, upon reading these diary entries, I attributed my father's adversarial reactions to remnant paranoia from his mental illness. On second thought, I attributed them to normal social dynamics when a newcomer joins an established group, a variant of hazing. More accurately, I accepted hazing as normal, but I questioned whether my father's reactions to this hazing crossed the boundary of normality. I leaned toward concluding that his reactions indeed crossed the boundary; remnant mental illness, paranoia, distorted the intent of his colleague's hazing.

Moreover, as I read these entries, with their paranoiac undercurrent, I paid particular attention to my father grousing about his boss, George Wilcox. Of course, that grousing is not atypical. But, it would be atypical if my father considered Wilcox an ersatz father subject to desertion and vengeance, as he had considered his previous boss, Huntington Cairns. Fortunately, the diary remained silent about this possibility, which I found reassuring.

On a more positive note, my father expressed a much healthier undercurrent of contentment as he resolved the conflict between his pecuniary necessity of getting a job and his literary aspirations. Despite his grumbling about Shepard's, my father accepted the job without corrosive personal misgivings. "As for myself, I feel that my connection with the company rests on a different foundation. Right or wrong, I took the job as one which would pay me a salary which would tide me over the transition from law to letters. I look upon any job as stultifying, as bound to be so. I actually don't know of a better job for my present purposes." Rhetorically, he referred to a union of routine employment, his job at Shepard's, and creative activity, his writing: work by day, write by night, so to speak. "To make my routine employment at Shepard's subserve my creative projects was on my mind when I came to the Springs. My aim now is to bring about a union, to merge routine employment with creative activity. The union of the routine with the creative may symbolize a fusion of diverse facets of my own personality, the termination of the ancient, troublesome schism. I am not seeking to play magazine editors off against Shepard's. I want to be in relation to both. I want to draw a salary from Shepard's and to draw acceptance, publication, random checks, a literary reputation from the monthlies and quarterlies.

"My writing doesn't exactly require secrecy, but it requires solitude; and I certainly prefer not to gab about it. The idea of throwing a screen of secrecy around my writing is less important than throwing a screen of privacy around my leisure so that I have time for reflection, complete idleness, writing.

"Maybe I have been hiding my writing from a conviction of the enmity of my colleagues. But isn't this comparable to a lad's hiding his testicles? My hiding action classifies these people about me as enemies and as swine. The truth is that all my experience points to the mob's hostility to 'high emprise,' to creative activity, to that which surpasses their own mediocrity. Nonetheless, at present, my satisfaction with hiding my light, my real interest, my distinguishing characteristic, my vital asset, is diminishing. Even my tendency to regard those around me as guardians of mediocrity and as destroyers of individuality is undergoing a change. The fact is, I'm pretty satisfied. I'm alive. I'm healthy. I'm as happy as one can get here below."

Needless to say, I smiled as I read this last sentence; my father was happy, content with his decision to relocate in Colorado Springs, to work at Shepard's, despite his misgivings about the nature of the job and annoyance at many of his professional colleagues. Moreover, he always seemed happy to find me sitting in his apartment studying when he came home from work.

In addition, I smiled because I remembered my happiness at suddenly having a father living in town, readily available for paternal companionship. Plus, he allowed me to use his car for social occasion during the week. My life was beginning to resemble the enviable lives of my high-school friends whose families were not broken by divorce. The resemblance was not exact, however, for I could not attend social functions with father and mother by my side, nor could I go on family vacations with father and mother. My happiness was still constrained by the stigmas of their broken marriage and his mental illness. Nonetheless, I felt newly content.

But, amidst his contentment, my father continued to skirmish with Suzanne. On the one hand, he parried what he perceived as her attacks on him. On the other hand, he treated her as a dear companion and confidante. The diary entries portray a testy but enduring relationship.

"Suzanne was here today. She made me a grand dinner. She didn't sleep well on the eve of coming to see me. She wasn't as at ease with me during the day as usual. Naturally, that affected me, so we weren't as at ease together as usual. It seemed to me that Suzanne was doubtful of herself. She would make a good meal so as to prove herself in that department. Underlying her approach to me was this thesis: value lies not in the person per se but in his or her usefulness, performance.

"She would like to imply that I must make myself worthy of her by having my writing published. However, if I should enjoy the success of publication, Suzanne would feel even more unworthy than she now does. The suggestion that I must prove my worth by achieving publication is a ruse designed to take the focus off of her own worthiness by raising a question about mine.

"I didn't urge Suzanne to see the vacant apartment down the street from mine on Cascade Avenue, as I had planned. I am sure that I can get her when I want her. She feels better being wanted than if she were stuck in a routine of limited means and household drudgery. It is better for both of us to postpone marital commitments. As she left this evening, Suzanne was distracted—appeared uncertain which way to turn."

Later that evening, after Suzanne's departure back to Denver, my father wrote Suzanne a letter. "The way in which I opened my letter was in keeping with the ultimate argument I intended to make. I opened with the most objective down to earth, realistic description of a fire, its discovery and its extinction, which is imaginable. The objectivity of my recognition of the fire lends credence to my appraisal of the other force which is ranged against me. I want Susanne to see what she is doing. I want her to gauge the drift of her maneuvers, to bring the motivation of her moves within the focus of her conscious vision. It isn't far from the truth that I defend myself less to make myself worthy of her than to make her drop her grenades and become worthy of me. I serve notice, too, that whether she joins me or doesn't, I will go on living and go my way.

"I went on to reproach her gently for her animadversions against the Springs. In just so much circumlocution as needed to sugar-coat the medicine, I pointed out that her attacks on the Springs are attacks on me, blows aimed at my self-respect. When she says Colorado Springs is a poor place to work, she is belittling me, belittling my choice. I take issue with her there. I want to force her to come with me, for me, whatever the consequences may be.

"Then I took cognizance of the difference between small towns and big ones. I did it in such a way as to make for realistic clarity and for Suzanne's willingness to accept what I said. My remarks were such as to stress the essentials and to strip away the superficial glitter. What counts is the resident.

"From there I moved onto an unusually frank *apologia pro vita sua*. I catalogued what could be charged against me, saying 'I know I'm poor as a church mouse, that I'm poorly paid, that I have no profession, that I have wooed editors without success.' I didn't list my assets at all. I ignored all that could be put down in my favor. I simply noted all the liabilities to be reckoned with and, in effect, said 'So what?' I didn't go on to say 'Still I am worthwhile. Nevertheless, I amount to something. Just the same, I am worthy of you.' I left an ellipsis.

"I defended myself; nothing more. I apologized for my life and existence, using 'apologize' in the sense of justifying. What should make Suzanne sit up and take notice is that I defended against her attacks on me. I do not strike out to cut away the props of her self-esteem. Rather I say nice things about her. I recognize her good qualities. I reinforce the props of her self-esteem. I fortify the foundations of her ego. Funny thing: I praise Suzanne, but she can expect scant praise from those who hitch their wagon to the star of fashion, froth, and show. Those people will quibble and question and cavil, but seldom compliment.

"But here is the sad part. I feel it necessary to plead for my life. Suzanne, my closest companion, threatens my life. I have to plead with her to acknowledge my right to live and live my own way. I don't plead with Suzanne to marry me, to join me here, to come and live with me. That is secondary. When she is willing to accept me as I am, then we shall have established our relations on a new and realistic basis, on a new and healthier basis. There are no ifs, ands, or buts. The clarity of my perception of the situation will make for perception on Suzanne's part. Besides, I am not only clear about what I see; but I am convinced of the rightness of my vision, of what is and what should be.

"I ask Suzanne to give credit where credit is due: to essentials, to me. At the same time, I expect the gilt and trappings for what they are, tinsel show. I advance

The Springs

my own banner, but, in addition, I pull down on the star to which Suzanne and so many have hitched their wagon.

"Both Suzanne and I may be moving toward a new relation toward each other. She is militant. So am I. For each of us, the opposite sex is a threat, or has been. Today's visit may have been a highly significant encounter. I could scarcely wait to drive her back to Denver, for her to go. While returning to Colorado Springs, one of the favorite songs of my father, one of the songs of my boyhood, ran through my mind: 'There will be a hot time in the old town tonight.'"

The next day, my father continued to analyze his frustrations with Suzanne. Indeed, they seemed to preoccupy his subconscious and conscious thoughts, threatening his contentment at work. "Today, I worked in a trance, a sleepy, half-waking state. My own relations with Suzanne may have contributed to the sadness which invaded my benumbed mind. Quite likely, I am angry, furious at myself for clinging to her and not throwing her overboard for some local floozy who would be more amenable to my wishes and desires. I am angry with myself for being subordinate to Wilcox, for clinging to Suzanne, for turning the treadmill of Shepard's. I rage at the editors who postpone, procrastinate, and temporize. I equate their pusillanimous refusal to recognize my merit with Suzanne's fearful reluctance to cast her lot with me. It probably is better for me that Suzanne should stall. Certainly I do not want my problems complicated by matrimony.

"Oddly enough, I do not feel drawn to Suzanne in the sense that I feel she is necessary to me sexually. The future is beyond cool, rational calculation. However, sexual drive will be a factor of negligible importance. I don't need Suzanne so. I can conquer her sexually; sexual conquest isn't a summation of what I have in mind. I even repel the alternative of sexual conquest, shove it into the background. I want to conquer Suzanne's mind; batter down her respect for the prevailing shibboleths; command respect for my views. After that, sex is a consummation—rather than a conquest. I see women as physiologically (for the moment, that only) in need of sexual union as much as men.

"Quite possibly I shall give up Suzanne. It may be I shall disengage, simply quit fighting to impose my views, and leave Suzanne to the hollow victory and empty relationships in subservience to social dictates. After all, it probably is foolish to expect her to throw over the ingrained, ground-in habits and attitudes of a lifetime. Better to leave her to herself; better to work out my destiny by forgetting Denver, forgetting Suzanne, forgetting law. Better to cut loose from the hampering forces of the past. Now that the call of the flesh is less insistent, the time for trampling on fetters has arrived. This does not mean a dramatic severance of relations. I shall return to Denver for Christmas. After that, to hell with Denver. My seven years there were just a wasteland. How few friends did I reap during my sojourn there? Very few. Indeed, I can scarcely claim any Denver friends. Of course, she may be able to triumph over her past and join me. But the likelihood is that that is asking too much. She stands to lose money, security, status."

Despite his negativism, my father continued his social life with Suzanne. Several weeks later, he wrote: "I took Suzanne to dinner, a hockey game, a cocktail lounge Saturday. She looked her best, her very best.

"Sunday, our relationship may have been pitched on a new level, a level of maturity exceeding anything previously existent. Besides that it may have been, it was, my leadership which established the new order, a new order of closer rapport, of greater dominance on my part. I was surprised that Suzanne liked my latest story, *Tribute to Tomkins*, as well.

"In my letter to Suzanne this evening, I spoke jocularly of being Napoleon. I signed, even, as Napoleon. I say I am king and she is my queen. Josephine. There are other meanings, which she may gather, probably will.

"The difference in our ages is a factor which, I feel sure, has bothered Suzanne. I referred Saturday or Sunday to the difference in ages between Napoleon and Josephine. I told Suzanne she was neither too young or too old, too hot or too cold. This is about as far as I can go in bringing the subject into the open, airing it. Ah yes, I also told Suzanne how Napoleon had added a few years to his age when applying for a license to marry Josephine."

Up and down, up and down. My father's relationship with Suzanne vacillated between its high points and its low points—in a manic depressive sort of way. Although he continued to visit her every Sunday, the separation during the rest of the week must have stressed them both. From reading the diary entries, I sensed tension in their communications, which were mainly by letters written back and forth. For even the most gifted writers, this mode of communication is imperfect: statements are misconstrued, facial expressions are invisible, clarifying explanations are muddled because of the two- or three-day lag imposed by the postal delivery system.

During this period, my father occasionally mentioned Suzanne to my brother and me. However, we never saw her, spoke to her, or communicated with her.

We knew that she lived in Denver and worked for the Colorado Ski Country trade association. Now and then, I would enter my father's apartment while he spoke to her (in French) on the telephone. He would quickly terminate the conversation. At Christmas, she would send each of us, via our father, a modest gift, usually an artistic knick-knack of one sort or another that we usually set aside in his apartment. Our father thanked her on our behalf. She simply was not a part of our lives. And, in retrospect, I suspect that my father preferred it that way.

Another year passed. My father had settled into the routine inherent in his role as an editor at Shepard's. His contentment waxed and waned, admittedly with less waxing and more waning, for he had not yet fully shed his anger, his frustrations, his mental fragility. Familiar demons arose now and then, but my father seemed less distraught by their presence. He seemed to be coming to uneasy terms with the demons of his past and present.

Three diary entries in 1962, two years after the move to Colorado Springs, demonstrate the waning phase of my father's contentment. Basically, he was depressed—not clinically, but certainly non-clinically. He was despondent over his meager salary and how that affected his relationship with Suzanne. And, he was despondent over his general dissatisfaction with the prevailing social mores, which were so different from his own. I sympathized with my father; his despondency was most likely painful. But I also considered his depression to be a normal reaction to discouraging or stressful life events.

"I am beset by problems, but I do not feel either desperate or defeated. I am terrifically pinched monetarily. Psychological factors of great importance are pushing themselves up from below. In consequence of the underground, geological upheaval my relations with Suzanne are threatened. They may continue, but they will never be the same.

"At home, my creativity is at a low ebb.

"At the office, my luncheon engagements with colleagues become more and more unsatisfactory. Many of them are motivated by hatred, jealousy, fear, and suspicion. They are the chief victims of these forces which dominate them. Wilcox seems to be leaving me pretty strictly alone. All the men, indeed, are fairly deferential. The women seem to tense up in my presence like a female pheasant endeavoring to attract the male. Besides that, all the females appear curious whether I will fall for one of them, make a play for one of their number: which one, on what basis?

"My situation appears to me to be that of one surrounded by enemies. Indeed, I have no doubt that such is the case. The difference wrought by three years is that the enmity surrounding me does not seem inordinately dangerous. My hostile neighbors suffer more from their saturating hostility than I do. They are to be pitied. During the height of my illness I had the same perception that I was surrounded by enemies. And that viewpoint was partially responsible for sending me to the hospital. In that regard, it was about three years ago this spring that I saw Dr. Walker for the last time. I have no feelings now, of a need to return to him in order to achieve some sense of direction.

"I want to be paid more. If an employer will disburse more shekels because of my so-called productivity, that is fine. Actually, I guess I am a bit embarrassed that any piddling skills are appreciated but not my insights, values and creativity. I still pride myself on what I have produced in response to the inner impulse to produce. It is unlikely that I ever again will have a decent income to spend. For that reason, it may be that I should go my way and let Suzanne go hers, for her satisfactions depend more than mine on getting and spending.

"What I most despise in myself is my proficiency at the piddling shores by which the ignorant masses set such store. That which the crowds admire, I deplore. When thousands cheer, I weep with shame. Thus do I set myself apart from the leprous mob. Can I ever find a degree of rapport with others?

"There was a time when I labored to understand the technical niceties of legal, political, diplomatic, and economic problems. Now I refuse to waste time considering the proper arrangements within the existing legal, moral, religious, cultural framework. My present concern is with the proper framework, and so detailed learning, fine distinctions, argumentative casuistry is of no significance. I take such a dim view of historic values, institutions, folkways, that I repudiate and reject everything. I am conscious of such revulsion as to feel nausea. Yet I lack the will to give any of myself for anything in the approved tradition. It is not for me to vomit up everything and long for Heaven, but neither can I embrace the dirty formalities with their worn, gray aspect of a railroad station.

"I wrote Suzanne. I tend, in my correspondence, to be hoping against hope for our continued association. I mix positive appreciations in with this skepticism. It may be that after the present crisis the two of us will have achieved a better, more realistic, more appreciative rapport than we've had until now.

"In last night's letter to Suzanne, I told her to address my letters to Mr. E.E. Smith. I didn't ask her, I told her. It is probably a fair summary of the crisis in our relationship to say that I am asking for, am demanding of her, that she accept my leadership, that she submit to me, that she acknowledge my masculinity and superiority more definitely and conclusively than heretofore. It is not for her to question my strength or my mastery.

"Heretofore, Suzanne has liked to strike the pose—as if that were necessary for the maintenance of her self-respect—that she plays tricks on me and hasn't really surrendered herself and her future and her fortune to me. It is a fact she hasn't accompanied me down here. When Suzanne has given, she has felt the need to protect herself with the disclaimer of giving and with the pretense she is taking.

"What has caused our personal crisis is that Suzanne has wanted to serve two masters: convention and me. If anything, convention has come first. My present tack may be calculated to force her to choose. Quite likely other factors also are forcing her toward the fateful, fairly final decision.

"In no way have I shown any lack of kindness, consideration, love. While I have masked the fact that the re-orientation needed is her own, that has been mainly a matter of tact.

"Maybe the long drawn-out compromise course of living in different cities is coming to an end. Maybe Suzanne's tutelage is to give way to a grown-up acceptance of her role to be with me, to help me, to find her satisfaction in my happiness. For that matter, perhaps I finally have become aware that my role calls for bringing her here, supporting her, cherishing her."

Several days later, his frustrations again bordered on depression: "After spending the day with Dean and Curtis, I wrote Suzanne. I ask her if I am welcome to come see her next Sunday. Instead of assuming I am welcome (as I usually do), I assume that I have given Suzanne reason to be unhappy with me, an excuse for feeling wronged. I assume demands on her part and denial on my part. On these assumptions, I am a naughty boy. Will the assumptions I make be so obvious as to induce contradiction? Can Suzanne contradict me? Are my assumptions vestiges of delusions or valid insights?

"This makes me wonder about the possibility of marriage to Suzanne. Would it be possible for her to be happy in the absence of the usual bourgeois satisfactions: comfortable living quarters, new clothes to show off, money to spend? As important, or more so, would I be happy in a bourgeois set up? Is a compromise possible, leaving to Suzanne the pothering with money, the showing one's self at public gatherings, the property manipulation?"

I seldom witnessed any manifestations of my father's frustrations. The only noteworthy occasion emanated from my choice of an undergraduate college to attend. For both my parents, it was axiomatic that my brother and I would attend college; there was no debate about that. But there was a serious debate about where I would go. Influenced by my mother, I had decided as a young teenager that I would attend an Ivy League school, preferably Harvard. My father, however, argued that I could never afford such elite colleges and that I should seek nomination to a service academy such as the Air Force Academy in Colorado Springs, because all expenses were paid by the Government. Stubbornly, I applied only to Harvard, Yale, and Swarthmore; I didn't apply to any schools in Colorado but, as a backup, I applied for a Boettcher Foundation Scholarship, which paid all expenses for attending any institution in the State of Colorado.

On the fateful day in April, I received letters from each college offering me admission with full financial aid—tuition, housing, the works. And I won a Boettcher scholarship. I told my father the next afternoon while riding in his car: "Good news. I'm going to Harvard on full scholarship." He pulled over to the curb, turned off the engine, and slammed his fist against the dashboard. He was livid. "Do you think you're too good to attend a school in Colorado? You know we can't afford Harvard." I replied defensively: "But Dad, they've offered me a full scholarship. It will cost us nothing." "You're a disappointing fool. You're on your own. I can't help you financially." So my course was set: off to Harvard, on my own financially, with only occasional gifts of about $50 from my mother, who was no better off financially than my father.

After that altercation, the topic of my choice of colleges never arose again. Notably, my father never mentioned it in his diary. Rather, the ensuing diary entries continued in his more personal vein: sparring with colleagues at work and with Suzanne at home. However, the intensity of these interactions gradually dwindled as my father adapted to his new environment. He perceived less antagonism by his colleagues and more acceptance by Suzanne.

Thus, as time passed, my father's mental health seemed to improve. The pace was slow and uneven. Relapses occurred now and then: he would react irrationally to a colleague's remark, a store clerk's comment, Suzanne's perceived recalcitrance. Nonetheless, with little doubt, his health was improving, albeit slowly.

In late summer, 1962, I left Colorado Springs for college in Massachusetts. Of course, this move changed my relationship with my father. No longer would I stop by his apartment after school, no longer would we go fishing or ice skating on a Saturday, no longer would he present me with his latest short story to read. But, the 2000 miles separating us did not stop my father from sharing his opinions with me. He wrote me two and sometimes three letters each week, long letters with fatherly advice about this and that: the worthy qualities of a man, the absurdity of bourgeois values, the beauty of a Colorado sunset. I treasured the letters; they connected me with my father, my home. Intending to re-read them some day, I stored the letters for more than thirty years but ultimately discarded them prior to an overseas move. Now, of course, I regret that decision.

Remnants

After moving East to attend college, I saw my father much less often. However, during my occasional return visits to Colorado Springs over the next several years, I could see that he was changing, settling into a somewhat conventional life style. Get up, walk to work, eat lunch at a nearby diner with co-workers, walk home, eat dinner alone, telephone Suzanne, work on a manuscript, write in his diary, go to bed. I suspect that enjoying an evening glass of armagnac belongs on that list as well. Although he wasn't wealthy, he earned enough money to buy a new car every two or three years and take an annual summer vacation to places as far away as Mexico.

All of that does not mean that my father settled into a less confrontational life style. In his diary entries, from 1962 to 1964, his quarrel with "bourgeois" standards persisted unabated, but the intensity of his overall anger at the world subsided. He wrote primarily about numerous less global quarrels: altercations with neighbors about noisy televisions, arguments with insurance companies about disputed claim payments, annoyance and outright disdain for working conditions at Shepard's. Noticeably, his anger was becoming more focused on specific events and individuals, not on society as a whole. In the diary, he chronicled various interactions with colleagues at work, doctors, editors, and Suzanne that became less vituperative, less combative, less aggressive. Occasionally, remnants of his mental illness arose in these narratives, as he conjoined these interactions with his traumas of the past. But by-and-large, the pace of this evolution in his temperament was steady, albeit slow and gradual.

Our father-son relationship was changing as well. He began treating me more and more as a young man, not a callow teenager. When he took me to lunch during my visits over the Christmas holidays or summer vacation, we usually went to nice restaurants instead of a casual diner. Because I had told him about sipping fine amontillado sherry during Friday afternoon "low table" at Harvard, my father began ordering cocktails to precede the meal. We both enjoyed them. Likewise, when I visited him in his apartment, he would usually offer me a small glass of armagnac. I reveled in this sophisticated adult world.

Our conversations were primarily one-sided. I usually dominated them as I described my experiences at Harvard, in Boston, New York, and so forth. He listened patiently, with occasional gibes at formal education or an editorial rejection of his latest short story. Otherwise, he seldom spoke about himself. Indeed, my self-absorbed descriptions of my new life beyond the confines of Colorado Springs left few openings for him to speak about himself. Consequently, I learned little about his new job, his relationship with Suzanne, his personal life in general during these visits.

In the course of a particularly stressful period midway through my sophomore year, my father suggested (via one of his frequent letters) that I see a counselor, a therapist. At first, I resisted; the stigma of my father's psychiatric counseling posed a major barrier. Nonetheless, distraught, I sought counseling at the student health service. The counselor quickly arrived at a conclusion: "you need a girlfriend." Obediently, I asked the single female in my calculus class for a date, and our relationship blossomed for the remainder of the academic year. The counselor was right, for I felt much, much better.

In the fall of 1964, my junior year, I entered into another particularly stressful period. At the outset of the semester, I encountered the foremost source of stress: my girlfriend from the previous spring—my foundation of emotional stability—had terminated our relationship, obeying strict orders from her father. Apparently, he held me responsible for her loss of Harvard scholarship support because of bad grades last spring semester and the cancellation of a planned vacation trip to Europe with her parents due to contraction of mononucleosis shortly after her return home for the summer. Fortunately, I had no such misfortunes. Nonetheless, as the fall semester progressed, I became less and less satisfied with my academic performance; most of the courses were quite difficult, and I was over-extended in extracurricular musical activities. Ultimately, I took a leave of absence for two semesters to "reset." During this interlude from Harvard, I returned to Colorado, where I got a laboratory job at the University of Colorado in Boulder. The pay was meager, I had only about $400 in savings from the previous summer, and I needed a car.

Again, my father stepped in to help me—but in a very different way this time. Acknowledging my need for a dependable car, my father offered me his 1962 Pontiac in exchange for my $400 in savings, a fraction of its worth, and wished me well. Of course, I accepted. My father had stepped in to rescue me financially, for which I was very grateful. We seldom spoke about my leave of absence or the financial rescue, nor in his diary did my father mention them beyond a few words: "I feel sorry for Dean."

At about the same time, the diary chronicled changes in my father's situation as well. The Shepard's management structure changed when a younger man, Todd Campbell, replaced George Wilcox as my father's supervisor. My father liked and respected Campbell. Campbell, in turn, was supportive of my father's professional development, preparing him for advancement in the company's hierarchy by reassigning him several times to introduce him to various aspects of the company's operations. Along the way, my father was given regular pay raises and several promotions that elevated him into mid-level leadership roles. In short, he became an established member of the company's workforce, slowly building up seniority. He continued to lash out at Shepard's for one reason or another and to squabble with his co-workers. However, I got the impression that these squabbles were vented in silence to my father's diary or letters to Suzanne, not in vociferous disagreements at work, and certainly not to me. All in all, I suspect that to his colleagues he appeared reasonably content with his lot at Shepard's.

I must amend that last assessment slightly. For reasons not made clear in the diary, during this time period, my father applied for jobs at two other organizations, both of them publishers of law books. The publishers invited him to interviews back East, at their expense. However, on both occasions, my father alienated his hosts from the start. At the outset, he must have said something that seriously irritated them. In fact, both publishers terminated the full-day interview after only an hour or so, sending him back to Colorado empty handed. Predictably, my father asserted that the interviewers were intimidated by his superior qualifications and threatened by his strength of character. He posits their thoughts: "We don't want a man like this around. He'll expose us for what we are, meaningless servants to a bourgeois enterprise." I confess to smiling when I read these job interview postmortems, not in *Schadenfreude* but in love for my father.

Speaking of love, during this period, my father's relationship with Suzanne had its usual bumpiness, but it seemed to stay on track. At least until she announced her plans to retire. This announcement caught my father off-guard, but from an outsider's point of view, it could have been expected. She was, after all, approaching retirement age, 65. The diary entries in November, 1964, meander from one familiar topic to another, but they concentrate heavily on Suzanne, telling the story of her announcement.

"Last Sunday, I learned of Suzanne's plan to be away from Colorado for a few months next year. She spoke about the possibility of her taking out an annuity for retirement. She also spoke of Phoenix as if it or Tempe might be her future home. I tend to think of her remarks, of such remarks, as intended to sound out, to explore, to verify my response, my reaction. Is he afraid he'll lose me? Would he prefer to be rid of me? Does he have his eye on my money? Does he feel able to get along without me? Would he, perchance, follow me and so acknowledge that this woman calls the tune? Well, if she pulls out on me, goes to Arizona to live, I'll be able to get along.

"There is no doubt that I regard her plans for the future, the vacation, possibly a move to Arizona and all, as posing a serious threat to the continuance of our relationship. I do not suppose that it can survive. For her there may be other men, older men, richer men, retired men with the same amount of time on their hands as she has on hers. For me there may be other women. But, I have no yen to find a younger woman. I have been and still am satisfied with Suzanne. If Suzanne persists in her plan to leave me, temporarily, I shall be equal to bearing the loss. It could well be that she is trying to force me into a new relationship which would cede dominance to her. That she cannot do. I shall not plead, shall not promise her hegemony if she steps or comes back.

"Am I powerless to prevent what she proposes? Should I exert myself to keep her from vacationing? I could make a counter proposal that we take a honeymoon. That wouldn't work. Suzanne may feel as impelled to leave me as Margie did before her. It may be that she doesn't feel adequate to a marriage relationship with me, doesn't feel adequate to a continuance of the status quo. It is impossible for me to remedy such a compulsion to leave, such a felt inadequacy.

"Whether Suzanne goes or stays, my last three letters have spelled out for her any idea that she ought to help me. Any idea she may have that she should live off me is ill-founded. She must be willing to do things for me. Her satisfaction in a relationship with me, marital or otherwise, will depend in part on yielding to me. She has been denouncing my reaction to her remark about 'Dutch dates.' She made the remark for the purpose of showing how tolerant she had been of my impecuniosity. My delayed reaction was to question her tolerance, my vulnerability, her need for tolerance. Indeed, it seemed to me that I was trying to validate and rationalize and justify the relationship which had existed between us these past years. Do I see Suzanne's announced plans for leaving me temporarily as an attack on me and as an attack on the whole basis of our relationship? I should do more for her! It could well be that Suzanne is continuing the unfinished battle against papa by taking aim at me. Papa didn't love her enough; didn't do enough for her. Neither do I. She'll run away from me as, years ago, she left France, *la patrie*, papa.

"Well, my course is clear. Let her go as she plans. Wish her Godspeed. Let her see and let me see how we fare apart. In the meantime, I have served notice on her that I do not feel guilty about my treatment of her. I do not agree that our past relationship was faulty, unrealistic, lacking. She is free to terminate our companionship, free to repudiate it."

Within a day, my father changed his tune. "It could be that her plan has had an impact on me already. It may have more effect on me as her departure comes closer. Yet, I doubt that I will feel crushed by her going away. Her move is understandable. It is not desertion. I can get along without her for those months. I will have to do some adjusting, of course. I won't be going to Denver on Sundays. I will miss those trips, burdensome as they sometimes seem now. Other women appeal to me, but their appeal is more limited than that of Suzanne.

"I believe I will push Suzanne to marry me this Christmas. No harm in trying. We'll finance a trip to Santa Fe some way. We could drive to Taos and Santa Fe, maybe Albuquerque. We could stay two days, say, at Taos, two at Santa Fe. That arrangement would cost Shepard's only 1½ days of my time. Suzanne could still take her trip to Arizona, but take it as Mrs. Smith. Ah, we shall see."

The Man I Didn't Know

Christmas came and went, and my father never mentioned asking Suzanne to marry him as he had planned. Maybe he couldn't overcome the inertia to pop the question. Or, maybe he asked her to marry him, but she demurred. In any event, their relationship continued essentially unchanged into the new year, when she retired. Then, as she had planned, Suzanne went to Tempe for an extended vacation.

Without Suzanne nearby, my father underwent a period of adjustment. Early on (January, 1965), he wrote of sadness. "Sadness overtook me today, as grumpiness did on Tuesday, but to a considerable extent I have been free from symptoms, from emotion, from a sense of desperation or difficulty." He was "down," so to speak. And, he focused his funk on his interactions with colleagues at Shepard's, where he was undergoing a routine training program.

By serendipity, the training assignments placed him in contact primarily with women. And, that lightened his mood considerably. Noticeably, and perhaps predictably, during Suzanne's absence, my father wrote much more extensively about interactions with women at work. He introduced new names that add additional texture to the narrative: Lila, Mrs. M., Millie, Edna, et alia. Collectively, they brought him face-to-face with the pleasures, challenges, and underlying tensions inherent in working with members of the opposite sex. As a bachelor, he undoubtedly attracted attention, and as a man, he undoubtedly enjoyed the attention. But, this attention required him to make some adjustments in his relationship with women.

"It is probably a good thing for the development of my mental health to be spending, as I am now, six weeks working with women. It has been on my mind for quite a while that there were special extra problems for me in relating to women. It could be, too, that women find it difficult to get on with me. My concern in relating to women seems to be that of pulling away, pulling away from mama, rather than trying to reunite with the earth. This pulling away, holding aloof, is what makes some of the women feel hurt and angry.

"In general, my reserve precludes a chummy palsy-walsy relation. Mrs. M., who seems to me to be pretty scatter brained, sad, hostile is one whom I hold at bay. She may be uneasy with me, not being able to find a handle whereby to manipulate me. It may bother her, too, that I keep Mary Lou, her partner, within the range of my attention. Hence I tend to prevent an *à deux* setup. We are always three. Today, my contacts with Lila, who strains to see me, were few and fleeting. I like it best that way. I am embarrassed when she tries to make an impression. It is my guess that I was involved in Mrs. Swanton's illness today, in Mrs. K's malaise while I was working with her.

"It may puzzle the women that I put work before the manifest opportunity to play with them, to play at sexual stimulation doomed to disappointment. It may puzzle everybody that I rank higher in their estimation for holding aloof. I say 'holding aloof,' but that course isn't a conspicuously willed, calculated matter. It simply is my way. At that, I laugh and tell stories. I enjoy their company. We work together in good humor. I esteem them. I do not depreciate them. Yet, I seem to make no move to catch them, to bring them closer, to tie them to me. We enjoy ourselves now. When we part, we both are free, as free as if we had never met."

As I read these entries, I thought back on my father's scheme for vengeance against women: engender dependence and then desert by withholding affection. He wrote about that five or six years ago, during his evident mental illness. Now, while reading the diary, I detected traces of this scheme in his relationships with women at work: flirt but hold aloof, engender dependence and then desert. They were unhealthy. Perhaps I overreacted, but this concerned me, because it implied incomplete recovery from the mental illness that had plagued him years earlier. Remnants remained.

Despite his professed newfound enjoyment in working with women at Shepard's, I remember that earlier in life, before the war, my father's relationships with women seemed far healthier, far more normal, mainly because they involved sex. For example, in Minneapolis, the Elfstrand twins awakened his adolescent libido, cavorting sexually in bed with the young Eldon Jones. As a cocktail-quaffing bachelor in Washington, D.C., he assuredly had opportunities to nourish his libido. And, before shipping off to war, my father most certainly enjoyed his new wife.

In that wartime context, after I was old enough to understand such things, my mother explained that during the war years, the prevailing ethos encouraged soldiers to impregnate their wives before leaving for war. If they did not return, at least they had left a legacy, a successor to propagate the American way of life. Accordingly, my father performed his patriotic duty; he rose to the occasion, resulting in my conception. I smiled embarrassingly at that story. But, my smile evaporated at the next aspect of the story. In the same discussion, my mother commented that my father gave her a copy of Nathanial Hawthorne's *The Scarlet Letter* as he departed for Europe. I had read the book about a shamed adultress and understood the significance of this unwelcome gift.

The distraction posed by female colleagues at work most probably took my father's mind off of Suzanne. Presumably, they continued to communicate regularly by telephone and letter. But, he no longer mentioned her regularly in the diary. And, when he did, the entries were short and to the point: usually brief comments on a phone call or a letter. For example: "I talked to Suzanne today by phone. She was glad to hear from me. Besides, my call gave substance to the words Suzanne has used in speaking about me to her friends." Or a week later: "I called Suzanne this morning about 9:30. She was waiting for my call, but said she was expecting a call from her friend Lou Alta. It may do Suzanne good to know I can get along without her as well as she can get along without me." Few entries exceeded the length of these two examples.

The most extensive entry about Suzanne involved a dream, which my father views as a "hopeful" dream. I view it as an anxiety dream, triggered no doubt by Suzanne's mention of a friend, Lou Alta, who I assume was male.

"Yesterday, I dreamt I was at the Broadmoor in a dine and dance room. Suzanne and I sat at a table a space or two removed from another couple. We decided to move together, and then somehow there were more than four of us. There were introductions. There was some talk in French. A short young fellow asked Suzanne to dance and led her off. Everybody got up to dance. There was no partner for me. I went out towards the men's room. My pockets were empty. The keys to my new Dodge were missing. I went to the lost and found department downstairs. Sure enough. I got them there.

"In yesterday's dream, the guy with whom Suzanne went off to dance so happily resembled Mike, the son of the caretaker of the apartment building in which she has been living. The woman clerk at the lost and found desk at the Broadmoor showed me a thin, wide, brown key case deluxe. I shook my head and spied the old, worn black case I use daily. I picked it up.

"The dream is a hopeful one. While others dance, I gain the keys to the car, the keys to the kingdom. Paradise regained.

"I doubt that I felt any loss in not having a dancing partner. Suzanne and I have almost never danced together. Now she goes on a vacation and will be the guest of folks who would like to see her dance and be gay. They will encourage her to be frivolous."

This dream added to my concerns about remnant mental illness, because it added another element of my father's scheme for vengeance against women: infidelity, the rationale for desertion. Once again, I may have overreacted, over-interpreted. After all, I am convolving the conscious with the subconscious, the real and the dream. But, my antennae were raised, receptive to signals of lingering PTSD.

I soon detected a faint signal of another element in my father's scheme, the element of withdrawal in another dream. My father detected it as well.

"I dreamt I was in bed with Edna C., a big-breasted married woman who works at Shepard's. I fondled her breasts. I lay on top of her in a position for intercourse. My penis lay at the entrance to her sex organ in readiness to go, but I went no further than that.

"I left the woman—the place of the forgoing scene was not indicated—and went to see Curtis. As I walked up the road, uphill, I saw a bright light in a small window in Dean's room. Mom was home and up. I decided not to visit Curt.

"Then the scene shifted back to Edna, but this time it was fairly clear the setting was the farmhouse which was my childhood home. My brother Forie came in. It seemed that he had come in from milking with the characteristic odor imported to a person by milking by hand. I said 'Good morning' in an earthy voice. He replied but not enthusiastically. He didn't like the idea that Edna had spent the night with me. A third person was present, but I know not whom.

"The woman who figured in last night's dream endeavored several times, when I was new at Shepard's, to impress herself upon my attention. There were several collisions or near collisions in the 'stacks.' I got the idea, rightly or wrongly, that she was acting less for herself than for her sex. I made no attempt to make the collisions a big event. Since then, the two of us have gotten along easily but distantly. In my recent training tour, I learned the gal has a decidedly limited mind. Often I avoid close acquaintance with the man or woman whom I suspect has a mediocre or threadbare mind. Even so, this little Edna has had a warm space in my heart. Her big breasts almost surely are part of it. They almost surely are not all of it, although her face is plain, manlike. The other big-breasted dames, one of whom courts my notice, have no such special place as does this Edna.

"I have seen Edna's husband, just seen him, never met him. It may be a distortion at work but he resembled a blank. Even so, I withheld myself in the dream because the girl belongs to another. I can be over her, as an office boss, say, or even a lover, but to give myself to her is *verboten*. Is this a vestige of my old illness, my quest for revenge, or is it a realistic conforming to the social necessities of our situation? Am I really more realistic than she?

"Last night's dream illustrates that the 'triangle concept,' so common in American life, is a distorting, frustrating factor in my own individual makeup. It is a blighting concept. Thus, a man is seen as always standing between the male and a female. A woman is seen as a barrier to close, friendly, loving relations with another man. In that regard, the mother may be seen as walling off father from son. Does the sense of blockade against closeness also operate to impede integration of a dual or split personality?

"During my recent training tour, I observed Dave's close, curious relationship with such married women as Millie, Madge, Virginia S., and Virginia K. However, isn't that a frustrating situation? It cannot eventuate in a bedroom act. Or do I ascribe too much importance to sexual intimacy? What profiteth a man, what profiteth a woman, to come close together but only so close?

"Yet, to return to me, what I need to jettison is the sense of being blocked, the sense of being bound to give way in favor of another. The sense of a social block against sexual expression should not have such a seeming importance as to prevent closeness not destined for fruition in a bedroom. I tend, I guess, to think of the relations with a woman as destined by nature to reach fulfillment in only one way: sexual intercourse.

"The significance of last night's dream may be that I am moving toward freedom, a sense of freedom, toward liberation, emancipation."

In this erotic dream, my father stopped short of consummation, withholding from the woman. Rhetorically, my father questioned whether this withholding was a vestige of his old illness, exactly the same question I asked myself about him. Perhaps it was a vestige of his scheme for vengeance, a very persistent remnant. I saw this through two different lenses. Pessimistically, I perceived indications of this scheme in subsequent diary entries; occasionally my father told of giving boxes of chocolate to select women (generate dependence), but he consistently stepped back from romantic entanglements (desert by withdrawal of affection). Optimistically, I perceived my father as a thoughtful colleague, thanking co-workers with boxes of chocolate but stepping back from romantic entanglements out of loyalty to Suzanne. I remained unsure.

While my father was exploring relationships with women at work, I was exploring relationships with college women in Boulder and Denver. I became especially close to a high-school flame, Nancy, who was a sophomore at the University of Denver. A bit too close, in fact. In March, 1965, her doctor announced: "Young lady, you're pregnant." We decided to get married right away, less than a month later. When I delivered the news, my mother responded by welcoming her prospective daughter-in-law. My father responded far more stoically, uttering "What did you expect?" End of conversation.

In June, Nancy and I drove back to Cambridge, where Harvard took us under their protective wing, and the baby boy, Curtis, was born. Nearly two years elapsed before my father saw his grandson. En route from Harvard to Stanford, where both Nancy and I would be students, we stopped for several days in Colorado Springs. My father was quite cordial but was an uneasy grandfather, not inclined to cuddle or "kitchy-koo."

Shortly after her graduation from Stanford, Nancy bore another son, Corey, and our young family was now complete. Again, it was another two years, when we were en route to Sweden for my postdoctoral studies, before my father saw the second grandson. During the days before our departure, my father saw his grandsons on several occasions. And again, he usually seemed uneasy whenever he was with them. However I do remember a very touching moment, when my father joyfully hoisted two-year-old Corey into the air and asked *"är du en svensk pojke?"* I had learned rudimentary Swedish in preparation for our trip, so I knew that this translated to "Are you a Swedish boy?" I asked my father how he knew Swedish, and, with a broad smile, he replied that "in Minnesota, everybody knows Swedish." As it turned out, after our departure, he never had the opportunity to see them again.

Curiously, my father never mentioned our marriage or either grandson in the diary. In that private realm, we as a family didn't exist. My initial reaction to these omissions was disappointment. I considered various explanations: he was embarrassed by such young parents of his grandchildren; we simply weren't suitable topics for his self-interested diary ruminations; we triggered distraught memories of his own young family that he chose to suppress. As I've gotten to know my father through his diary entries, I'm inclined to suspect the latter explanation.

As my father's attitudes towards work, women, society in general mellowed, so did his writing style. The diary entries became less didactic and more descriptive of everyday encounters and events. They commented on myriad interactions between him and his colleagues and possible managerial changes at Shepard's. But, unlike earlier entries, they were not hypercritical; they were more "matter of fact."

Although the stories and the diary became less intense, my father still wrote about moments of anger, of insecurity, of mental instability. Metaphorically, they resembled sporadic, minor eruptions of vented pressures below the surface, akin to erratic Yellowstone geysers. Stated more directly, the illness was subsiding, but it was not yet in complete submission. For example, his rage erupted during an altercation with a neighbor over her noisy television. Notably, my father attributed the eruption to underlying pressure generated by Suzanne's departure.

"I am amazed at my reaction to my neighbor Amanda's playing of her TV set late last night. I pounded on the floor in protest and that pounding was symbolically equivalent to pounding her skull. For the moment, this grotesque personality and dwarfed physique symbolizes all I know of Bad Mama. Thereafter I had anxious, fearful moments. In infancy there was obvious danger to giving a clear cut overt manifestation of Bad Mama.

"Never before that midnight confrontation with Amanda had I noticed the traffic noises so much. I suspected that all that roar of motors and changing gears had been unleashed by my enemy. What counter measures do I fear? The worst possible: those which affect my health, my livelihood, my home. That I hate and fear is on the liability side. That I dared to give a loud, clear testimony of my emotions, that is on the credit side.

"Why was I so angry and so fearful last night? I see manifestations of Bad Mama (or Bad Papa) all around me. Shepard's is Scroogelike. Bad Papa. Suzanne has left me to revel in sunny climes. Bad Mama. Do I hate all women or only those who appear to be Bad Mama? I took out on Amanda some of the animus I bear Suzanne. It isn't exactly a case of equation. It is rather a matter of confusion."

I remember vaguely my father complaining about his downstairs-neighbor's television in one of his letters. So this passage came as no surprise, nor did his anger, vented by banging on the floor. Many people, including myself, may have done the same thing to silence a noisy downstairs neighbor. But my father's analysis of the event in the diary concerned me. He couldn't simply bang on the floor to communicate "Turn it down!" or knock on her door to protest the loud volume. For him, it wasn't that simple. This angered response laid bare remnants of his mental illness, remnants visible in the diary but otherwise invisible to me. Of course, diaries provide a venue for expressing and analyzing private thoughts; that is their therapeutic value. And, of course, I was intruding on his privacy by reading his diary. Regardless, I felt compassion for my father when I read his analysis of this not unusual altercation between neighbors in tight living quarters. For him, the present was inextricably bound to the past.

This bondage of present and past was manifest further in my father's ongoing adverse relationship with doctors. As I read further in the diary, I came across two further examples. In these entries, my father recounted his visits to two doctors for checkups—one physical and one psychiatric—ordered by his health insurance company. The first was with a doctor that specialized in physical examinations for insurance companies, Dr. Everett Crouch.

"This morning I am to have a physical exam by Dr. Crouch at the behest of the insurance company. He has the same first name that I do, as did my father. I don't look forward to this examination, this judgment of my naked body. Is this doctor my father? Is this examination an inquiry into my guilt? Has father returned to life to confront me in my nakedness and judge of my guilt for his sudden death? If so, I accuse my accuser of relegating to me a disapproved status. I excuse my hate by pointing to his hate, which cast me into an inferior status.

"I saw Dr. Crouch. I am ill-impressed with him as an individual. He resembled a child going through a bag of tricks as an adult looked on. He acted as if the examination were being conducted by me. It was a moral rather than a physical test. In a sense I was testing him. Even so, I sweated under the arms. I was evidently nervous about the affair. We examined each other, I guess. He gave the impression of trying to catch me in a crooked scheme. All his patients think about is money, he said. He stretched the examination out till it lasted an hour.

"At one time he said, rather hopelessly, 'You're all right.' I have tried to fathom that remark 'You're all right.' It came like an admission, a grudging, reluctant admission. In my case, getting the insurance I've applied for depends on the supposed effect of my nervous breakdown 16 years ago."

Several days later: "I had my VA examination. It was a 'current evaluation' of the present effects of my nervous breakdown. It baffles me whether the VA medical staff concentrated on a physical examination of me or, rather, focused on the extent of my recovery from my nervous breakdown. It would seem that Dr. Crouch's examination ought to suffice so far as my physical condition is concerned.

"What is the significance of the examination? I scarcely care whether I qualify for the extra insurance or don't qualify. In that respect, the rendezvous meant little. Yet I once belonged to the VA. I once was a patient. I am going back. Have I done well since I left the VA hospital? God, have I done well! I have come through fire and water. I have stood alone. I feel that I have accomplished wonders. And still much remains to be done.

"Dr. Lewis Overholt, the psychiatrist, was a man whom I tended to see as an older man, older than me. Maybe he really was about my own age. In dress and demeanor he was older. His name reminded me of Old Overholt whiskey and the picture that goes with Old Grandad. It also reminded me of Ernie Oberholtzer, a Minnesotan twenty-five years older than me. This is to say, he reminded me of my father.

"For the most part, I treated Dr. Overholt rather brusquely. I kept to the point. I had the impression of a degree of falsity—of the deliberate presentation of himself as a slow, ineffectual stumbling, bumbling fellow. I was in no hurry, was not impatient. He laboriously scribbled notes of my replies to his questions. As we went along, I think, the guy gained confidence in me. He felt more at ease. He began by asking my age, as if I might feel vulnerable about that. Several times he expressed his willingness to forego questions and to let me volunteer questions or information.

"I said 'My job is not a tremendous one, but it is what I do.' I spoke as I was trying to correct an impression on his part that I cut a wide swath in whatever I did. He asked me my height at one time. I told him 'About average height.' In answer to a question about my history of psychiatric treatment, I gave him a frank, precise, concise, detailed account of it from beginning to end. In general I spoke frankly, freely, forcefully, good humoredly. I named names. So far as I know, I never once struck a pose.

"At times, I disregarded the back of the chair and sat with my back to the wall. I turned my eyes on the doctor. As it were, I evaluated him. Also, I let my eyes roam around the room and its paucity of simple, severe furnishings. Strange, his facial expressions, the way he fluttered his eyelids, reminded me of Nobel Shadduck, who is now a lawyer in the town I sometimes call my home town. Also, he vaguely reminded me of a hog rooting for corn in a manure pile, as Fred Winner, a Denver lawyer, used to.

"I let Dr. Overholt know I didn't particularly care what he reported. My attitude wasn't particularly friendly. It is true I sat with my back to the wall part of the time, but I wasn't hostile. I asked nothing of the guy until, at the end, I showed him the callous on my heel (my Achilles heel) and asked his advice about that. I gave scarcely more than he asked."

Like medical professionals in general, Dr. Oberholt evoked anxiety during my father's psychiatric evaluation. Indeed, my father revealed a scar from his wartime experiences when he sat with his back to the wall. This is a defensive position in combat that allows an unobstructed vantage point of the lurking danger that may enter the place at any moment. I infer that my father perceived consciously or, more probably subconsciously, Dr. Oberholt as a threat to his safety, as a lurking danger. Despite my father's overt improvement, these occasional episodes—these minor eruptions—manifest tenacious remnants of his PTSD.

What is it about the medical profession that makes my father so anxious? I thought about two possible causes. The first cause emanates from my father's experiences in the mental hospital where, in his illness, he wrestled continuously with the medical staff, the ones who routinely administered insulin- and electro-shock therapy. The second cause can be traced to my father's role in the Dachau trials. As a member of the JAG legal staff in the first trial, *USA v. Martin Gottfried Weiss, et al.*, he would have interacted first-hand with Nazi doctors who committed atrocious medical experiments on prisoners. These included infecting inmates with malaria and then testing various antidotes, submerging inmates in ice water to test the body's endurance to cold, introducing infectious diseases to skin and other tissue, feeding inmates only salt water, performing liver biopsies without an anesthetic, and withdrawing air from a confined area to test endurance limits in conditions that approached a vacuum. The tribunal proceedings (and numerous popular books) describe these experiments in sufficient, gruesome detail to repulse even the most hardened reader. Latent memories of these interactions alone could pervert my father's trust in the medical profession.

But, there is another factor compounding the intensity of these traumatic interactions with members of the medical profession. The Nazi perpetrators were Germans speaking German, as did his mother. Many years ago, my father told me that he was particularly disturbed during the war because the malevolent enemy, the Nazis, spoke German, the language his mother spoke. A confusing, abnormal linkage between evil and mother may have formed: a linkage that took numerous bouts of shock therapy and sessions of psychoanalysis and many years of time to mitigate—but not expunge totally.

At the time, my father wrote briefly about these doctor's appointments but not about the analyses in his letters. They were addressed to me, not to me and my wife Nancy—that is, not to us as a married couple. With time on my hands, this snub could have irked me, but my attentions focused sharply on the rigors of Harvard, with precious little time to dwell on such petty matters. I simply shared the letters with Nancy, and she read them with interest.

In one of those letters, he mentioned a potential job offer from the insurance company, United Services Automobile Association (USAA), without providing any further details. But, off and on in his 1965 diary entries, he expanded on this possibility. His commanding officer in the war, Col. Cheever, was president of USAA, and in several exchanges of letters, Col. Cheever raised the possibility of a job for my father. Details of the position were not discussed precisely, although my father inferred that it would be some type of executive assistant to Col. Cheever. This imprecision bothered my father; he questioned whether the job would be a sinecure, whether the other senior employees would resent him. Regardless, the job would provide a more generous income and an opportunity to establish a new career in San Antonio. Importantly, in my father's mind it would catalyze marriage to Suzanne, whom he assumed would accompany him. Hope springs eternal.

In March, 1965, Col. Cheever visited Colorado Springs briefly, providing an opportunity over dinner to discuss the job offer in more detail. However, the conversation proved to be little more than irrelevant chit-chat, with only vague references to the exact nature of the job. My father was dissatisfied and frustrated. Nonetheless, he remained guardedly hopeful.

"No word from Charlie. He may be testing my power to hold out against him. This interval of silence may be a testing time. I will not be found wanting. I have thought about going to San Antonio to work quite a lot today. It has seemed a desirable thing to do. Perhaps the idea has been that I am going to go down there and, so, the sooner an agreement is reached, the better. Maybe it would be more realistic to look at it this way. It isn't at all sure that I will go to San Antonio to work for USAA. Therefore, the longer definite decisions are delayed, the better. Let me hear from a few more manuscripts. Let's see what is in store at Shepard's.

"In wartime, Charlie had me ordered to San Antonio. It isn't so easy this time. In wartime, Charlie could be more sure of his authority. Now he would outrank me, but would I be dazzled by his rank? Scarcely. If I am to view the thing soberly, therefore, it may be best to down-grade the opportunity at USAA.

"I have made it fairly plain to Charlie that if I come to San Antonio, Suzanne comes with me. I can't be pointed out as an eligible bachelor, or even as a bachelor. It is my guess that Charlie regards me married as a less desirable employee than unmarried. Would Suzanne stand between the two of us?

"'Blue moon, now I'm no longer alone without a dream in my heart, without a love of my own.' That is one song which flitted through my mind today. The other is the Island Song from South Pacific."

The diary entries during this period interlace my father's dreams about this potential new career and more mundane interactions with colleagues—primarily female—at work. Indirectly, they also convey how Suzanne's absence had weighed heavily on my father. He wrote about it only occasionally, but the impact came across unambiguously. He missed her.

Then came the happy news: "Suzanne called. She is back from Arizona."

The diary continues for another several months with little change in content. During this period, Col. Cheever never formally offered the job at USAA, and my father never followed up with a formal application. The opportunity continued to linger unresolved. Concurrently, my father applied for reinstatement into a Civil Service job. The Civil Service approved my father's application for employment, but no federal agency showed any interest in hiring him. So, that opportunity never materialized either. My father resumed his routine visits to Suzanne in Denver every Sunday, although he seldom mentioned her in either the diary or letters to me. Again, they took separate vacations; she went to visit her son in Wisconsin, and he went to San Francisco. And, as usual, editors rejected many more of his stories than they accepted.

On a positive note, Shepard's promoted him to a position one step up in the hierarchy, which increased the number of female staff members under his supervision. Predictably, this resulted in a corresponding increase in sexual tension in the workplace.

As my father's attentions turned from himself, from his troubled childhood, from his quarrel with society, to his workplace, the diary entries became shorter. They contained fewer philosophizing rants about the bourgeois values of the herd, less extensive analyses of dreams and daily interactions with colleagues. And, my father referred seldom to my brother or me; we had both moved out-of-town for college and saw him only on vacations. In a way, my father's life, his mental health, was approaching normality, although it was marked with occasional aberrations, usually involving women.

"Today in the stacks, I was hurrying along one aisle. As I entered an interesting aisle, I suddenly found Lila S. in my path. We didn't collide, but, for some reason, I took advantage of the confusion and her proximity to slide my hand along the bare forearm with which she was supporting her bosom. In this way, did I signal to her that she attracted me sexually? My act was done ever so quickly. It was almost a reflex. Yet it must not have been necessary for me to balance or steady myself. It was a meeting of the flesh, a highly personal gesture. Why that particular gesture? I did not touch or feel her bosom. I simply ran my bare hand along her bare forearm from elbow to wrist or vice versa. Was that friction movement symbolic of the friction movement of the sex act? If I, the actor, don't know, could she? Later when I met her again, near her desk, she seemed in a state of satisfaction, high good humor. Frank H. witnessed the sudden encounter. So probably did the girl called Viola.

"It surprises me a little that I made any gesture of affinity. Lila S sometimes repels me. Her bad breath has repelled me at times. Her personality has made me shrink from her at times. My gesture was not possessive, as an embrace would have been. Or, in its sudden, sly way, was it even more bold and possessive? Was the gesture one of entry, aggression, or was it one of withdrawal? Lila is married, and my gesture may have signified my recognition of that fact, my awareness of onlookers, etc. It was over almost as soon as it began. I write of this episode at length. Yet it was not one which lingered in my consciousness long during the work day.

"Millie, who is not a friend of mine, asked me today 'What are you looking for? Trouble?' Looking her squarely in the eye, I replied 'No, I'm looking for you.' It was as if my words were to convey this meaning: 'I know you're no friend of mine, and your enmity causes me no fear. I do not seek your enmity, but I do not fear it either.' My words may even have meant: 'I would like your friendship, but I do not fear your enmity.'"

Good grief. When I read about this encounter, I was appalled. Nowadays, my father could have been fired for that gesture or even charged with assault; no excuse would be good enough. I had never known my father to misbehave with women. At most, he once told me that "sometimes women like to be pushed around." I never took that comment seriously at the time. Indeed, as a teenager in the "old-west" side of Colorado Springs, I grew up in a male culture that revered, cherished, and protected woman, as, supposedly, did our pioneer forefathers. The ethos derived from the hardships of taming the land, building a homestead, raising a family. For the male pioneers, a wife at his side was a most treasured asset as they faced these challenges of settling the West.

I cannot retrospectively pinpoint anybody's specific contributions to my cultural upbringing regarding women. Clearly, my father must not have contributed significantly to the "pioneer ethos." Although he adopted Colorado as his home, he retained his upper Midwest cultural attributes. I suspect, rather, that my mother, her mother (my maternal grandmother), and her four siblings (my grandmother's brothers and sisters) played significant roles in this regard. They and other relatives on her side descended from pioneers who established a family compound in Colorado Springs in the late 1800s. As a child, I would listen to their tales of the family's past. Although I remember few details of these historical stories, I assume that they influenced my cultural development. As did neighbors, who also derived from pioneer families and told about their histories as they migrated to the "wild West." My brother and I are products of that heritage.

A year passed with little further drama. The most consequential event was Suzanne's leaving for another vacation in 1966. And, once again, my father was to be tested during her absence. My father expressed sadness without Suzanne nearby, but he also expressed emerging contentment with his job at Shepard's. "I have begun to wonder whether this trouble in my throat is a 'lump in the throat,' a physical spasm expressive of a profound and settled sadness. The watering of the eyes, especially the left eye, might be tears. Why, though, should this sadness make itself known right when I seem to be less agitated and restless than usual? Loneliness is no worse than seeking companionship from those unable to give it. Do I seek something? If so, what? Have I perchance found what I've been seeking? Is loneliness so terrible when one gives without asking? During Suzanne's absence, I shall be working five days per week with people.

"What hits me hardest, seemingly, is the idea of being deserted. That parallels a childhood experience which must have been truly frightful. I was left alone — and, indeed, I thenceforth had to survive alone. When I left Margie here in the Springs and went to San Antonio to prepare for my departure overseas, I suffered great anxiety and depression. I wonder if Suzanne feels the same way and is anxious to return. In infancy, maternal desertion can be fatal. But I am a man. If my sweetheart should desert me (which isn't likely), I should be able to carry on without experiencing the tension, fear, anxiety which is appropriate to the child's but not the man's state. Nor should I as a man hate a deserter with the intensity appropriate to the child's status. Here in the Springs, I may have deliberately created a vacuum, an isolation ward. Here I suffer to show I can survive. I can get along without parents. On that basis, I have kicked all possible parent figures in the teeth. Maybe it is time for me to cease hiding myself away like a hermit.

"This type of thinking, the idea of being surrounded by hostile forces, of being in the midst of enemies, of being deserted is the type which landed me in the hospital. The idea of being surrounded by enmity signifies pretty intense enmity in one's self. What is there that brings all hostility to the surface now? What is there that makes my present situation parallel that of 1949 when I went to the hospital and that of some period in my childhood? It is my guess that when father died unexpectedly, mother withdrew figuratively but nonetheless realistically. The situation in 1949 bore a closer parallel to that of childhood than does my present setup. Still a parallel exists."

But, this year, my father also took a vacation. "With Suzanne gone for the coming weeks, my ability to stand alone will be tested further. I went on vacation to California alone. What did I do? I did what I seldom, if ever, do here. I went sightseeing; took in theater and ballet; went to lectures; made gustatory excursions; went shopping in a big way; sat by the sea; sat by the bay; rode buses, streetcars, cable cars; lived in a hotel. Oh, I went to Chinatown, and I visited the Wells Fargo museum. I savored it more thoroughly than most tourists."

"The vacation did me good, with or without Suzanne. I came back feeling less of a rebel. I take responsibility. It may be I feel less in rebellion and more in command. To be in rebellion is to feel trapped, enslaved. One beats up the walls of his cell and screams in rage. What surprises me is that I seem gradually to have been going over from an 'employee psychology' to a 'boss psychology.' Little by little, I identify less with those who are supervised and more with those who do the supervising."

Once again, the diary reveals a subtle transition in my father's personality. He perceives himself as less a rebel and more a leader, a supervisor. Ten years ago, my father perceived himself as a leader, a messiah. But those perceptions were quite different; they were delusional constructs characteristic of his mental illness. In contrast, his present-day perceptions are realistic correlates of his promotions up the managerial ladder at Shepard's. They occur understandably during the transition from an "employee psychology" to a "boss psychology." Basically, he is becoming a company man.

The transition in my father's interactions with women was less subtle. His musings about co-workers of the opposite sex at Shepard's probably fall within the boundaries of normality for both men and women. Nonetheless, I found them discomforting for two reasons. First, I tensed up when his flirtatious encounters became physical or overtly suggestive. They portended trouble. Second, I sympathized with Suzanne. I realized that she had rebuffed his proposal to join him in Colorado Springs and, therefore, had no formal claim to his fidelity. Nonetheless, I couldn't suppress feelings of defensive loyalty to her. Simply put, through our initial brief encounters in Madison and many diary entries, I had become fond and protective of her.

Importantly, despite my discomfort with his flirtatiousness, I sensed that my father stood on the cusp of mental health, of recovery from mental illness. His diary entries still expressed occasional remnants of the past, but for the most part, they expressed contemplations that might be considered normal. He began to resemble the man I knew as my father. Cautiously, I read further in the diary, the final volumes, hoping that my senses were right.

The Return

In early June, 1967, my father returned to his home in Minnesota for only the second time since he joined the army. The previous visit was in 1952, nearly twenty-three years earlier, shortly after his hospitalization. Now, he expressed anxiety about meeting his brother and sisters again. Although they exchanged letters once or twice a year (usually just Christmas cards) their relationships had become shallow over time. Curiously, he expressed little anxiety about meeting his mother again. In fact, he seldom mentioned the pending visit with her when discussing and planning the trip in his diary entries.

I was in Colorado Springs for the week before my father was scheduled to leave. He shared his travel plans with me: drive to Minnesota by way of the Black Hills in South Dakota and spend one or two nights at a motel along the way. If he was excited or anxious, I couldn't tell. It appeared to be just another vacation. However, in retrospect, I concluded that I misjudged the excitement of the pending trip.

An Ellis Worth story, *A Visit to the Governor*, prompted me to that conclusion.[13] In that tale, he recounts a man's trip back to Minnesota to visit his family. Excerpts tell of his excitement. "It was knee-deep in July

---

[13] "A Visit to the Governor," *Snowy Egret* 31, no. 1 (1967). Pp. 18-20.

when I hit the highway northward-bound. The winter wheat had already been harvested, but I could smell it. The odor of it still lingered. It permeated the air. When I got further north, where they grow spring wheat, No.1, Dark Northern, there might be some of those immense fields of standing grain I knew as a boy. Good heavens, what would I do then? The dusty, nose-filling aroma of ripe and ripening wheat might be overwhelming, over powering, all pervasive. I worried. I was afraid of that scent; well, if not afraid exactly, leery.

"The odor grew stronger as I went along. The Black Hills were behind me. It wasn't an unpleasant sensation. I liked the smell, the invisible pungency, except that it was unsettling, exciting, intoxicating, on the order of a stimulating drug or that unearthly poppy-weed. I don't know why. I was born in July, in the middle of the harvest-season. My father, who died when I was ten years old, was a farmer. My fondest recollections of him were those harvest-scenes when he held an old-fashioned three-tined pitchfork in his hands. He was short and solid and blue-eyed, much as I am now. When he came into the house from the fields, he was as aromatic as a straw stack or a granary, redolent of the creased, nutty kernels he'd let run through his hard, sun-browned, sweaty hands.

"Delirious with the sight and smell of the rich, dark, ruddy-red grain, I set my course eastward across the Grain Belt to the city of lakes and Swedes and shopkeepers. I didn't even stop to fix myself and my gaze momentarily upon father's monument or, farther on, my own birthplace. All, all this land, his land, was my land. Not just two specks of it. All was mine to swim in. He, my father, was in this very air which tickled my nose, filled my lungs, and unaccountably brought tears to my eyes.

"As I approached the flour-milling metropolis which had been Mother's home almost from that cold day of Father's demise, long ago, my fever subsided. It is a good thing, too, for there's no place for wildness in the traffic of a big city. That is a crime the time-set, red, green, amber, signal-control lights could never understand, much less forgive. Something there is, too, in a metropolis that doesn't like the serene sweetness of alfalfa or the heady fragrance of grain."

I assume that my father experienced the same euphoria when driving through South Dakota en route to the farm in Minnesota, as the familiar smells and grandeur of the upper Midwest evoked pleasant memories of his youth. The pending visit to his family also must have evoked memories, but they were probably less than euphoric. He hadn't seen them for a long time; he had changed, they had changed, the rural environment had changed. It's easy to imagine a somewhat guarded atmosphere as they reacquainted themselves. It's also easy to imagine that old stereotypes quickly emerged. The older brother was still the hard-working farmer; my father was still the good-for-nothing dreamer; his mother was still the inattentive widow. The calendar years had changed, but little else—at least in their relationships with each other.

Afterwards, he wrote in the diary: "On my recent visit to my childhood home, mother seemed almost speechless, mute. Was she repeating 'Nothing I could say would please you?' Yes, I think so. She was striking a pose of impugned innocence. Father had rejected her by dying; I by leaving Minnesota. She has been wrongly rejected.

"I can see that my childhood surroundings were anything but a bed of roses. Mother probably was so insecure, so in need of praise, compliments, declarations of love that she couldn't bring herself to love her children. In fact, never once did she say she was glad to see me. Nor did she ever say anything else which would convey the same idea. Probably I was quite as mute about feeling any enjoyment in the visit. It is slight wonder that I grew up mixed up.

"In a letter I received from mother since my return home, she said 'It was good to see you, even for such a little while.' When she finally says 'It was good to see you,' she adds to it the 'little while,' meaning the little while I cared to see her. I had a sort of hands off attitude. Don't try any pretense on me. I don't trust you.

"I feel I have changed immensely in the past five years. In what way? Am I healthier and more mature? Do I now accept life and accept the world?"

My father's visit to Minnesota, to his family, to the farm of his childhood, marked a significant milestone in his path from mental illness. He returned to the farm not in despair, as in 1952 after his discharge from the hospital, not in angry rage, as in the diary entries from five to ten years earlier, but in reconciliation. He reconciled childhood memories with present-day reality. To be sure, he still harbored unpleasant feelings towards his mother, but they lay within the boundaries of normality. I base my judgment mainly on the diary entries, for outwardly, I didn't detect any overt change in his demeanor. He was still "dad," as he recounted noteworthy experiences during his visit: huge meals, going to town with his brother, watching a baseball game with his brother-in-law, visiting his favorite fishing and frog-catching spots, and so forth.

Shortly after my father returned, I visited the family farm for the first (and only) time, while driving with Nancy from Colorado Springs to Cambridge. In those early days of the interstate highway system, a stopover in Minnesota provided a welcome relief while driving cross-country often on two-lane highways, and it provided an opportunity to introduce Nancy to my father's family members, whom I hardly knew myself. We had a pleasant two-day stay, dominated by massive meals three times a day made of food grown on the farm. Conversations were primarily about farm matters such as the weather, crop health, chicken egg-laying productivity, and the like, with little mention of my father, although he had been there less than a month earlier. For the most part, his mother, my grandmother, remained quiet, and when she spoke I had difficulty understanding what she said because of her thick German accent. After we left, Nancy and I, of course, rehashed the visit and quickly agreed that my father's family were good people: pleasant to visit and certainly attentive to both of us.

Retrospectively, I thought about my father's childhood in Minnesota, his experiences on the farm. I envisioned the image portrayed in the diary: a tragic Minnesota farm boy beset by ravaging demons. I had become familiar with this image. But, I had also become familiar with an alternative image in the Ellis Worth stories: a happy Minnesota farm boy at one with his environment. Indeed, despite the grousing about his mother's reticence (and other shortcomings), my father must have had fond memories of the farm. More than once, I witnessed tears in his eyes when he reminisced about childhood on the farm. I always looked away in embarrassment. This persistent disconnect between the diary and the fond memories continued to perplex me. Stated metaphorically, some piece is missing from the puzzle.

Stumped by this inconsistency in these contrasting images of my father as a child in Minnesota, my mind drifted to his experiences in the war. I know so little about them, but I strongly doubt that there were many fond memories. As I mentioned earlier, he never spoke to my brother or me about the landing at Normandy, the siege of Bastogne, the tribunals at Dachau. At most, he mentioned that he had participated in the liberation of Luxembourg and that Col. Cheever had been his commanding officer. Other than that, nothing. Our mother told us more about my father's time in the army than he did, and that wasn't much.

Likewise, my father rarely wrote about his military experiences. Looking back, neither he, in the diary, nor Ellis Worth, in the stories, describes significant wartime events. Although my father acknowledged his recognition as a war hero, the French *Croix d'Guerre* et cetera, he seemed to have expunged a significant fraction of his military details from his consciousness. There are no extensive memories on record. There are simply discontinuities, blank spaces in the chronology of his life.

I reflected further on my hypothetical explanation for these military discontinuities. Recapitulating earlier thoughts, I surmised that this curious cutout stemmed from the shock therapy administered during his hospitalization. Ellis Worth describes daily insulin shock treatments and an unknown number of electroshock episodes in *The Eldon Jones Sextet*. And, my father told me on several occasions that his back had been broken twice from the electroshock treatment.

The Man I Didn't Know

I am a neuroscientist by profession, so it should come as no surprise that I delved into the science underlying shock therapy, looking for explanations of how it works—what it does to the brain that ameliorates symptoms of depression and schizophrenia. In textbooks and scholarly articles, I found detailed accounts about its physiological effects: low blood sugar, altered neurochemistry, seizures, et cetera. More to my interest, I found that both insulin- and electro-shock induce memory loss, that is, amnesia. Significantly, memories of past events may be lost: retrograde amnesia in scientific terms. Usually, these memories return with time—but not always. Although some accounts considered memory loss a side effect, others considered it the primary therapeutic effect. For that matter, some articles consider memory loss a direct consequence of the trauma underlying PTSD. Regardless, retrograde amnesia caught my attention, because it conforms to the gaps in my father's wartime chronology.

I posited that retrograde amnesia explains why my father never mentioned certain wartime experiences. His traumatic memories from the war were expunged by the shock treatment, and they did not return. He had few conscious recollections of his traumatic experiences at the Dachau trials or, for that matter, at the Siege of Bastogne. That's why he seldom spoke or wrote about them. I surmise further that eradication of those memories opened the doors to recovery from his acute mental illness.

This hypothetical explanation made sense to me at a superficial level, and I accept it. But, it raised a scientific issue. What distinguishes the memories that were lost from those that were not lost? The physiological architecture of the traumatic wartime memories must differ from the traumatic childhood memories and myriad non-traumatic memories. Unfortunately, the physiology of memory formation and retention simply isn't known at the fundamental level of inquiry needed to answer this question, to explain my father's illness.

My posit raised another issue. If one month of daily insulin shock and several bouts of electroshock erased traumatic memories from wartime but not childhood, perhaps the childhood experiences were not so traumatic after all. During the initial several years of the diary, my father commented regularly about emotional injuries inflicted on him by his parents. Were they really so injurious? Their memories apparently were not targeted by the shock therapy. Maybe the childhood injuries, perceived abandonment by his father and inattention from his mother, were a construct of psychoanalysis. The important point is that those childhood memories were not lost, unlike the traumatic wartime memories; they were different physiologically.

Pursuing this logic a bit further, I pondered whether my father could have recovered from his mental illness without the aid of a psychiatrist. Would the shock treatment and the presumed loss of traumatic wartime memories have sufficed? I suspect that most medical professionals would insist that he needed psychiatric help. They are probably right. I acknowledge the soothing benefit of talking about personal matters with an attentive listener, a psychiatrist. Moreover, I acknowledge the benefit of a well-trained psychiatrist's help in disentangling the convolution of father, mother, German-speaking Nazis, and traumatic wartime atrocities. Although I profess skepticism about the therapeutic benefit of symbolic interpretation of dreams, I accept the importance of psychiatric counseling in the treatment of mental illness like my father's.

During this time of thoughtful reflection, it dawned on me that I had come upon a coherent theory that explained my father's illness. The childhood trauma inflicted damage that might warrant psychiatric attention at some point in time but not debilitating damage. My father emerged from childhood to lead a normal life. Until World War II, that is. The wartime trauma — interacting with German-speaking Nazi perpetrators of medical atrocities and whatever else occurred on the battlefield — inflicted damage, much worse damage resulting in acute mental illness (PTSD). Shock therapy expunged the toxic memories, enabling my father's escape from the pernicious grasp of acute insanity. But, he was not fully healed. Recovery, the return to normality, required the help of psychiatrists and the passage of time. His psychiatrist, Dr. Walker, could not attend to damaging memories of wartime trauma; shock therapy had taken care of that. But, Dr. Walker could attend to less damaging memories of childhood trauma, thus helping my father readjust to society, reestablish mental equilibrium, reset his life.

Of course, I am not a psychiatrist, so my explanation lacked a specialist's authority. But, as a medical-school neuroscientist, it made sense to me. It filled the gap in the timeline of events leading up to the transition from a seemingly stable young man to a patient under suicide watch in a mental hospital. I took satisfying comfort in this explanation.

With that satisfaction came the realization that reading the diary had introduced me to the father I didn't know, the man who was struggling to overcome the devastating impacts of trauma inflicted in early childhood and later in wartime. My memories of him were now set in that more complete context. He was a father chasing dreams, dreams of fulfilling the needs of his growing children, of becoming a successful writer, of achieving financial comfort, of marrying the woman he loved. I recognized this father, for his dreams were not unlike my own at his age. They were not unlike those of many men. We all fulfilled our dreams in quite different ways, of course. But, we all share the same blend of gratification and, yes, disappointment as we reach the age of retrospection. At least, I speculate that we do.

Well, enough speculation. Back to the diary; the story is not yet complete.

After my father's trip to Minnesota, the diary was gradually coming to an end. The entries were less and less frequent and noticeably shorter. The final entries of 1967 narrate several interactions with male and female colleagues.

"Today, I took George Rice and Margaret Rogers to lunch. I was rather detached. Conversation lagged. George and Margaret did most of the talking. The occasion for the lunch was to give Margaret a ride in my new car and to launch George on his vacation. There was no effort to exploit the conversational potential of the shop. This lunch will increase the mystery which surrounds me. The more I expose myself, the more significant I seem.

"Various people will try to pump Margaret about today's lunch. She herself may compare notes with George. Leona will be glad I invited Margaret. She won't be jealous. George's colleagues will be satisfied I invited George rather than them. One expectation I have had from the beginning is this. Margaret's tendency to look to me for a romantic overture will be blighted."

Next week: "I took Doc Lawson and Leona to lunch today. This lunch, like the one for George Rice and Margaret, was a means for giving expression to my love of mankind in general and these guests in particular. They both enjoyed the occasion, as did I. I kept the conversation from turning to shop talk.

"My aim, so I think, in taking Doc as well as Leona was to relieve any embarrassment, to preclude any supposition that I was courting Leona, a married woman. Also, I like the idea of having had George and Margaret together to still any supposition that I might be wooing Margaret. Maybe my main aim in each case was to show my affection for the women. I needed the man to show that I could control that affection. Or did I need the man to show that I no longer fear a triangular situation? In neither of these two occasions did I feel any urge to push the other man out of the picture and seize the woman. The man may not have been primary, but he was not a competitor.

"Friday, Thelma paraded herself before me and, I thought, insinuated a sexual relation between us (she is married). Thelma has a tenseness of bearing as if withholding what she offers. She says nothing suggestive or provocative, however. Millie likes to come over, ostensibly just to be near me briefly. Edna craves a close relationship with me, maybe more social than sexual. Occasionally she says something which assumes I desired her sexually, which means she feels a certain desire for me. Indeed, quite a few of the women probably give the editors a feeling I am the one. Right now, George has a pretty exclusive relation with Fern, Ruby, Mrs. Ives, and the Mexican girl. That relation makes his job more palatable.

"The men, strangely enough, seem rather to interpret me via the women's reactions to me than to interpret me directly. They, the men, see the women coming over to me repeatedly, attracted yet mystified. The women are very anxious to please me. I ignore overtones in dealing with my visitors. I attend to the business they bring. Impersonal is the word for my attitude, yet attentive, polite, prompt. I ask nothing from them, seek nothing, am glad to help but no one more than another.

"George and the other editors cannot be unaware of the yen of these women, of the half-formed sexual relation between them and me (never to be fully formed). They feel jealous, rebellious, cantankerous. Yes, I think that the hostility that George bears toward me has a triangular formation. He hates the primacy I possess vis-à-vis the females around. He feels vastly inferior but locked in a triangular prison with me. His hate and his feeling of inferiority go together. I am papa. Maybe I fear being papa, his papa.

"The great change of attitude towards women—indeed, towards the world in general—which has taken place in me during the past seven years is a change from rebellion, protest, and complaint to assent, or an even more positive position than assent. Now, I affirm; I accent the positive. I embrace life. I intone the everlasting play. Life is okay. I am not persecuted or reviled. The world is good to me and to others. At least I seek to affirm, to try to visualize the environment as fairly promising."

The difference between these entries concerning women from 1967 and those written five to ten years earlier is remarkable. Indeed, my father's attitude towards women had evolved from belligerence to acceptance, from torment to contentment. During the years of mental illness, he had disparaged women disrespectfully, equating them with his unloving mother. Shortly after the move to Colorado Springs, my father's relationship with women became more flirtatious — occasionally somewhat prurient. Now, in these final diary entries, my father's relationship with women seems less flirtatious, more respectful, more mature, so to speak. He enjoyed their company. Despite occasional discomforting sexual overtones, his interactions with women at work now appeared innocuous; they were, refreshingly free from the anger and disaffection prevalent in the entries written five to ten years earlier and from the occasional raunchiness in the entries written two or three years earlier. Stated simply, my father now found enjoyment with women, an enjoyment that I have found all of my life.

Where was Suzanne during all of this? In the diary entries of these last several years, Suzanne was seldom mentioned. This did not come as a great surprise, because my father had begun to write less and less about her after settling in Colorado Springs. However, her nonappearance in the diary certainly did not presage her nonappearance in his life. As usual, he travelled to Denver every Sunday to be with Suzanne, and, on several occasions when I was visiting him in Colorado Springs, I overheard his telephone conversations with her. They were in French. I don't speak the language, but I recognized his terms of endearment ("*mon petit choux*," "*mon chérie*") and his warm smile when he spoke them. Without a doubt, Suzanne remained an important, romantic part of my father's life.

Several noteworthy events during this time were documented in the diary. For example, Col. Cheever eventually offered my father a job as his executive assistant at USAA. That would require moving to San Antonio. But, my father turned it down, choosing to stay in Colorado Springs where he could pursue his writing ambitions. Furthermore, he wasn't convinced that Suzanne would accompany him to Texas. In addition, McGraw-Hill bought Shepard's and introduced computers to the operations. At that time, this meant noisy keypunch machines, stacks of key-punched cards, and a new corps of computer operators. As far as I could tell from his occasional comments about the new machines—where they were located, how to store the voluminous punch cards, et cetera—my father adapted to these new developments with little apparent difficulty. And, the new McGraw-Hill management team promoted him again, with a modest pay raise.

With the increased pay raise, my father took more adventurous vacations. Not to Paris or Rio de Janeiro, but to less expensive places in Mexico. On one occasion (summer 1968), he went to La Paz, located in Baja California. He wrote me several picture postcards describing his pleasure at sitting on the hotel veranda, smoking a Cuban cigar, looking out at the ocean.

At Shepard's, my father had risen in the ranks and, by 1969, had become an associate editor, one step away from editor-in-chief. He had earned respect from his colleagues, the acceptance that he had so long desired. In letters and telephone calls, my father would tell me about occasional spats at work, at home with noisy neighbors, and unappreciative editors. But by-and-large, he was at peace with the world. That is how I remember him.

With one final one-paragraph entry on June 8, 1969, the diary came to an end. "Today, I went to Charlie

Grebenstein's funeral. I asked Nick DeLeon if I could ride with him. Then George Rice joined us. Nick and George are two who have tended to consider themselves outcasts. Now here I show a personal interest in them. Moreover, I do not go to Charlie's funeral merely to escape work. I go out of consideration for the guy, out of respect."

The story of my father's descent into and return from the maelstrom of mental illness also had come to an end. He appeared to have lost interest in the diary. It had served its purpose, ostensibly as a therapeutic tool for rebuilding his mental health. Now it was time for me to pack them back into their boxes for indefinite storage.

But, there was one surprise left. In one of the boxes, three small magazines were stuck to the bottom cardboard due to water damage. I pulled them loose, tearing pages but not beyond readability. Two of them contained Ellis Worth short stories that I had read previously in manuscript form. To my surprise, however, one small magazine, *Orion Magazine*, contained an article by E. Smith that I had not seen before, *A Blessing in Disguise*.[14] My father had written this under his own name, not his pen name. This short article proved to be a personal reconciliation with his mental illness and a fitting conclusion to this chronicle.

****

A Blessing in Disguise

Between fifteen and twenty years ago, things were going along smoothly for me—I thought. I had a good-looking, talented wife and two healthy young boys, one in school and the other not yet old enough for

---

[14] Everett Smith, "A Blessing in Disguise," *Orion Magazine* 15, no. 125 (1970).

that. We lived in a fine Maryland suburb of the nation's capital. I had an excellent job as Assistant General Counsel for one of Uncle Sam's agencies. My wife and I seemed to be getting along well. A host of people envied both my present and my prospects.

We had neighbors in to dine. We would go to the concerts in Coolidge Auditorium and were invited to musical homes to participate and listen to quartets. I could, on occasion, escort distinguished visitors through the museums, around the Capital and to Mount Vernon and historic Virginia. At the theater, especially the summer theater, we laughed, relaxed and, during intermissions, rubbed elbows with famous generals, career diplomats, well-known politicos, and the leavening mass of threadbare government clerks and awestruck tourists. At clubs in warm weather we partook of the bounty of the Sunday evening smorgasbords on the lawn. In any gathering of families our sons stood out for their rosy-cheeked health and high-spirited glee.

Well, that was long ago, and everyone expects things to change with time. Ah yes, but the course of my life was altered radically by a wholly unexpected event, an illness which, though exceptionally severe, was a blessing rather than a misfortune. A nervous breakdown befell me and required a year's hospitalization, deep-shock therapy, considerable expense and, after my release from the hospital, close to nine years of psychiatric consultations at intervals which lengthened as time went on—and more expense.

When I got out of the hospital, my wife had left me. Now we're divorced, and I have not remarried (nor has she). I have kept in close contact with my children, both in college now, but I had to move from the great political metropolis to a small western city in order to do it.

I'm no longer in the government service. I'm no longer a lawyer. All these changes, though brought about by my illness, did not take place suddenly. For the most part, they worked themselves out gradually with plenty of assists from chance. Now I earn a modest living as a minor executive in the local unit of a giant publishing house which has its headquarters in New York City.

The transitions have not been sudden, no, nor have they been easy, nor exactly triumphant. There has been some stumbling en route; and some "agonizing reappraisals," as the statesmen say, have been necessary. For all one can tell, the past may repeat itself in these respects. Yet I value my present success more than the appearances which were the envy of my acquaintances long ago. I accept my present with less fear and more confidence; and, as for the future, I trust its uncertainties more than I once relied on its promises.

Have my sons suffered from my illness and its consequences—a "broken home" and my financial reverses? They have suffered, of course, and they have benefited too. The balance is in their favor, I'm sure. They were never abandoned by either parent. I never missed a visit once I managed to get to the West. Want never laid its frightful hand on them; poverty has not been their lot. They've had their share of parental love, concern, and guidance. In recovering my health—in making my agonizing reappraisals—I gained insights and emotional resources which were passed on to them. Their formal education, too, has been and is of the best. One goes for science and the other for art (as their old man bows to literature, which we shall see later). I've done more for them because of my illness and recovery from it than I would have been able to do otherwise. I shall not try to prove that last statement by a recitation of details and a multiplicity of incidents, but I know it to be true.

Though I have not remarried, it isn't because I feel "once burned, twice shy." No. I have a girlfriend I cherish and have known for more than ten years. We realize, though, that I have no backlog of savings nor reserves of life insurance. My salary barely suffices to cover my living expenses and relatively small contributions to the support and education of my boys. We both realize that, and we accept the fact as Margaret Fuller accepted the Universe. We're happy together. I suppose I would be willing to take a chance on marriage, but my gal is more realistic. My compulsory retirement is less than a full decade away now, and what will I, would we, live on then?

By availing myself more of my legal training and experience I might have been able to earn more in recent years (and in the productive span which lies ahead). I preferred to do as I have done. My "dumb job," if that's what it is, has left me free to do something I always wanted to do. Most of my life I was ignorant that such a frivolous, nonsensical thing was important to me. I wanted to write, and to write at all costs, whether money came my way in the process or not. Up to now, it hasn't.

Much of my life I had a keen sense of the value of money, economic security and all that. I still do, but maybe that sense is less keen now and more healthy. Certain it is that nothing less than a shattering illness could break through the thick wall of my ignorance of essentials, through my self-deception, and compel me to pick up the pieces of my life and start all over again in a new location, with a different family status, with a different type of livelihood and a changed mode of living, with a new hobby which is more than a hobby, with a feeling of liberation from the strait-jacket of conformity and convention and stereotyped partying. It took a severe illness, protracted hospitalization, and years of outpatient treatment to beat into my brain that emotional security is at least as important as economic security—and to force me into a realization of other essentials of that nature.

As a lawyer, my focus was always on behavior. Now I can take motivation, the underside of the iceberg, into account. Previously, I recognized aesthetic as well as monetary values, but emotional considerations seemed as silly as sentiment in business or imagination in government. Nor was I alone by any means in that respect. To write a legal opinion or a memorandum of government or business procedure, as so many do, is to write, I suppose, but it is to write with scarcely a trace of individuality, without a spark of imagination. For the scrivener, as a poet would say, Romance is on the town and Art a vagrant.

As it is, I have written, and I have been published here and abroad. I began by writing articles and then essays, mostly for free, some for a pittance. For example, as autobiographical essay of which I was and am very proud—the title is *Once upon a Farm*—finally found a publisher, but that excellent little Long Island quarterly is no more. I say the magazine was first rate (as it was), but it didn't—probably couldn't—pay its contributors.

Fiction I have written under a pen name. More than a dozen of my stories have been published, all in the academic, literary, no-pay, low-pay periodicals. I certainly have no complaint about the meager financial returns my writings have brought. I have done what I have wanted to do. That is a precious emotional return. If that has to be all I get, it will be. If I can pick up a penny here and there for writing what I choose, so much the better. Commercial fiction, however, is not my long suit, and I know it. I can't write it, and I don't try.

Of all the achievements of my lifetime so far (aside from what I have been able to do for my children, which is paramount), I am proudest of my published short stories, but, as I've said, I've done those under a pen name. Few—only one or two—of my friends know how I spend my spare time. I don't broadcast what I'm doing. My social life is minimal. My hermitage is on an old-time ranch. Are these strange quirks? Ah, but I'm proud of my military record in World War II also, but I don't go around bragging about that either.

Is this account of the turning point in my life so bristling with the first-person pronoun and so saturated with egregious egoism and braggadocio that it contradicts absolutely my secrecy about my leisure-time activity and its fruits? Yes. Does that contradiction in my nature or conduct seem strange, too? If so, I can only say, "No wonder. I'm a strange fellow, as all must know by now"

And if I seem to "sing of human unsuccess in a rapture of distress," I do. It is, oddly enough, because I'm made that way—and thanks to my illness and recovery, I know it, and I'm satisfied to be so.

****

My father died from a heart attack at age 61 on December 19, 1972, less than a year after this story was published. He was preceded in his death by his father, who died in 1920 from a heart attack at age 57, and his mother, who died from natural causes at age 85. In his coat pocket, my father had a bottle of nitroglycerin tablets. Apparently, he had been experiencing angina prior to the attack. In the trunk of his car, he had 36 gift-wrapped presents—one for each of the Shepard's staff members reporting to him. In his mailbox over the next two months after his death, he received thirteen rejection letters from various editors. But rejection is relative. His obituary in *Fine Arts* magazine expressed fulfillment of my father's dream: acceptance as a writer.[15]

> Dean O. Smith has informed *Fine Arts* of the death of his father, Everett E. Smith who enjoyed writing for *Fine Arts* on the arts and the law. "He was frequently seen climbing the mountainous trails surrounding Colorado Springs. Recently, he had become quite fond of Spanish culture (having always been a Francophile) and took yearly vacations to the most un-American spots in Mexico that he could find. At the time of his death, he had over thirty-five short fiction stories published plus a dozen or so professional articles. He also had manuscripts for two novels and nearly fifty unpublished stories. He published mainly in small magazines. *Fine Arts*, incidentally, was one of his favorites. He was always quite proud to see his articles appear in its pages." For this and other information about our friend the editors of *Fine Arts* extend the deepest sympathy to Dr. Smith and to his other son, Curtis who is a professional musician and teaches piano for the Department of Music at Colorado College in Colorado Springs. Our thanks also to Dr. Smith for taking time to write to us from the Technical University

---

[15] Fine Arts Magazine, "In Memorium: Everett E. Smith," *Fine Arts* 20, no. 932 (1973).

of Munich, where he is a scientist currently involved in medical research.

I should like to add a final thought to this obituary. Sentimentally, I miss the father I knew.

www.ingramcontent.com/pod-product-compliance
Lightning Source LLC
Chambersburg PA
CBHW031100080526
44587CB00011B/754